CompTIA Network+
Certification Guide

The ultimate guide to passing the N10-007 exam

Glen D. Singh
Rishi Latchmepersad

BIRMINGHAM - MUMBAI

CompTIA Network+ Certification Guide

Commissioning Editor: Vijin Boricha
Acquisition Editor: Heramb Bhavsar
Content Development Editor: Abhishek Jadhav
Technical Editor: Swathy Mohan
Copy Editor: Safis Editing
Project Coordinator: Jagdish Prabhu
Proofreader: Safis Editing
Indexer: Priyanka Dhadke
Graphics: Tom Scaria
Production Coordinator: Nilesh Mohite

First published: December 2018

Production reference: 1131218

Published by Packt Publishing Ltd.
Livery Place
35 Livery Street
Birmingham
B3 2PB, UK.

ISBN 978-1-78934-050-1

www.packtpub.com

`mapt.io`

Mapt is an online digital library that gives you full access to over 5,000 books and videos, as well as industry leading tools to help you plan your personal development and advance your career. For more information, please visit our website.

Why subscribe?

- Spend less time learning and more time coding with practical eBooks and videos from over 4,000 industry professionals

- Improve your learning with Skill Plans built especially for you

- Get a free eBook or video every month

- Mapt is fully searchable

- Copy and paste, print, and bookmark content

Packt.com

Did you know that Packt offers eBook versions of every book published, with PDF and ePub files available? You can upgrade to the eBook version at `www.packt.com` and, as a print book customer, you are entitled to a discount on the eBook copy. Get in touch with us at `customercare@packtpub.com` for more details.

At `www.packt.com`, you can also read a collection of free technical articles, sign up for a range of free newsletters, and receive exclusive discounts and offers on Packt books and eBooks.

Contributors

About the authors

Glen D. Singh is a cyber-security instructor, consultant, entrepreneur and public speaker. He has been conducting multiple training exercises in offensive security, digital forensics, network security, enterprise networking and IT service management annually. He also holds various information security certifications, such as the EC-Council's Certified Ethical Hacker (CEH), Computer Hacking Forensic Investigator (CHFI), Cisco's CCNA Security, CCNA Routing and Switching, and many others in the field of network security. Glen has been recognized for his passion and expertise by both the private and public sector organizations of Trinidad and Tobago and internationally.

> *I would like to thank my parents for their unconditional support and motivation they've always given me to become a better person each day. Thanks to my family, friends, and students for their continued support, the people at Packt Publishing for providing this amazing opportunity, and everyone who reads and supports this amazing book.*

Rishi Latchmepersad is a Tier II data center engineer in the IP team at Air Link Networks, a medium-sized, Miami-based ISP that provides a number of video, co-location, and dedicated internet access facilities for numerous customers in the western-hemisphere. Rishi works alongside his team to manage the core IP network, managing infrastructure in a multi-vendor environment across several geographically diverse sites. Before taking on this role, Rishi worked at the University of the West Indies to develop a small network management solution (NMS) to measure several KPIs across a network by employing small probes in the network.

About the reviewer

Rishalin Pillay with over 11 years of cybersecurity experience has acquired a vast number of skills consulting for Fortune 500 companies while participating in projects involving the performance of tasks associated with network security design, implementation, and vulnerability analysis.

He holds many certifications that demonstrate his knowledge and expertise in the cybersecurity field, including CISSP, CCNP Security, CCSPA, MCSE, MCT, A+, and Network+.

Rishalin currently works at a large software company as a senior cybersecurity engineer.

Packt is searching for authors like you

If you're interested in becoming an author for Packt, please visit authors.packtpub.com and apply today. We have worked with thousands of developers and tech professionals, just like you, to help them share their insight with the global tech community. You can make a general application, apply for a specific hot topic that we are recruiting an author for, or submit your own idea.

Table of Contents

Preface

CompTIA-certified professionals have always held the upper hand in the IT industry. This book will be your ideal guide to passing and achieving this certification efficiently, learning from industry experts and implementing their practices in order to resolve complex IT issues.

This book will focus on networking concepts; readers will learn everything from network architecture to security, network monitoring, and troubleshooting. This book will not only prepare readers conceptually, but will also help them to pass the N10-007 exam.

This guide will also provide practical exercises at the end of every chapter, where readers can ensure that they understand the concepts fully.

By the end of this book, readers will leverage this guide and the included practice questions to boost their confidence in appearing for the actual certificate.

Who this book is for

This book is intended for readers wanting to pass the CompTIA Network+ certificate. Rookie network engineers and system administrators interested in enhancing their networking skills would also benefit from this book. No prior knowledge of networking is required.

What this book covers

Chapter 1, *The OSI Reference Model and the TCP/IP Stack*, covers both the OSI reference model and TCP/IP stack, and the purpose of network port numbers, protocols, and network design (topologies). Furthermore, the reader will be introduced to IP addressing and subnetting, the fundamentals of routing and switching concepts, and cloud technologies.

Chapter 2, *Network Ports, Protocols, and Topologies*, discusses the importance of network ports on a system and the different protocols that are used in networks. The reader will also learn about network design using diagrams that are known as network topologies.

Chapter 3, *Ethernet*, explains the fundamentals of Ethernet and its importance on a network. This chapter also covers the sub-layers of Ethernet and how each sub-layer interacts with other components and protocols on the network.

Chapter 4, *Understanding IPv4 and IPv6*, delves into the different classes of IP addressing and their assignments. The second half of this chapter will teach the reader how to break down an IP address block into smaller subnetworks for better efficiency.

Chapter 5, *Routing and Switching Concepts*, covers the properties of network traffic, segmentation, network performance concepts, how traffic is routed between networks, and how switching works.

Chapter 6, *Wireless and Cloud Technologies*, explains the fundamentals of wireless technologies and configurations. The second half of this chapter will discuss cloud technologies and their uses.

Chapter 7, *Network Components*, describes the different types of wired media and their connectors and determines the appropriate placement of networking devices on a network.

Chapter 8, *Network Virtualization and WAN Technologies*, helps the reader to understand how virtualization technologies can be used in a network infrastructure and its benefits, while exploring network storage technologies and wide-area network technologies and concepts.

Chapter 9, *Business Continuity and Disaster Recovery Concepts*, focuses on network uptime and ensuring a high availability of network resources. It provides an insight into business continuity and disaster recovery concepts, ensuring that proper network documentation and topology diagrams are available and secured. Concluding this chapter, the reader will be able to use appropriate tools to scan and monitor a network to prevent and mitigate security risks.

Chapter 10, *Network Identity Management and Policies*, discusses how access works on a network and introduces methods for ensuring that it is secure for users and organizations. We will then dive into discussing identity management, policies, and best practices.

Chapter 11, *Network Security Concepts*, focuses primarily on understanding the different types of cybersecurity threats and network attacks, securing a wireless and wired network infrastructure using best practices and mitigation techniques.

Chapter 12, *TCP/IP Security*, focuses on the vulnerabilities in the TCP/IP design and how an attacker can take advantage of weaknesses in the layers of the TCP/IP stack to leverage an attack and exploit these vulnerabilities further. The reader will learn how to adopt best practices and apply security to the TCP/IP stack.

Chapter 13, *Organizational Security*, covers a number of aspects of organizational security, providing the reader with information on physical security concepts, such as the purpose of physical devices and access control methods and concepts. This is important when it comes to helping to restrict unauthorized access to the physical network infrastructure and its components.

Chapter 14, *Troubleshooting a Network*, teaches the reader how to troubleshoot using a systematic approach involving a variety of methods, using the appropriate network security tools to identify and mitigate various network security threats, and troubleshooting both a wired and wireless network infrastructure and network services.

To get the most out of this book

In this book, we need the following:

- PC with working Internet connection
- Wireless router

Download the color images

We also provide a PDF file that has color images of the screenshots/diagrams used in this book. You can download it here: https://www.packtpub.com/sites/default/files/downloads/9781789340501_ColorImages.pdf.

Conventions used

There are a number of text conventions used throughout this book.

CodeInText: Indicates code words in text, database table names, folder names, filenames, file extensions, pathnames, dummy URLs, user input, and Twitter handles. Here is an example: "Using the show ip arp command on a Cisco IOS device, we can once again see the current ARP entries."

A block of code is set as follows:

```
0 AND 1 = 0
0 AND 0 = 0
1 AND 0 = 0
1 AND 1 = 1
```

When we wish to draw your attention to a particular part of a code block, the relevant lines or items are set in bold:

```
[default]
exten => s,1,Dial(Zap/1|30)
exten => s,2,Voicemail(u100)
exten => s,102,Voicemail(b100)
exten => i,1,Voicemail(s0)
```

Any command-line input or output is written as follows:

```
$ mkdir css
$ cd css
```

Bold: Indicates a new term, an important word, or words that you see on screen. For example, words in menus or dialog boxes appear in the text like this. Here is an example: "Select **System info** from the **Administration** panel."

Warnings or important notes appear like this.

Tips and tricks appear like this.

Get in touch

Feedback from our readers is always welcome.

General feedback: If you have questions about any aspect of this book, mention the book title in the subject of your message and email us at customercare@packtpub.com.

Errata: Although we have taken every care to ensure the accuracy of our content, mistakes do happen. If you have found a mistake in this book, we would be grateful if you would report this to us. Please visit www.packt.com/submit-errata, selecting your book, clicking on the Errata Submission Form link, and entering the details.

Piracy: If you come across any illegal copies of our works in any form on the internet, we would be grateful if you would provide us with the location address or website name. Please contact us at `copyright@packt.com` with a link to the material.

If you are interested in becoming an author: If there is a topic that you have expertise in, and you are interested in either writing or contributing to a book, please visit `authors.packtpub.com`.

Reviews

Please leave a review. Once you have read and used this book, why not leave a review on the site that you purchased it from? Potential readers can then see and use your unbiased opinion to make purchase decisions, we at Packt can understand what you think about our products, and our authors can see your feedback on their book. Thank you!

For more information about Packt, please visit `packt.com`.

1
The OSI Reference Model and the TCP/IP Stack

The Internet—the largest computer network in the world today, is constructed from several protocols and protocol suites that work together to allow users (like you and I) to communicate across the globe. A protocol is simply a rule, or a collection of rules and conventions, that a device (such as your computer) follows in order to communicate with other devices around the world (which follow those same rules). A protocol suite is simply a collection of these rules, which work together to allow complex applications on networking devices (for example, web browsers on your computer) to communicate with billions of other devices around the world, through an assortment of networking equipment and media:

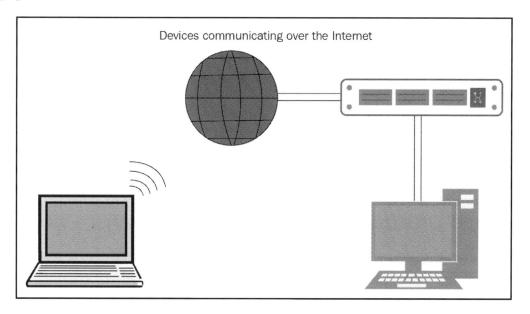

Devices communicating over the Internet

In this chapter, we will discuss two protocol suites in particular that have largely influenced the internet as we know it today:

- The **Open Systems Interconnection** (**OSI**) reference model
- The **Transmission Control Protocol/Internet Protocol** (**TCP/IP**) suite

Although these two protocol suites possess significant differences between them, they both serve as important blocks in the foundation of the internet, and, as such, they both continue to exist as important concepts that budding Network Engineers and System Administrators must understand and appreciate if they wish to become exceptional in their careers.

By understanding these two protocol suites, professionals add an important tool to their arsenal of network troubleshooting weaponry; namely, a systematic, step-by-step approach to be followed in the diagnostic processing of any networking issue, which both simplifies and speeds up the process of pinpointing the root cause of an issue and the rectification of the situation. These suites allow both equipment vendors and Network Engineers to segment the operation of a network into several discrete modular parts or layers, and deal with each layer individually. This allows us to focus on a single part of a system at a time, thus greatly simplifying the development and troubleshooting of networking equipment.

To illustrate this concept in a real-life scenario, consider the following situation—you're a System Administrator in a small IT firm. It's 4 o'clock on a Friday evening and you're excited to clock out and start your weekend. Suddenly, your Syslog Server starts sending emails to all the administrators in your team, complaining about a reachability issue regarding a particular server in your datacenter. Your co-workers immediately begin to panic, knowing that several employees have already left and that they'll likely be working late on a Friday evening. However, since you've mastered your protocol suites, you immediately locate the server and begin troubleshooting the issue from the Physical Layer upwards, quickly locating a disconnected cable to the server and saving your team a lot of troubleshooting time and stress:

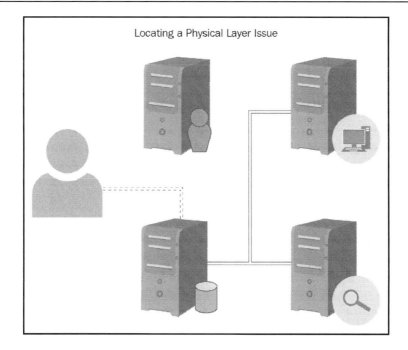

Locating a Physical Layer Issue

For the rest of this chapter, we will first discuss the OSI reference model, delving into a bit of its history and the combination of factors and entities that led to its development and subsequent publication in 1984, before discussing each of the seven layers of the developed model in detail, explaining the purpose of each of the layers and illustrating how each of the layers interact to effect communication between devices across a network. We will then introduce the TCP/IP protocol suite, comparing and contrasting it to the OSI reference model, and similarly explaining and illustrating how each of the layers plays a vital role in transmitting messages across a network. Lastly, we will conclude this chapter with a set of practice questions, which will allow you to test how much information you've retained about the content we've covered in this chapter.

The OSI reference model

Development of the OSI reference model began in the late 1970s in response to the amalgam of proprietary, non-interoperable networking equipment and protocols that vendors were creating at that time. Networks had to be built entirely out of equipment from a single vendor, since networks built from equipment from different vendors could not easily be interconnected. The OSI reference model was thus designed as one solution to this interoperability problem. The development of this model was fueled by two teams—one from the **International Organization for Standardization (ISO)**, and the other from the **Consultative Committee for International Telephony and Telegraphy (CCITT)**. The aim of the model was to become a global framework for protocol development, allowing a diverse array of networking and computing architecture to easily interconnect and communicate.

The standard describing the model, titled ISO/IEC 7498-1, was initially published in 1984, with a second edition succeeding it in 1994.

 You can download and view the actual ISO standard at `https://standards.iso.org/ittf/PubliclyAvailableStandards/s020269_ISO_IEC_7498-1_1994(E).zip`.

The OSI reference model described by the standard consists of seven layers:

- The Application Layer (layer 7)
- The Presentation Layer (layer 6)
- The Session Layer (layer 5)
- The Transport Layer (layer 4)
- The Network Layer (layer 3)
- The Data Link Layer (layer 2)
- The Physical Layer (layer 1)

With this model in mind, protocol developers create their protocols for a specific **N** layer. At this particular layer, termed layer N, a protocol may communicate with other protocols at the same layer, but may not communicate with protocols at other layers directly. A protocol at layer N only utilizes the services provided by the layer following it (N-1 layer), and provides its services to the layer preceding it (N+1 layer):

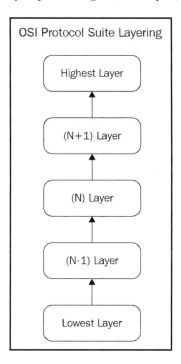

At each N layer, protocols act on several bits of data, specifically:

- **Protocol Control Information (PCI)**: Information communicated among entities at a specific N layer
- **User Data (UD)**: Data transmitted between entities at a specific N layer on behalf of the entities above them at layer N+1, for whom they are providing services
- **Protocol Data Unit (PDU)**: A unit of data specified in a protocol at a layer N, consisting of both PCI and UD
- **Service Data Unit (SDU)**: Some information that is preserved through the lower layer N when transmitted between entities at the higher N+1 layer

Relationship between the Protocol Data Unit (PDU) and Service Data Unit (SDU)

To understand the relationship between this data, consider the following diagram of data being passed down from the upper layers to the lower layers during transmission of data from a sender to a receiver.

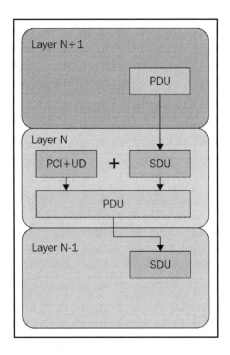

Data is passed down from a higher **Layer N+1** to the current **Layer N** and becomes an SDU at the current layer. Layer N then adds its bits of PCI and UD (if present), and combines all of this data into a new PDU, which is to be passed down again to the lower **Layer N-1** to become a new SDU at that lower layer. This process is termed encapsulation, as each SDU is encapsulated (contained) in a new PDU at the lower layers.

This process of encapsulation continues until the data reaches the lowest layer (the Physical Layer), at which point the data is transmitted over transmission media as a signal until it reaches the intended recipient. Then, the reverse process of decapsulation occurs. During this decapsulation process, protocols at each layer strip off the PCI and UD that are applicable to their layer, and pass the remaining SDU upwards to the higher layers, thereby delivering the data required by the upper layers and thus providing their services to the higher layers.

To understand this concept, consider that Alice, existing at Layer N+1, in this example wants to mail a letter to her friend Bob also existing at Layer N+1 in another country. Alice writes her letter, places it in an envelope, and hands it to the mailman for delivery. The mailman existing at Layer N collects the envelope from Alice and adds it to a pouch of other envelopes that are destined for that country, ensuring that it has all of the necessary information that the other mailmen might need. He then hands the pouch to the team responsible for airmail existing at Layer N-1. This airmail team then places the pouch in a box, ensuring that it has all of the information that their own teams need, and delivers the box to the destination country. The airmail team in the destination country then reads the addressing information that they need, removes the pouch from the box, and passes it up to the mailman in their area. The mailman, in turn, reads the address on the pouch and removes the envelope from the pouch, finally delivering just the envelope to Bob.

In this example, Bob has no idea about the pouches and boxes used to deliver Alice's letter; he only reads the actual letter that Alice has sent. In the same way, higher-level protocols in protocol suites are independent of the protocols below them, allowing certain protocols to be updated or changed without requiring the protocols at other layers to be changed as well.

Additionally, by using this layered OSI model, functionality of a complex networking or computing system can be broken up and grouped into each of the layers, with similar functions being collected in a single layer. This allows an engineer to easily describe the workings of that system by beginning at either the top or bottom or the model and working their way to the other end, describing the function or group of functions provided at each layer as they move through the model.

This concept becomes incredibly important to an engineer or administrator during the troubleshooting process. Rather than randomly trying things in an attempt to diagnose and solve issues on a system, engineers and administrators are now able to begin at one end and work through protocols at each layer, thereby developing a logical methodology for troubleshooting. CompTIA refers to this as the top-to-bottom, or bottom-to-top, troubleshooting methodology.

In the next section, we will discuss each of the layers of the OSI model in detail, which will help you understand which protocols can be grouped into which layers, and thus determine the steps to take in troubleshooting the protocols comprising a system.

The seven layers of the OSI model

The following diagram illustrates the seven layers of the OSI model. Communication between peer protocols (protocols at the same layer in different systems) is established using the same processes of encapsulation and decapsulation that we discussed previously. Remember that protocols may communicate with protocols in remote systems at the same layer, but not with protocols in different layers of those remote systems. PDUs are therefore exchanged between corresponding layers in remote systems referred to as open systems in the OSI model through physical media interconnections, allowing networking and computing devices to communicate all the way around the world:

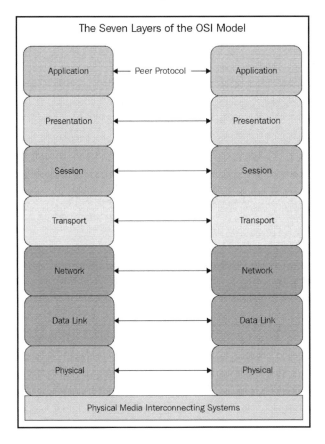

Professionals and students alike have come up with several mnemonics and acronyms to help them remember the names of each of the layers. One such mnemonic is **All People Seem To Need Data Processing**, with the first letter of each word in the mnemonic corresponding to the first letter of each word in the OSI model. Feel free to make up your own method of remembering these layers!

Before delving into descriptions of each of the individual layers, it is important to distinguish between two important terms that often arise in discussions of protocol stacks—**connection-mode** transmissions and **connectionless-mode** transmissions. In a connection-mode or connection-oriented transmission, an association must first be established between two or more peer protocols before data can be transferred between these peer protocols. In contrast, in connectionless-mode transmissions, data may be transferred between peer protocols without a prior connection establishment.

Now, let's explore what each of these layers are actually responsible for.

Application Layer

The Application Layer (layer 7) is the highest layer in the OSI reference model (although you may sometimes hear coworkers joke about end users being the theoretical eighth layer). This is the layer that most end users of networks and systems are familiar with, as it is responsible for directly providing services to application processes or programs that we use on a day-to-day basis. This layer also encompasses any other services that are not provided by the lower layers. This includes functions of programs, as well as end users (the people using these devices). As the highest layer in the model, the Application Layer provides the means for processes and end users to access and interact with the OSI protocol stack. Applications and protocols that we utilize in our machines (such as web browsers and email clients) are categorized in this layer. Devices such as desktop computers, mobile phones, and special layer 7 or Application Layer firewalls operate at this layer. Common protocols at this layer include X.500 (used to provide electronic directory services) and X.400 (a message handling system).

Presentation Layer

The Presentation Layer (layer 6) follows, and is responsible for how information is represented while it's being transferred between Application Layer entities. This method of data representation is called the **transfer syntax**. Remember that lower layers in the protocol stack provide services to upper layers in the stack. In this case, the Presentation Layer makes a set of transfer syntaxes, which are available to the Application Layer. This layer therefore provides services such as encryption (ensuring that data is not easily readable while being transferred), decryption (making the data readable again), and translation of data between different structures. One protocol that exists at this layer is the X.216 protocol (the presentation service).

Session Layer

The Session Layer (layer 5) is the next layer in the OSI model. This layer is responsible for providing presentation layer protocols with a means to organize and synchronize their communication. This layer allows protocols above it to establish session connections, to exchange data in an orderly fashion, and to finally tear down or release the connection. Additionally, this layer may provide other services such as exception handling services (generating error dialogues when problems occur with the connection). An example of a protocol that exists at this layer is the X.215 protocol (the session service).

Transport Layer

Below the Session Layer is the Transport Layer (layer 4). This layer in the model is responsible for the transparent transferring of data between protocols at the session layer, providing a reliable and cost-effective means of transferring data from the preceding layers. This layer determines how best to utilize the available resources below it (the network services) in order to meet the performance demands of the session layer protocols above it. The Transport Layer assigns transport addresses to each Session Layer protocol that requires its services, and then uses these addresses to establish communication between Session Layer protocols. This communication may be connection-oriented or connectionless, and may allow multiple connections to the same Session Layer protocol. This layer may additionally provide services such as data segmentation (the breaking up of large chunks of data into smaller pieces), the generation of acknowledgements (providing a message when a chunk of data is delivered), and data reordering (ensuring that data is processed in the correct order on the receiving side). Examples of protocols at this layer include X.224 (the connection-mode service protocol) and X.234 (the connectionless-mode service protocol).

Network Layer

The next layer in the OSI reference model is the Network Layer (layer 3). This layer is responsible for providing the means to establish, maintain, and tear down network connections between network devices and computing systems in an interconnected system. It provides a means to transparently transfer data between transport layer protocols in different machines. This transportation of data is facilitated by network addresses, which uniquely identify each end system in an OSI interconnected system. The OSI model stipulates that network connections at this layer must be point-to-point (from a single system to only one other system), although it supports complex physical networking configurations.

Additionally, the Network Layer provides services for routing and relaying (moving data around networks and subnetworks), and error detection and recovery. Devices that operate at this layer include routers and layer 3 switches. Examples of protocols at this layer include the **Intermediate System to Intermediate System (IS-IS)** intra-domain routing protocol and the **End System to Intermediate System (ES-IS)** routing exchange protocol.

Data Link Layer

The Data Link Layer (layer 2) is the next layer in the reference model. This layer is responsible for the provision of both connection-oriented and connectionless communications among network protocols, through the transfer of data link SDUs. The connections in this layer are also facilitated by addresses called (unsurprisingly) data link addresses. These addresses provide a means for Network Layer protocols to identify each other, and to establish data link connections between themselves. In addition to setting up these connections, the data link layer also provides error notifications, sequence control (ordering of bits of data), and **Quality of Service (QoS)** parameters. These QoS parameters may allow a network protocol to specify certain requirements, such as the minimum throughput (speed at which data is transferred across a link) or the maximum tolerable error rate on the link. This layer can be further segmented into two sub layers—the **Medium Access Control (MAC)** and the **Logical Link Control (LLC)** sub layers. The LLC is responsible for providing addressing, flow control, error detection, and identification of which Network Layer protocol is utilizing the services at the Data Link Layer, while the MAC controls how hosts access the physical media. Devices that operate at this layer include switches and bridges. One example of a Data Link Layer protocol is the X.212 data link service protocol.

Physical Layer

Lastly, at the very base of the OSI model, exists the Physical Layer. This layer provides the electrical, mechanical, and functional methods to move the actual bits of data (the 1s and 0s that encompass data in its raw forms) between networking and computing devices in order to facilitate the transparent transmission of bit streams between Data Link protocols. This movement of data is supported by various forms of media (both wired and wireless). Examples include copper cables or wireless channels. Data being transmitted across these various forms of media may flow in either half-duplex mode (in one direction at a time) or in full-duplex mode (in both directions simultaneously). Devices that operate at this layer include hubs and repeaters.

Communication using the relay system

Together, these seven layers work in tandem to facilitate communication across end systems. The top four layers (the Application, Presentation, Session, and Transport Layers) are generally considered to be the upper layers, while the lower three layers (Network, Data Link, and Physical Layers) are considered to be the lower layers. It is important to note that not all seven layers are required to be implemented on all of the devices that are present in the network. Some devices simply act as relay agents, supporting the lower layer protocols, while not decapsulating and processing the upper layers:

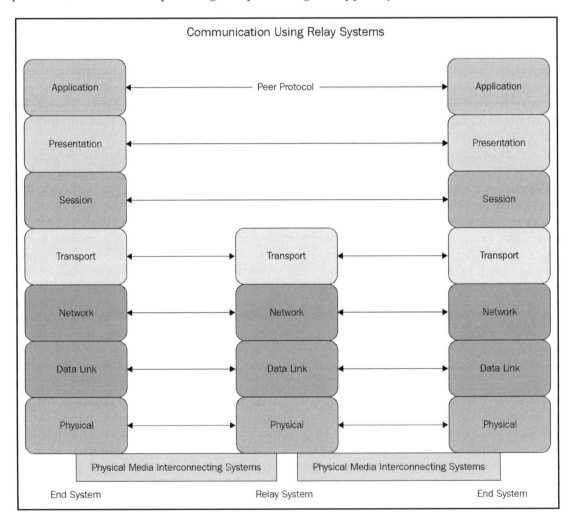

To illustrate the preceding diagram, consider that the two end devices being used are computers. Applications (such as web browsers) run on these computers and communicate at layer 7, but data for those applications may pass through relay devices that cannot run these applications. These relay devices may be equipment such as routers (devices that read addresses at the Network Layer and move packets between networks) or switches (devices that read addresses at the Data Link Layer and move frames between their ports). Routers, switches, broadcast domains, and collision domains will be discussed in depth in later chapters.

Now that we've explored the seven layers of the OSI reference model and described how systems exchange data using the processes of encapsulation and decapsulation, let's take a step back and establish some context for what we've learned. The OSI model, while being an important tool for explaining concepts and helping professionals develop methodical approaches to troubleshooting, is not widely implemented in the industry today. The reasons for this are numerous, but the most important factor is the existence of a second suite of protocols called the TCP/IP protocol suite or, alternatively, the IP suite. However, the distinctions between both models is often blurred, and many professionals combine the concepts of the OSI reference model with the devices and protocols that are in use today.

 You can read more about the battle between the OSI and TCP/IP models at https://spectrum.ieee.org/tech-history/cyberspace/osi-the-intern et-that-wasnt.

In the following section, we will examine this ubiquitous IP suite and consider how it compares to the OSI reference model.

The TCP/IP protocol suite

The IP suite, also called the TCP/IP protocol suite because of two of the key protocols in the stack, TCP and IP, is described in RFC 1122. The **Internet Engineering Task Force (IETF)** frequently publishes these technical documents related to the internet in the form of **Request For Comments (RFCs)**.

 You can read the entire RFC 1122 at https://tools.ietf.org/html/rfc1122.

In this RFC, the TCP/IP suite is defined as consisting of four layers:

- Application Layer (layer 4)
- Transport Layer (layer 3)
- Internet Layer (layer 2)
- Data Link Layer (layer 1)

We can immediately notice some key differences between both models. The OSI model we discussed previously consisted of seven layers, while this TCP/IP model consists of only four. The Presentation and Session Layers of the OSI model have been absorbed into the Application Layer, while the Physical and Data Link Layers of the OSI model have been combined to form the Link Layer here. The Internet Layer corresponds to the Network Layer of the OSI model, while the Transport Layer remains unchanged. This simplified structure of TCP/IP was actually a key factor in its dominance over the OSI model.

However, in spite of these differences, many of the concepts we discussed in the OSI reference model are also applicable to the TCP/IP suite. Applications still utilize the concepts of encapsulation and decapsulation that we discussed previously, and protocols at a particular layer still communicate with protocols at that same layer in end hosts (called **internet hosts** in the RFC). In the following section, we will dive into these layers in more detail, and show you how the applications we use every day utilize the TCP/IP protocol suite to transmit data to and from applications on other hosts across the internet.

The four layers of the TCP/IP protocol suite

The following diagram serves to illustrate the four layers of the TCP/IP protocol suite and to build upon the knowledge we gained during our study of the OSI reference model to illustrate data flows through each of the layers during the process of encapsulation. At each layer, data is passed down to the layer directly underneath and becomes an SDU or payload at that lower layer. A header, containing information that this lower layer requires, is then added to the SDU/payload, before the process is again repeated for the layer below it. Once the data reaches the Link Layer, it is transmitted across physical media before the reverse process of decapsulation begins:

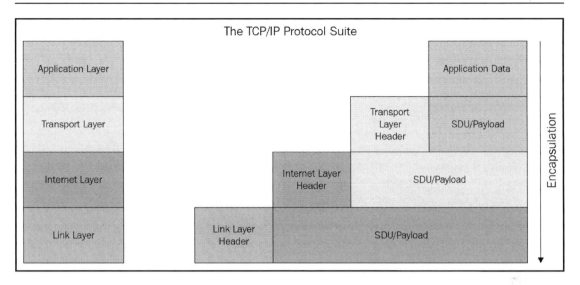

Let's briefly discuss each of the layers that comprise the TCP/IP protocol suite:

- **Application Layer**: At the very top of the protocol stack exists the Application Layer. The programs that we use every day on our desktop computers and mobile devices exist at this layer. For example, every time you request a web page in your browser, you use the **Hypertext Transfer Protocol** (**HTTP**) or **Hypertext Transfer Protocol Secure** (**HTTPS**) protocol. Protocols at this layer create data that needs to be transmitted to or received from other internet hosts.

- **Transport Layer**: The Transport Layer exists just below the Application Layer, and serves to provide the means for Application Layer protocols above it to transfer data. Devices such as desktop computers and mobile devices also run Transport Layer protocols. There are two well-known protocols at this layer—TCP and the **User Datagram Protocol** (**UDP**). TCP provides connection-oriented transmission of data, requiring a connection to be set up between internet hosts before data can be transmitted, but also providing features such as reliable, in-sequence delivery of data. UDP, on the other hand, is a connectionless protocol that does not require any setup before data can be transmitted, but also does not offer features such as guaranteed delivery of data. Applications access the services of Transport Layer protocols (and, by extension, lower layer protocols) through logical ports. For example, the HTTP protocol uses the well-known TCP port 80. The concept of logical ports and which protocols are associated with which well-known ports will be discussed in more detail later.

- **Internet Layer**: The Internet Layer exists just below the Transport Layer, and provides the service of moving data from the Transport Layer across networks, using forms of internet addressing. IP has become the most utilized protocol at this layer, and you are certain to deal with IP addresses from both version 4 of the protocol, IPv4, as well as version 6, IPv6. Other protocols that exist at this layer are the **Internet Control Message Protocol (ICMP)** and the **Internet Group Management Protocol (IGMP)**. Devices that operate at this layer include routers and layer 3 switches.
- **Link Layer**: At the bottom of the TCP/IP protocol suite, we will find the Link Layer. This layer operates only on the local segment that a host is physically connected to, and is responsible for delivering data between devices that are connected in the same local segment/network. Protocols at this layer include the **Address Resolution Protocol (ARP)**, Ethernet, and the **Neighbor Discovery Protocol (NDP)**.

Now that we've covered the services that each layer in the TCP/IP protocol suite provides, let's see how applications can use these layers to actually communicate.

Communication using the TCP/IP protocol suite

The communication using the TCP/IP protocol suite can be seen in the following diagram:

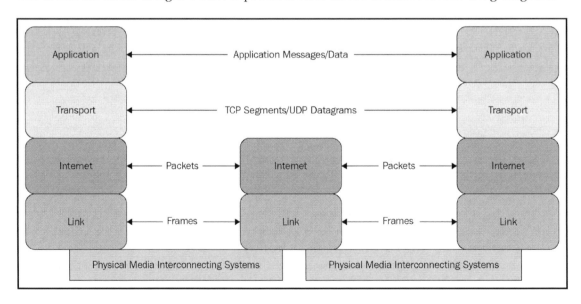

This preceding diagram combines all of the concepts we discussed previously. For a host to transmit messages, application messages/data are encapsulated down the protocol suite. At the Transport Layer, PDUs being transmitted between hosts are commonly called TCP segments or UDP datagrams, depending on which Transport Layer protocol is being used. At the Internet Layer, PDUs are termed IP packets, or simply packets, while PDUs transmitted between Link Layers are termed Ethernet frames, or simply frames, which are then transmitted out the wire as bits (or grouped together to form bytes). The following screenshot shows how **Wireshark**, a popular tool used to analyze protocols, categorizes data according to protocols that have been arranged in the same layers we have discussed:

```
> Frame 730: 356 bytes on wire (2848 bits), 356 bytes captured (2848 bits) on interface 0
> Ethernet II, Src: Micro-St_01:19:90 (30:9c:23:01:19:90), Dst: GemtekTe_fa:97:78 (1c:49:7b:fa:97:78)
> Internet Protocol Version 4, Src: 192.168.1.53, Dst: 93.184.216.34
> Transmission Control Protocol, Src Port: 56933, Dst Port: 80, Seq: 356, Ack: 974, Len: 302
> Hypertext Transfer Protocol
```

Summary

In this chapter, we've covered the OSI reference model and the TCP/IP or IP suite, explaining why these models are significant in the field of networking and how data is actually transmitted across networks by using protocols implemented at the different layers. In the next chapter, we will discuss how communication occurs on a network in more depth by using the various network ports, protocols, and topologies.

Questions

1. How many layers constitute the OSI reference model?
    1. 4
    2. 7
    3. 5
    4. 1

2. A technician is troubleshooting a connectivity problem on a host machine and his manager asks him to troubleshoot using the bottom-to-top methodology. What layer of the OSI model should he start at?

    1. The Data Link Layer

    2. The Network Layer

    3. The Application Layer

    4. The Physical Layer

3. An engineer has captured the following output from a host machine:

```
∨ Transmission Control Protocol, Src Port: 56933, Dst Port: 80, Seq: 356, Ack: 974, Len: 302
      Source Port: 56933
      Destination Port: 80
      [Stream index: 14]
      [TCP Segment Len: 302]
      Sequence number: 356     (relative sequence number)
      [Next sequence number: 658     (relative sequence number)]
      Acknowledgment number: 974     (relative ack number)
      0101 .... = Header Length: 20 bytes (5)
   >  Flags: 0x018 (PSH, ACK)
      Window size value: 252
      [Calculated window size: 64512]
      [Window size scaling factor: 256]
      Checksum: 0x9905 [unverified]
      [Checksum Status: Unverified]
      Urgent pointer: 0
   >  [SEQ/ACK analysis]
   >  [Timestamps]
      TCP payload (302 bytes)
```

Which layer of the OSI reference model is this output most applicable to?

    1. The Transport Layer

    2. The Network Layer

    3. The Application Layer

    4. The Session Layer

4. A network architect has designed a plan for connecting hosts in a new office, but he has realized that he needs to provide more physical ports for these hosts. Which of the following layer 2 devices would be most appropriate to provide these ports?
   1. A router
   2. A switch
   3. A hub
   4. A WAP

5. Which sub layer of the Data Link Layer controls which host is allowed to access a shared Ethernet link at a particular point in time?
   1. The LLC sub layer
   2. The MAC sub layer
   3. The IP sub layer
   4. The UDP sub layer

6. An engineer is examining frames from a particular host machine that is exhibiting issues on the network, and notices that headers from higher-level protocols are present in the frame. This is due to the process of:
   1. Decapsulation
   2. Connectionless transport
   3. Encryption
   4. Encapsulation

7. A security administrator has received notice that management wishes to block access to a particular application on port 80, but not interfere with other traffic communicating through that same port. What device will be most suitable to implement this rule?
   1. A router
   2. A switch
   3. An L7 firewall
   4. An L3 firewall

8. A network administrator is analyzing TCP traffic in an effort to better understand connection-oriented transmissions. What types of PDUs should he be analyzing?
   1. Frames
   2. Datagrams
   3. Segments
   4. Packets

9. The leader of the fiber team has just called to report that a truck has pulled down overhead cables in a particular area, and that services will be interrupted until splicing works can be completed. What layer of the OSI model can this be best classified as?
   1. Physical
   2. Application
   3. Transport
   4. Network

10. An engineer has purchased a wireless repeater that works by simply retransmitting the bits that it receives over its coverage area. What layer does this device most likely operate at?
    1. Network
    2. Data Link
    3. Application
    4. Physical

Network Ports, Protocols, and Topologies

2

In this chapter, we will dive a bit further into understanding how communication occurs on a network and what makes a particular type of message unique. As you have learned about the different layers of both the **Open Systems Interconnection** (**OSI**) reference model and the **Transmission Control Protocol/Internet Protocol** (**TCP/IP**) protocol suite from the previous chapter, you will have realized each layer helps both the upper and lower layers with adding some important information to the **Protocol Data Unit** (**PDU**) and, in return, help with the communication of delivering the message between devices:

OSI Model	PDU	TCP/IP Stack
Application		
Presentation	Data	Application
Session		
Transport	Segment	Transport
Network	Packet	Internet
Data Link	Frame	Network Access/Link
Physical	Bits	

Here, we'll focus on providing a better understanding on the port numbers that reside at the Transport Layer of both the OSI model and the TCP/IP stack, and we'll discuss various network protocols at the Application, Transport, and Internet Layers with their functionalities and various network topologies.

In this chapter, we will discuss the following topics:

- Network port numbers
- Network protocols
- Network topologies
- Introduction to Ethernet and its evolution

Let's dive in!

Technical requirements

The technical requirements are as follows:

- Windows machine
- Ping utility through Windows Command Prompt

Network port numbers

The term **ports** or **network ports** usually means the physical interfaces or ports on a device, such as a router, switch, server, or even a personal computer. A physical port also known as an interface is the connector on a local system such as computer where an Ethernet cable to attach which connects the device to the rest of the network. However, even though these are the physical ports, there are also logical ports within an operating systems or a device. You may ask yourself, *how does a physical port exist within a computer, server, or network appliance such as a router or switch?* Here, we are going to further break down the concepts of these logical ports or what are known as network ports.

To get started, we will use a simple analogy to help you understand the fundamentals of logical ports on a system. Let's imagine you own an organization; at the organization's headquarters, a single building with many floors, there are elevators for easy access to the upper floors. Each floor is occupied by a unique department and its respective staff members. Each day, the employees use the elevators, which transports them to their relevant department and back. Let's imagine the physical building is a computing system such as a server; there are doors at each relevant department, and the employees of the organization are different types of network traffic entering and leaving the system on a daily basis.

Now let's put all the piece together and get everything working in harmony. Each time an employee (network traffic) enters the building (operating system), they take the elevator (Transport Layer), which delivers the employee to their respective doorway (logical port) at their department (service/protocol at the Application Layer). From this analogy, you may have realized each type of network traffic (employee) enters their relevant department using a doorway; this doorway is a logical port existing within the operating system (building) and won't be visible to any entity outside of the system.

Each type of network traffic is sent to a specific logical port for further processing before it's delivered to the Application Layer. Chapter 1, *The OSI Reference Model and the TCP/IP Stack* discussed the details of each layer, such as what happens to the PDU (data, segments, packets, frames, and bits) as it moves up or down either in the OSI reference model or the TCP/IP stack. At this point, you may be wondering the following:

- *Who manages and regulates the port numbers?*
- *How many logical port numbers are there?*
- *Where can I get more information about a specific port?*

The **Internet Assigned Numbers Authority (IANA)** is the governing body that manages and regulates **Internet Protocol (IP)** addresses and port numbers assignments. According to the Service Name and Transport Protocol Port Number Registry of IANA, there are a total of 65,535 ports. Each of which are either TCP or **User Datagram Protocol (UDP)** port types; however, there are some ports which are both TCP and UDP types.

The ranges of the ports are categorized into three simple categories for easy identification:

Port Ranges	Category
0-1,023	Well-Known Ports
1,024 - 49,151	Registered Ports
49,152 - 65,535	Private/Dynamic Ports

To get further information on the assignments of port by IANA, you can visit: https://www.iana.org/assignments/service-names-port-numbers/service-names-port-numbers.xhtml. **Internet Engineering Task Force (IETF)** defines the procedures for managing the service names and port numbers by RFC 6335. Further information can be found at https://tools.ietf.org/html/rfc6335.

Now that we have a clear understanding of the roles of ports on a system, let's dive a bit deeper in defining some of the well-known ports and their purposes on a network.

Network protocols

A **network protocol** defines the rules and procedures in which data communication occurs among devices over a network. Without predefined rules or procedures, the messages traversing a network would be without any particular formatting and may not be meaningful to the recipient device. To further discuss the importance of having protocols on a network/system, we will use the following analogy to provide you with a real-world situation compared to network protocols.

Let's imagine you work for an organization, ACME Corporation, and within the company there are many policies and procedures that govern the handling of day-to-day transactions and activities within the organization. One of the most important procedures is the emergency evacuation plan. If there's an emergency within the organization, the procedure documents the rules and guidelines each employee must follow to ensure they are escorted safely out of the compound to the assembly point while the health and safety officers conduct their checks before allowing anyone to re-enter the compound. If proper procedures and guidelines didn't exist within ACME Corporation, people would be attempting to exit the compound in a haphazard manner, which may result in further safety issues. With procedures and guidelines, the employees would evacuate in a systematic manner.

This is the same concept that is applied to a network. There are many different protocols that use a network to communicate with another device. Each protocol has their own uniqueness in which the information is formatted and the rules and procedures it follows while traveling on the network until it is received by the intending recipient and process upward on the OSI reference model or the TCP/IP stack.

 The ISO OSI is simple a reference model and it not actually implemented on a system; however, network professionals use this model mostly during network and security discussions and troubleshooting concepts. The TCP/IP stack is implemented in all network-related devices.

Now you have understand the concepts of network protocols, let's discuss some of the popular protocols with their respective port numbers and their importance on a network.

Protocol types

In this section, we are going deeper into discussing various types of protocols and their characteristics. We are going to cover the functionality of **Internet Control Message Protocol (ICMP)**, TCP, UDP, and IP.

ICMP

On a network, whether on a **Local Area Network (LAN)** or a **Wide Area Network (WAN)**, host devices will be communicating to exchange data and information among one another and sometimes an error can occur. Let's imagine you are sending a packet to a server on the internet, and, while your computer is initializing the connection between itself and the remote server, it provides an error stating, it is unable to connect. As an upcoming networking professional, you may wonder why both devices are unable to successfully establish a connection between themselves.

ICMP defined by RFC 792 is typically used to provide error reporting on a network. There are many types of ICMP messages that provide different actions and give feedback regarding whether an error occurred and the issue that exists.

ICMP message types

There are many ICMP message types; however, we'll be discussing the main ones, which will be very useful as a network professional.

ICMP Type 0 – Echo Reply

The Type 0 message is when a sender device is responding to an ICMP Type 8 – Echo Request.

ICMP Type 3 – Destination Unreachable

The Type 3 is given then a destination cannot be found or is simply unreachable by the sender.

However, the ICMP Type 3 gives a bit more details by adding a code to the message:

- Code 0—network unreachable
- Code 1—host unreachable
- Code 2—protocol unreachable
- Code 3—port unreachable

Therefore, combining the ICMP Type 3 message with a unique code gives you, the network professional, a better idea of the error on the network.

ICMP Type 5 – Redirect

An ICMP Type 5 message occurs when a default gateway device such as a router notifies the sender about the destination is directly connected to another gateway which exists on the same network. One reason for a redirect is that the second gateway device or router may have a better route to the destination or a shorter path.

ICMP Type 8 – Echo Request

The ICMP Type 8 message is used by a sender device to check for basic network connectivity between itself and the intended recipient device. Any device receiving an ICMP Type 8 message, responds with an ICMP Type 0 – Echo Reply.

ICMP Type 11 – Time Exceeded

Whenever a packet or message is sent on a network, a **Time to Live** (**TTL**) value is attached. The TTL value decreases after passing reach layer 3 devices such as a router along the way to the destination. If the TTL value reaches zero before arriving at the intended destination, the last router to change the TTL value to zero will send an ICMP Type 11 message back to the sender indicating the TTL expired and the packet has been discarded before reaching its destination. The -i parameter adjusts the TTL value on the ICMP message:

```
C:\>ping 8.8.8.8 -i 4

Pinging 8.8.8.8 with 32 bytes of data:
Reply from 179.60.213.149: TTL expired in transit.
Reply from 179.60.213.66: TTL expired in transit.
Reply from 179.60.213.66: TTL expired in transit.
Reply from 179.60.213.66: TTL expired in transit.

Ping statistics for 8.8.8.8:
    Packets: Sent = 4, Received = 4, Lost = 0 (0% loss),
```

Without adjusting the TTL value of the ICMP Type 8 message, the sender received an ICMP Type 0 message indicating successful transmission between both devices:

```
C:\>ping 8.8.8.8

Pinging 8.8.8.8 with 32 bytes of data:
Reply from 8.8.8.8: bytes=32 time=52ms TTL=120
Reply from 8.8.8.8: bytes=32 time=52ms TTL=120
Reply from 8.8.8.8: bytes=32 time=52ms TTL=120
Reply from 8.8.8.8: bytes=32 time=52ms TTL=120

Ping statistics for 8.8.8.8:
    Packets: Sent = 4, Received = 4, Lost = 0 (0% loss),
Approximate round trip times in milliseconds:
    Minimum = 52ms, Maximum = 52ms, Average = 52ms
```

 Further information of ICMP can also be found at `https://tools.ietf.org/html/rfc792`. Further information of all the ICMP message types can be found at: `https://www.iana.org/assignments/icmp-parameters/icmp-parameters.xhtml#icmp-parameters-codes-7`.

A simple and easy-to-use utility is **Ping**. The Ping utility harnesses the functionality of ICMP and provides meaningful feedback whether communication is successful, unsuccessful, redirected, the destination host or network is unreachable, and so on. The Ping utility is integrated into almost every, if not all, modern-day operating systems, from desktops to servers, and even mobile-operating systems.

The `ping` command can be executed in Windows Command Prompt or the Terminal of Linux-based operating systems. When a user initiates the `ping` command with a destination address, the Ping utility sends an ICMP Type 8 message to the intended destination. The syntax for checking basic connectivity is as follows:

```
ping <ip address or hostname>
ping 8.8.8.8
ping www.google.com
```

TCP

When you send a letter using your local postal service, have you ever wondered whether your letter reaches the destination successfully, whether it was prioritized within the processing system of the mail service for delivery, or *whether you would receive confirmation that your letter was delivered successfully?* Consider that, in a network, there are the same concerns with devices. If one device sends a datagram to another device, whether on the same LAN or a remote network, *what reassurance is given for the guarantee of the datagram (message) between the sender and the receiver?*

TCP defined by RFC 793 is a connection-oriented protocol that operates on the Transport Layer of both the OSI reference model and the TCP/IP protocol stack. It is designed to provide reliable transportation of the datagrams over a network. It provides reassurance by initializing a three-way handshake before communicating data between the sender and the receiver. Let's imagine there are two devices that want to communicate and use TCP to ensure their messages are delivered successfully. Let's use a simple analogy to further explain the **TCP three-way handshake**; we have two devices, Bob and Alice. Bob wants to exchange data with Alice but needs to ensure the data being sent is successfully delivered, so Bob decides to use the TCP to guarantee the delivery.

Bob initializes the TCP three-way handshake by sending a TCP **Synchronization (SYN)** packet to Alice indicating he wants to establish a session or connection. Alice, upon receiving the SYN packet, responds to Bob indicating she also wants to establish a session and acknowledges receipt of the SYN packet using a TCP **Synchronization/Acknowledgment (SYN/ACK)** packet. Bob, upon receiving the TCP SYN packet from Alice, responds with a TCP **Acknowledgement (ACK)** packet. Now the TCP three-way handshake is established, data can be exchanged between the two devices; with each datagram sent across the session between Bob and Alice, an ACK packet will be sent to confirm successful delivery of the message:

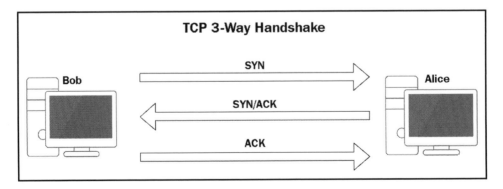

What if Bob sends a message to Alice and Bob does not receive an ACK packet from Alice? In this situation, Bob would retransmit the data again after certain intervals until an ACK packet is sent back to Bob. Another question you may have is—*how does TCP terminate a session gracefully?* Each device sends a TCP **Finish** (**FIN**) packet to each other, indicating they would like to terminate the session:

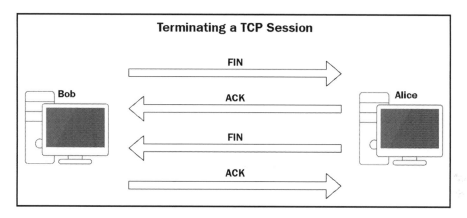

Furthermore, if we use a network protocol analyzer tool, such as **Wireshark** (www.wireshark.org), we can see the packet composition of each datagram passing across the network. The following exhibit is a capture using Wireshark during the writing of this book to demonstrate the TCP three-way handshake:

Source	Destination	Protocol	Length	Info
172.16.17.12	a1488.dscd.akamai.net	TCP	62	58930 → http(80) [SYN] Seq=0 Win=64240 Len=0 MSS=1460 SACK_PERM=1
a1488.dscd.akamai.net	172.16.17.12	TCP	62	http(80) → 58930 [SYN, ACK] Seq=0 Ack=1 Win=29200 Len=0 MSS=1412 SACK_PERM=1
172.16.17.12	a1488.dscd.akamai.net	TCP	54	58930 → http(80) [ACK] Seq=1 Ack=1 Win=64240 Len=0

Another benefit of using TCP is its ability to reassemble packets that may have arrived in an out-of-order fashion at the destination.

User Datagram Protocol (UDP)

UDP defined by RFC 768, is a connectionless protocol. This protocol also operates at the Transport Layer of both the OSI reference model and the TCP/IP protocol stack. However, unlike TCP, UDP does not provide any guarantee or reassurance of the delivery of datagrams across a network. Not all protocols at the Application Layer use TCP; there are many layer-7 protocols that use UDP.

You may be wondering, *why would an upper-layer protocol use UDP instead of TCP?* Let's do a brief recap of TCP; when devices are using TCP as their preferred Transport Layer protocol, for each message sent between the sender and the receiver, an ACK packet is returned. This means if a sender such as Bob, sends 100 TCP packets to Alice over the network, Alice would return 100 ACK packets to Bob. Let's imagine a larger network with hundreds or thousands of devices, or even the internet, where everyone would use TCP—the returned traffic in this case of the ACK packets would create a lot of overhead in the network and therefore cause a lot of congestion. This is a bit similar to having a roadway when the number of vehicles are increasing—this would cause traffic congestion.

Let's use another analogy—a lot of people globally use YouTube for many reasons. Imagine if the video traffic used TCP instead of UDP; YouTube has millions of users daily who stream content on the site. If each user were to send a TCP ACK packet back to YouTube on that very large scale, the YouTube network and even the internet would be congested with a lot of TCP ACK packets and would cause the network performance to degrade. Therefore, not all upper-layer protocols use TCP because of this issue.

The way in which UDP behaves is simply to send datagrams without any reassurance or guarantee of delivery of the message. When devices are communicating over a network, the path taken by each packet may be different than the other, and therefore may be received in an out-of-order sequence. UDP does not provide any mechanisms for reassembly of the packet, unlike TCP, which aids with the reassembly and reordering of the packets when they are received from the sender.

 Voice and video traffic uses UDP as the preferred Transport Layer protocol.

Comparison of TCP and UDP

The key differences between TCP and UDP are shown in the following table:

TCP	UDP
• Reliable • Uses acknowledgments to confirm receipt of data • Resends data of any of the packets are lost during transmission • Delivers the data in a sequential order and handles reassembly • Applications—HTTP, FTP, SMTP, and Telnet	• Very fast in delivery of data • Very low overhead on the network • Does not require any acknowledgment packets • If packets are lost during transmission, it does not resend any lost data • Does not send data in order or handles the reassembly • Applications—DHCP, DNS, SNMP, TFTP, VoIP, and IPTV

There are protocols that use both TCP and UDP, such as DNS and SNMP.

IP

During the course of this book, IP is mentioned a quite a lot, but *what exactly is IP?* IP, as defined by RFC 791, was created for operations in interconnected systems of packet-switched computer communication networks. IP operates at the Network Layer of the OSI reference model and the Internet Layer of the TCP/IP protocol suite.

However, IP has three main characteristics:

- **Connectionless**: The sender of the message does not know whether the recipient is available; the protocol sends the messages as is. If the message is successfully delivered to the intended recipient, the sender does not know whether the message arrives. Since IP behaves a bit like UDP, there is not session create prior to the data communication, which leads to the receiver not being aware of any incoming messages.
- **Uses best effort**: Best effort implies that IP is unreliable. Similar to UDP, IP does not provide any guarantee of the data between a sender and receiver. Furthermore, if any data is lost during the transmission, IP does not have the functionality to facilitate the resending of any lost packets.
- **Media independent**: The benefit of using IP is it's independent of the type of media being used for transporting the data between the sender and the receiver. At times, there are many different types of media between the sender and the receiver, such as copper cables, radio frequency, and fiber optic. IP datagrams can be transported over any media type; the data link is responsible for formatting the frame for each type of media as it leaves a device.

Protocols and ports

Here, we are going to discuss some of the well-known protocols at the Application Layer.

File Transfer Protocol (FTP)

FTP defined by RFC 959 is used to transfer files between systems either on a LAN or a remote network. This is beneficial to users who would like to simply upload, download, or even remove files from a remote system. FTP provides user authentication: a username and password combination as an extra layer of security.

Unlike some protocols, FTP uses two ports, port 20 is used for **Data** (data transfer) and port 21 is for **Control** (parsing of commands):

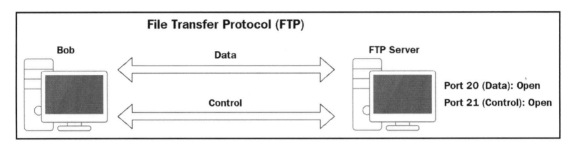

 If you're interested in setting up your own FTP server, check out an open source application called FileZilla (www.filezilla-project.org), which provides both an FTP client and and FTP server applications.

Secure Shell (SSH), Secure Copy (SCP), and Secure FTP (SFTP)

SSH defined by RFC 4250 to 4256 is designed to provide secure remote Terminal access over an unsecure network. To further understand how SSH works, I will provide you with a real-world scenario—a few years ago, I worked for a large telecommunication provider and part of my job was to monitor the entire network infrastructure and resolve any issue that may arise. TELCO provides services to multiple countries regionally; however, as an engineer, I was based in one location, which was their main operation center. Being at a single location and monitoring for any faults on the network made me wonder—*how am I to access the devices between my location and another country that may be experiencing an issue?* One of the main concerns was security, because my connection may be passing through multiple networks and we need to ensure the data-in-motion is keep confidential. The preferred choice was the SSH protocol; the remote device was configured to allow incoming SSH connections from authorized networks/persons, while the user (me) used an SSH client on my local system.

To put it simply, SSH is the preferred protocol of choice in any network environment, primary due to its mechanism to encrypt data between the SSH client and the SSH server. SSH operates on port 22.

 PuTTY (www.putty.org) is a free SSH, Telnet, and serial client application.

SCP provides a secure channel for transferring data, such as files, between two devices, whether these devices are on a local network or a remote network. Imagine you would like to transfer files between your computer and a remote server securely across a network and one main concern is confidentiality; all data being transferred is encrypted between the sender and the receiver. SCP provides this functionality for secure data transfer between devices. SCP uses port 22.

 WinSCP (https://winscp.net/eng/index.php) is a free application that supports SCP, SFTP, and FTP protocols.

SFTP uses port 22 to exchange data securely on a network, unlike FTP, which sends data in plain-text, a malicious user can see what's being sent across between the FTP client and the FTP server. To improve security, SFTP was developed to provide encryption between the client and server while providing the functionality of FTP. This ensures any data/files exchanged are keep confidential from others.

Telnet

Telnet provides remote terminal access between systems. However, unlike SSH, Telnet provides an unsecure connection. Therefore, making the communication between devices vulnerable to network-based attacks. The Telnet protocol operates on port 23.

 It's not recommended to use Telnet on account of security vulnerabilities.

Simple Mail Transfer Protocol (SMTP)

SMTP defined by RFC 821 and 5321 is designed for the transmission of email between systems. *Have you wondered what takes places when you send an email to someone using either an email client application or webmail?* To simply explain the process, when you send an email from your computer using an email client such as Microsoft Outlook or Mozilla Thunderbird, the client application sends the email to the email server, which has port 25 open. The email server will then forward the email to the intended recipient or to another email server that contains the recipient's mailbox. SMTP is used by both the email client and the email server for sending emails:

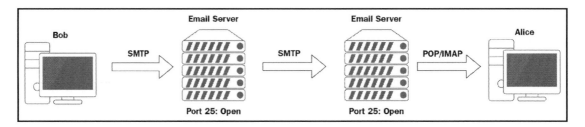

 All email server has port 25 open by default, as SMTP operates on this port. SMTP is used only to send email messages.

Domain Name System (DNS)

All devices on a network have a unique IP address, which allows communication among themselves. However, some networks may be very large, such as the internet, with a lot of devices. Since each device has an IP address, it would eventually become a bit difficult to remember each device's IP address. Let's imagine you want to visit www.facebook.com; this address is known as a host name, and we humans would open our web browser and simply enter www.facebook.com into the address bar within our web browser, and within a few seconds Facebook's website is presented to us. However, in the background, your computer will resolve the host name, www.facebook.com, to the various IP addresses which belongs to Facebook such as, 31.13.71.38:

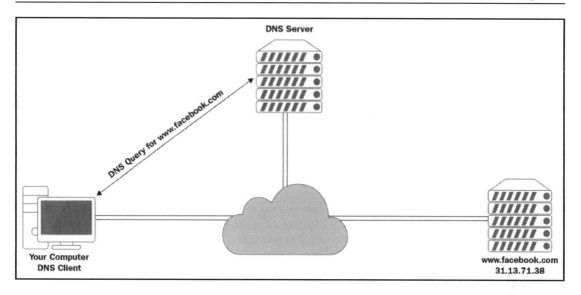

The protocol that is responsible for resolving hostnames to IP addresses is known as DNS. The DNS protocol operates on UDP port 53. However, TCP port 53 is used to exchange DNS entries between one DNS server and another; this process is known as **DNS zone transfer**.

 Further details on the underlying features of DNS can be found at: https://www.isc.org/community/rfcs/dns.

Dynamic Host Configuration Protocol (DHCP)

DHCP defined by RFC 2131 provides network/IP configurations to devices that make an initial connection to a TCP/IP network. Each device on a network requires some IP configurations; these are an IP address, a subnet mask, a default gateway (for communicating outside the local network), and DNS server (for browsing the internet using a host name). *Have you ever noticed whenever you're connected to a network, your device automatically receives those configurations and you can communicate with devices and other services?*

To explain further, when a host (**DHCP Client**) connects to a network, it looks for an available DHCP Server. It does this by sending the **DHCP Discover** packet in search of a **DHCP Server** on the network. Secondly, once a DHCP Server receives the **Discover** packet, it responds directly to the host with a **DHCP Offer** packet providing a potential offer of available IP configurations. Thirdly, the host will respond to the DHCP Server with a **DHCP Request** to confirm the usage of the IP configurations and finally, the DHCP Server sends a **DHCP** Acknowledgement back to host to confirm the request:

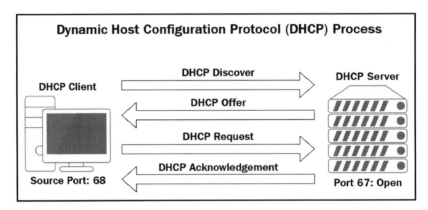

DHCP uses two ports; these are port 67, which is opened on the DHCP Server, and port 68, which used as the source port on the DHCP Client.

The following is a high-level overview of a DHCP Discover packet. Since the host doesn't know the MAC address of the DHCP Server on the network, the destination MAC address of FF:FF:FF:FF:FF:FF is used with a destination port of 67:

DHCP Discover Packet					
Source MAC Address	Destination MAC Address	Source Port Number	Destination Port Number		Trailer
AB:CD:EF:12:34:56	FF:FF:FF:FF:FF:FF	68	67	Payload	FCS

The following is an overview of a DHCP Offer packet; notice in this packet, the DHCP Server MAC address is now included, and therefore the DHCP Request packet can be sent directly to DHCP Server, as the host would have learned the DHCP Server's MAC address:

DHCP Offer Packet					
Source MAC Address	Destination MAC Address	Source Port Number	Destination Port Number		Trailer
AC:DE:F1:DA:44:11	AB:CD:EF:12:34:56	67	68	Payload	FCS

During the exchange of the DHCP messages, the source and destination IP address fields remain unassigned.

Trivial File Transfer Protocol (TFTP)

TFTP, which is defined by RFC 1350, is a simple network protocol that is used to transfer files between a client device and a Trival FTP server. TFTP operates on port 69 and does not require user authentication on the TFTP server. This makes it easy for network administrators and engineers to simply back up and restore network appliance's configurations.

There is a lot of free TFTP server software available out there on the internet, one of which I would like to recommend is SolarWinds TFTP server (www.solarwinds.com).

Hypertext Transfer Protocol (HTTP)

Whenever you want to visit a website, one of the first things you would do is open your web browser and enter the website's address and in a few seconds the web page loads up. The underlying protocol that is used to retrieve the web page is known as the HTTP. HTTP is defined by RFC 2616, 7230, and 7231 and uses request messages to retrieve a **Uniform Resource Locator** (**URL**) or, in other words, a website's address such as https://www.cisco.com/index.html. The client would send an HTTP GET Request message to the intended web server and the server would send a response back.

HTTP is a request and response protocol and, due to its design to transfer data in plain text, is an unsecure protocol.

Post Office Protocol (POP)

POP is designed to retrieve emails from an email server. However, POP operates on port 110 and by default, the emails are downloaded to the email client (such as Microsoft Outlook or Mozilla Thunderbird), then they are deleted from the server:

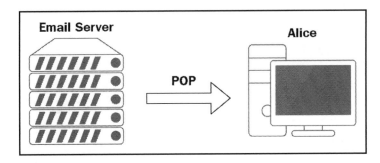

Network Time Protocol (NTP)

In my organizations, it's very important each system has the same time. Having to set the time on hundreds or thousands of systems in a network can be a challenging task. The NTP, defined by RFC 958, 1305, and 5905, is used to synchronize the computer time clocks. NTP uses a server-client model where the NTP Server, which operates on port 123, handles the association of NTP Clients. To explain simply, the time is set on the NTP Server, the NTP Clients then associates to the server, and the clients check whether their local clocks are the same as the NTP Server's; if not, they simply adjust their clock to match the time on the NTP Server's clock. Synchronization of time is very important in many organizations; one the benefits is proper timestamps on log messages, which may be generated from network appliances:

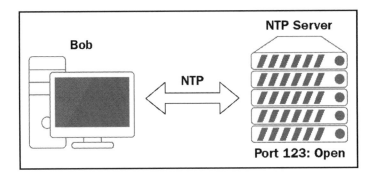

Internet Message Access Protocol (IMAP)

Another protocol that is used to retrieve emails from an email server is known as IMAP. IMAP operates on port 143 and, similar to POP, IMAP downloads a copy of the email messages from the server and the messages as access through an email client, such as Microsoft Outlook or Mozilla Thunderbird:

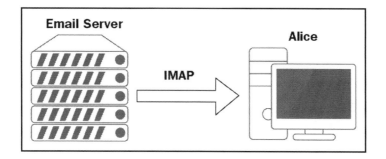

 IMAP does not automatically deletes email messages from the email server. To delete an email from the email server requires manual intervention.

Simple Network Management Protocol (SNMP)

SNMP operates on port 161 (managed device) and 162 (SNMP manager device). SNMP was designed to allow network/system administrators to manage network appliances such as routers, switches, firewalls, and servers over an IP-based network environment. This allows administrators to monitor and manage the network posture by observing the network performance, detecting and resolving network related issues, and planning for future network growth.

SNMP is made up of three components:

- **SNMP Manager** (installed on the client computer)
- **SNMP Agent** (configured on the managed device such as the switch and router)
- **Management Information Base (MIB)**

The following diagram is a simple topology outlining where are each components of the SNMP protocol exist on the network. As mentioned, the SNMP manager is an application of the administrator's computer and the SNMP agent is running on the network appliance such as the router:

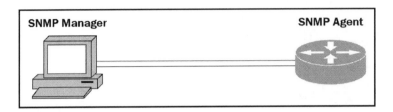

 Spiceworks (www.spiceworks.com) provides a free SNMP monitoring application.

Lightweight Directory Access Protocol (LDAP)

Within an organization, there's usually at least one **Domain Controller** (**DC**) to centrally manage all of the user accounts, user groups, computers, and even the group policies objects. In the Windows Server platform, there's a role called **Active Directory** (**AD**), which handles the management of user accounts (objects). This is like a database, with all of the users' information stored centrally for easy access and management.

Let's imagine an application or an operating system needs to query the user account information with the Windows Server AD service; the LDAP was designed to query and update such directory services. LDAP is not a directory standard but simply a protocol for providing the functionality to make queries and updates to the actual directory—in this case, the directory is the Windows AD platform.

By default, LDAP uses TCP and UDP port 389. However, a secure form of LDAP that uses **Secure Sockets Layer** (**SSL**) and **Transport Layer Security** (**TLS**) encryption is available; this is known as **LDAPS**, which uses port 636.

HTTP Secure (HTTPS)

HTTPS uses port 443 on the web server and provides a secure channel for HTTP communication between a client and a server. With HTTPS, the encryption is currently handled by TLS; however, in previous times, SSL was the dominant protocol for HTTPS encryption, but due to security vulnerabilities, TLS was developed and now is the successor:

Server Message Block (SMB)

SMB protocols uses port 445. The primary purpose of this protocol is to provide access to shared resources such as files, printers, and network shares.

Remote Desktop Protocol (RDP)

RDP was created by Microsoft, which operates on port 3389. This protocol is proprietary to Microsoft platforms and provides a **graphical user interface (GUI)** for remotely connecting to another system over a network:

Network topologies

A network topology is simply the orientation or the layout of objects that are interconnected for the purpose of communication or sharing resources. To put it simply, it's the network diagram displaying where devices are located, the type of media used to physically connect the components, the interfaces or the physical ports used, and the IP addresses of each device.

In the following section, we'll dive a bit deeper into understanding the characteristics and features of the different types of topologies.

Star

The star topology is simple and is used in most modern-day networks. The name star was derived from the from the actual layer of the devices; all of the clients or host devices are connected to a central network intermediary device such as a switch. The benefit is each client device can all access the network simultaneously; however, the intermediary device (switch) goes down, and the clients won't be able to communicate with one another:

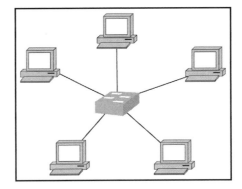

Ring

This type of topology got its name from observing the physical layout, as all of the devices are interconnected in a ring orientation. Whenever a host wants to send data or a message to another device, the data/message passes by each node along the way until it's delivered to the intended recipient:

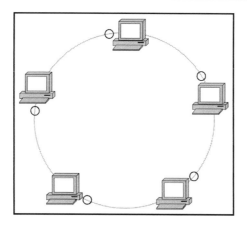

Bus

The bus topology is where all the computers or terminals are connected to a single cable. In older network designs, the bus topology was used, there was a centralized mainframe computer system with a single cable connected, leading to the other Terminal's machines. The main disadvantage of this topology is if the cable breaks, the entire network goes down:

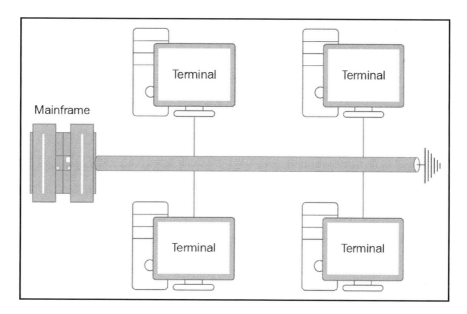

Hub and spoke

The hub and spoke model is quite simple. A lot of organizations that have multiple remote offices or branch offices use this type of topology. The headquarters location would contain all the main servers and network resources; this is known as the **hub**. The branch offices usually have a small number of employees versus the amount at the head office location. The branch offices would need to access the network resource at the hub—this makes each branch office a spoke, and each spoke is connected to the hub.

Therefore, if one branch wants to communicate with another, all traffic passes through the hub:

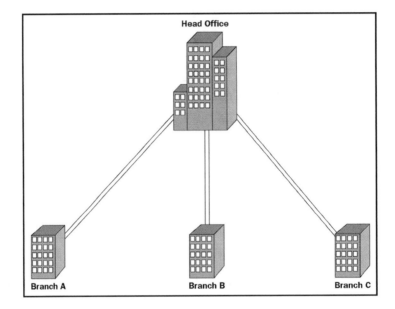

Mesh

In mesh topology, each node is directly connected to every other node on the network; this provides full redundancy should there be a network failure on any of the physical links. As more nodes as added to this topology, more links are needed, and this will eventually make the implementation and troubleshooting very complex. This design is very costly as more nodes are added to the design:

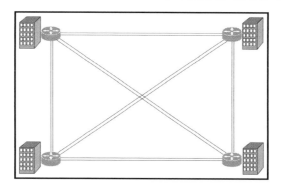

Hybrid

The hybrid topology contains at least two or more different types of topologies, such as combining a hub and spoke with a star topology:

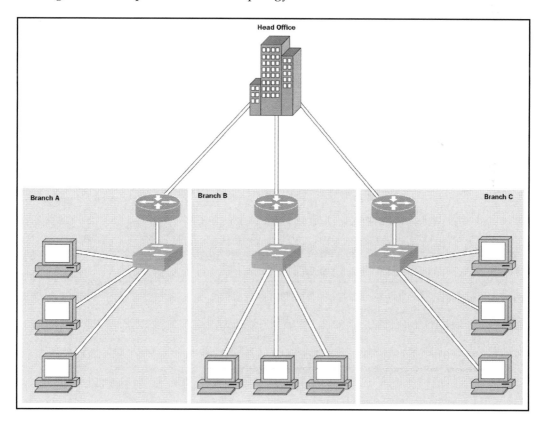

Tree

This topology starts with a root device and expands branches that contain more devices to form a hierarchy structure:

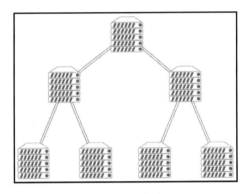

Types of networks

In this section, we will discuss the different type of networks:

- **Local Area Network (LAN)**: LAN is a small network within a home, an office or even a building.
- **Wide Area Network (WAN)**: The purpose of a WAN is simply to extend a LAN over a large geographic distance. Imagine you own a company—at the moment, it's only a single office location; however, as time passes, your business expands to another branch office in another city or country. Since the first branch has all of your main servers and network resources, it becomes the head office. The challenge is to allow the other branch office(s) to share the existing network resources from the head office to the other branch location. The solution is to implement a WAN connection between the offices:

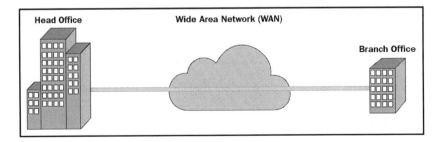

- **Wireless Local Area Network (WLAN)**: A WLAN is where either an **Access Point** (**AP**) or a wireless router is implemented on a LAN to provide wireless access to the resources on the LAN. This provides freedom of mobility to the users on the wireless LAN.

- **Metropolitan Area Network (MAN)**: A MAN is a network that is usually larger than a LAN but exists within a single geographic area for sharing resources. This type of network is usually found in cities.

- **Storage Area Network (SAN)**: SAN is a segment on your network that has high-capacity storage appliances. This part of the network is a high speed and specialized area that provides network access to storage.

- **Personal Area Network (PAN)**: PAN is used to interconnected devices on a personal or independent network. An example is having two Bluetooth-enabled devices connected to share a file.

Introducing Ethernet and its evolution

At times, we usually hear the term Ethernet when discussing networking, whether within a classroom or with network professionals, but *what exactly is Ethernet?* Here, we'll take a look at the fundamental characteristics and its functionality on a network.

In the previous chapter, we spoke about the OSI reference model and the TCP/IP stack. We've observed that layer 2 (Data Link Layer) is where the **Protocol Data Units** (**PDUs**) are either entering or exiting a system and layer 1 (Physical Layer) is the actual media used for transporting the bits. At these two layers, both the Physical and the Data Layers, we can find Ethernet:

OSI Model		TCP/IP Stack
Application		Application
Presentation		
Session		
Transport		Transport
Network		Internet
Data Link	Ethernet	Network Access/Link
Physical		

Ethernet, defined by IEEE 802.3, is a standard that defines how network communications occur, such as the encoding and decoding of a message, the synchronization of the flow of messages, the format for messages, and the size of each message. In `Chapter 3`, *Ethernet*, we'll be going even further into the operations of Ethernet and how it functions and helps devices communicate on a network.

Summary

In this chapter, we've taken a look at port numbers and their importance on a system. Without port numbers per services, a computer will have a challenge processing any messages it has received from a sender. For every port number, there's a service or network protocol that is mapped to it. Each network protocol handles the formatting and encoding of data in its own way and uses a unique port number for communicating with another device. So far, this chapter provided a better understanding in understanding and identifying network protocols and port numbers and understanding network design.

In the next chapter, we'll be covering Ethernet a bit more in-depth while providing the functions of its sub-layers and the fields within an Ethernet frame.

Questions

1. Which protocol exist at the Internet Layer of the TCP/IP stack?
    1. TCP
    2. IP
    3. UDP
    4. ARP

2. Which protocol sends a message without first establishing a session?
    1. DHCP
    2. TCP
    3. HTTP
    4. UDP

3. When a user opens their web browser, the browser is unable to reach `www.google.com`; however, you are getting success responses after you ping the IP address `8.8.8.8`. Which protocol may be affected?
     1. HTTP
     2. IP
     3. SMTP
     4. DNS

4. You're a network administrator at a local company, and the IT department has recently installed a new email server within the organization. Your task is to ensure all employees computers are configured to send email successfully. Which protocol would be used for sending email?
     1. POP
     2. SMTP
     3. IMAP
     4. HTTP

5. A company has a single location and, after a year, it is able to open another branch office far way. However, the manager of the company wants to extend their local network resources to the other location; what type of network connection is suitable?
     1. MAN
     2. PAN
     3. SAN
     4. WAN

6. As a network technician for a local company, one day you as task to copy files between two devices over the network. These files may contain sensitive information. Which is the preferred protocol you would use to ensure the files as transport safely?
     1. SCP
     2. FTP
     3. SSH
     4. HTTPS

7. Which layers of the OSI model does Ethernet operate? (Choose two answers)
     1. Physical
     2. Network
     3. Transport
     4. Application
     5. Data Link

8. Which the IEEE standard for Ethernet?
    1. 802.11
    2. 802.15
    3. 802.3
    4. 802.1Q

9. Which topology provides the most redundancy?
    1. Star
    2. Ring
    3. Tree
    4. Mesh

10. As a network administrator, you've notice the email clients on employees computers downloads the emails from the server to the email client and deletes it from the email server. Which protocol behaves in this manner?
    1. IMAP
    2. SMTP
    3. IP
    4. POP

Further reading

Read the following articles for more information:

- Check out the **CompTIA Network+ Cert (N10-007): Full Course and Practice Exam [Video]** at https://www.packtpub.com/networking-and-servers/comptia-network-cert-n10-007-full-course-and-practice-exam-video.
- To get more information on all the existing network protocols with their port assignment, you can visit the Internet Assigned Numbers Authority's **Protocol Registries** at https://www.iana.org/protocols.

3
Ethernet

In networking, it's very important to understand the functionalities of Ethernet, where exactly in the protocol suites it exists, and how it helps devices on a network communicate, as messages are passed from an operating system to the physical network infrastructure.

We'll take a step further into breaking down the operating of layer 2 of the **Open Systems Interconnection (OSI)** reference model and the Network Access Link Layer of the **Transmission Control Protocol/Internet Protocol (TCP/IP)** protocol suite.

In this chapter, we will cover the following topics:

- What is Ethernet?
- The sublayers of Ethernet
- Fields in an Ethernet frame
- Transmission types at layer 2, the Data Link Layer
- The **Content Addressable Memory (CAM)** table

What is Ethernet?

Whether you're new to the field of networking, studying for your CompTIA Network+ Certification, an enthusiast, or a seasoned network professional doing a refresher course, you'll encounter Ethernet. In this section, we will help you to better understand the characteristics and the responsibilities of Ethernet in a network.

To put it simply, Ethernet is a technology used in all modern day **local area networks (LANs)**. It is used to help with the logical communication of network devices over a wired network infrastructure with the use of various protocols. As mentioned previously, a protocol is a set of rules of procedures which are used to govern how information or data is passed within a system, along a network.

The **Institute of Electrical and Electronics Engineers** (**IEEE**) has created standards for Ethernet, known as IEEE 802.2 and IEEE 802.3, which define how Ethernet can be used within a wired network. Ethernet operates at both the **Data Link Layer** and the **Physical Layer** of the OSI reference model:

OSI Model		TCP/IP Stack
Data Link	Ethernet	Network Access/Link
Physical		

IEEE 802.2 and IEEE 802.3 define how **Protocol Data Units** (**PDUs**), such as frames and bits, are handled by both the Data Link Layers and Physical Layer as they are either passed down the protocol suite onto the network (sending) or vice versa (receiving).

Ethernet also defines and supports data transfer rates on networking devices interfaces, as follows:

- 10 MBps—Ethernet
- 100 MBps—Fast Ethernet
- 1000 MBps—Gigabit Ethernet
- 10,000 MBps—10 GB Ethernet

The sublayers of Ethernet

Let's talk a bit more about layers 1 and 2 of the OSI model, the Data Link Layer and the Physical Layer.

The Data Link Layer

The Data Link Layer (layer 2) of the OSI model is responsible for allowing the messages of the upper layers to access the network. It also controls how the data is placed onto the physical network (media), and handles error detection.

Within the Data Link Layer there are two sublayers, the **Logical Link Control** (**LLC**) sublayer and the **Media Access Control** (**MAC**) sublayer. Switches only operate at this second sublayer, as they are only able to read and understand frames containing MAC addresses.

 At the Data Link Layer, the PDU is known as a **frame**.

The LLC sublayer

The LLC sublayer typically moves the data between the software applications on a system onto the physical hardware components of a network, such as the **Network Interface Card** (**NIC**) or the media cables. When bits are received by the LLC, it helps with the reassembly process and passes them up to the upper layers of the protocol suite, such as the TCP/IP stack.

At this point, you may be wondering where exactly the LLC is located on a computer, switch, or even a router. The answer is quite simple—it is implemented in software within the firmware or the operating system of the local device. LLC is often described and referred to as the component driver software which interconnects the device's NIC to the operating system.

The NIC's driver software is what interconnects the physical hardware onto the operating system for communication on the network. The following diagram shows both the sub-layers of the Data Link Layer:

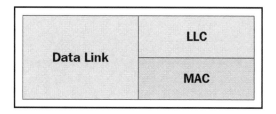

The MAC sublayer

The MAC sublayer defines the processes that enable the hardware components such as the NIC to access media (wire) on the network. MAC is responsible for handling data encapsulation and media access control.

The data encapsulation phase adds a layer 2 header, which contains the source and destination MAC addresses, inserting a preamble which is used for bit synchronization and helps any receiving devices identify the start of a bit. Finally, a trailer is applied to the end that is used for error handling during transmission of traffic across the network, as shown:

Frame					
Header					**Trailer**
Preamble	Src MAC: AA:BB::CC:DD:EE:FF	Src IP: 192.168.1.10	Src Port: 49,123	Data	File Check Sequence (FCS)
	Dest MAC: AB:CD:EF:12:34:56	Dest IP: 198.134.5.6	Dest Port: 80		

The second function of the MAC sublayer is to handle how frames access physical media, and how they are removed and pass upward to the LLC to the rest of the host system.

Fields in an Ethernet frame

Networking professionals need to have an idea of the fields within an Ethernet frame, as shown in the following screenshot:

Preamble	Source MAC Address	Destination MAC Address	EtherType	Data	FCS

The fields are as follows:

- **Preamble:** The Preamble is made up of seven bytes and the **Start Frame Delimiter (SFD)**, which is one byte. This is generally used for synchronization between the sender and the receiver devices on a network.
- **Source MAC Address**: The source MAC address field is made up of six bytes in length which is used to store the sender's MAC address.
- **Destination MAC Address:** Similarly to the source MAC address field, the destination MAC address field is also six bytes and contains the destination MAC address of the next device along the path to the final destination.
- **EtherType**: The EtherType field is two bytes, and is used to help identify various protocols which are used by the layers above the Data Link Layer of the OSI reference model.
- **Data**: The data field ranges between 46 and 1500 bytes per Ethernet frame. This field contains the data from the Application Layer of the protocol suite.

- **File Check Sequence (FCS)**: The FCS is four bytes and is used for error detection in the Ethernet frame. It contains a **Cyclic Redundancy Check** (**CRC**), which is a hash value of the frame itself. The sender of the frame would include this hash value before sending to the destination; when the frame is delivered, the recipient device calculates its own version. If the version calculated by the receiver matches the sender's value, there are no issues. However, if the CRC values does not match, the frame is dropped.

MAC addresses

In this section, we will discuss the format of the MAC address of an Ethernet frame. Let's take a look at a capture of an **Address Resolution Protocol** (**ARP**) message using the **Wireshark** tool:

```
∨ Frame 1276: 60 bytes on wire (480 bits), 60 bytes captured (480 bits) on interface 0
  > Interface id: 0 (Unknown/not available in original file format(libpcap))
    Encapsulation type: Ethernet (1)
    Arrival Time: Mar 17, 2015 16:42:58.622303000 SA Western Standard Time
    [Time shift for this packet: 0.000000000 seconds]
    Epoch Time: 1426624978.622303000 seconds
    [Time delta from previous captured frame: 0.000188000 seconds]
    [Time delta from previous displayed frame: 0.000188000 seconds]
    [Time since reference or first frame: 11.883034000 seconds]
    Frame Number: 1276
    Frame Length: 60 bytes (480 bits)
    Capture Length: 60 bytes (480 bits)
    [Frame is marked: False]
    [Frame is ignored: False]
    [Protocols in frame: eth:ethertype:arp]
    [Coloring Rule Name: ARP]
    [Coloring Rule String: arp]
∨ Ethernet II, Src: Vmware_f3:f2:f6 (00:50:56:f3:f2:f6), Dst: Vmware_b6:b5:48 (00:0c:29:b6:b5:48)
  ∨ Destination: Vmware_b6:b5:48 (00:0c:29:b6:b5:48)
      Address: Vmware_b6:b5:48 (00:0c:29:b6:b5:48)
      .... ..0. .... .... .... .... = LG bit: Globally unique address (factory default)
      .... ...0 .... .... .... .... = IG bit: Individual address (unicast)
  ∨ Source: Vmware_f3:f2:f6 (00:50:56:f3:f2:f6)
      Address: Vmware_f3:f2:f6 (00:50:56:f3:f2:f6)
      .... ..0. .... .... .... .... = LG bit: Globally unique address (factory default)
      .... ...0 .... .... .... .... = IG bit: Individual address (unicast)
    Type: ARP (0x0806)
    Padding: 000000000000000000000000000000000000
> Address Resolution Protocol (reply)
```

As we can see in the preceding screenshot, both the source and destination Ethernet (MAC) addresses are included. The MAC address is a 48-bit (six-byte) address which is hard coded into the NIC of a device. A MAC address consist of hexadecimal values ranging from 0 to 9, and from A to F.

IEEE assigns the first three bytes (24 bits) of the MAC address to a vendor. This part of the address is known as the **Organizationally Unique Identifier (OUI)**. The OUI helps network and security professionals determine the manufacturer of a MAC address.

Remembering the OUI value for each vendor can be a very challenging task; however, there are various OUI databases available online for anyone to query a MAC address. One notable database is the Wireshark OUI lookup tool, which can be found at `https://www.wireshark.org/tools/oui-lookup.html`.

The remaining three bytes (24 bits) of the MAC address are uniquely assigned by the vendor. By combining the OUI (24 bits) and the remaining portion of the address (24 bits), we'll get a unique 48-bit MAC address.

For example, the MAC address `00-E0-F7-58-1E-83` can be broken down as follows:

Organizationally Unique Identifier (OUI)	Assigned by the Vector
3 Bytes	3 Bytes
24 Bits	24 Bits
00-E0-F7	58-1E-83
Cisco Systems	Device specific

Using the command `ipconfig /all` on a Windows system will display the physical address, which is also known as the MAC address on the NIC:

```
C:\>ipconfig /all

FastEthernet0 Connection:(default port)

    Connection-specific DNS Suffix..:
    Physical Address................: 0002.165D.5D20
    Link-local IPv6 Address.........: FE80::202:16FF:FE5D:5D20
    IP Address......................: 192.168.1.2
    Subnet Mask.....................: 255.255.255.0
    Default Gateway.................: 192.168.1.1
    DNS Servers.....................: 8.8.8.8
    DHCP Servers....................: 192.168.1.1
    DHCPv6 Client DUID..............: 00-01-00-01-A4-39-DB-87-00-02-16-5D-5D-20
```

MAC addresses is also known as **burned-in address** (**BIA**) since they are usually hard coded into the NIC.

Transmission types at the Data Link Layer

There are three types of network transmissions at layer 2, the Data Link Layer. These are unicast, multicast, and broadcast:

- **Unicast**: In a unicast transmission, the frame is sent to only one destination MAC address or device on the network, as follows:

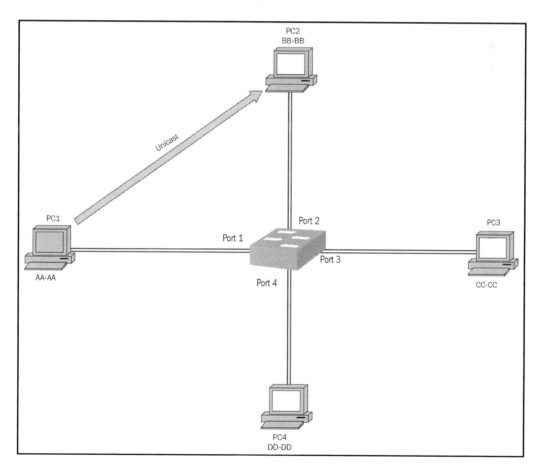

- **Multicast**: In a multicast transmission, a single stream of one or more frames is sent to multiple devices on the network. Multicast addresses take 01-00-5E as the first 24 bits of the MAC address:

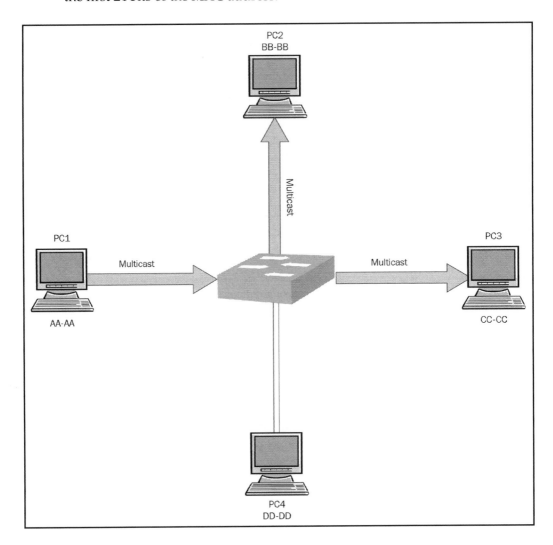

- **Broadcast:** A broadcast is a one-to-all transmission, where the frame originates from a single source device, but is sent to all devices on the LAN. In a broadcast MAC address all the 48 bits are 1, resulting in the address FF-FF-FF-FF-FF-FF:

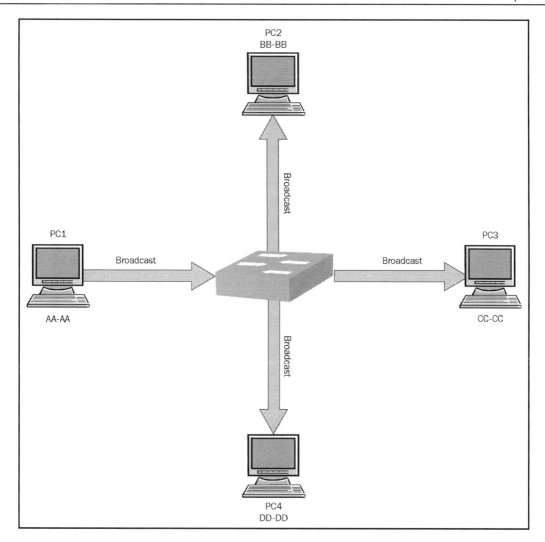

The CAM table

When a switch is powered on, it doesn't know where each end device is located on the network. Managed switches store the MAC addresses of devices in a special location called the CAM table.

To get a better idea of how the MAC addresses are stored within the CAM table, we'll use the following network topology to demonstrate:

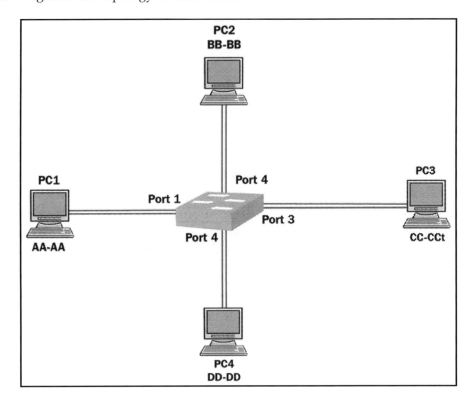

At this point, the switch has now been powered on and doesn't know which devices are connected to which interfaces/ports, since the CAM table is empty:

Content Addressable Memory (CAM) Table	
Interface	**MAC Address**
Port 1	
Port 2	
Port 3	
Port 4	

Let's assume **PC1** wants to send a message to **PC4**. **PC1** would build an Ethernet frame with its source MAC address as **AA-AA**, and **PC4**'s MAC address of **DD-DD** as the destination.

Once sent to the switch, the source MAC address is recorded on Port 1, as follows:

Content Addressable Memory (CAM) Table	
Interface	**MAC Address**
Port 1	AA-AA
Port 2	
Port 3	
Port 4	

Since the switch doesn't have an entry for **PC4** (**DD-DD**), it would send it out of all ports except Port 1 (as that's the receiving port). The devices connected to ports 2, 3, and 4 would all get a copy of the message, but only the device with the assigned destination's MAC address will respond, and all others will discard the frame.

When **PC4** responds to **PC1**, the source MAC address of **PC4** will be recorded under **Port 4** of the CAM table, as shown here:

Content Addressable Memory (CAM) Table	
Interface	**MAC Address**
Port 1	AA-AA
Port 2	
Port 3	
Port 4	DD-DD

In future, if **PC1** or **PC4** want to communicate with one other, the switch will forward the frames (message) directly to the interface of the intended receiver. A switch will only flood a message out to all ports if it doesn't know which device has the destination MAC address from the Ethernet frame header.

Switches usually remove entries within the CAM table after a period of time if no activity is detected on the interface or with the MAC address.

To view the entries within the CAM table on a Cisco switch, simply use the `show mac address-table` command.

The following is an example of a CAM table displaying the MAC addresses with their corresponding interfaces, which it received from the switch, and the associated **virtual local area network (VLAN)**:

```
Switch#show mac address-table
            Mac Address Table
-------------------------------------------

Vlan    Mac Address       Type        Ports
----    -----------       --------    -----

   1    0060.3e22.7b16    DYNAMIC     Fa0/24
  10    0001.43ab.3a54    DYNAMIC     Fa0/24
  10    0002.165d.5d20    DYNAMIC     Fa0/1
  10    000a.416b.d101    DYNAMIC     Fa0/24
  10    0060.3e22.7b16    DYNAMIC     Fa0/24
  20    000a.416b.d101    DYNAMIC     Fa0/24
  20    0060.3e22.7b16    DYNAMIC     Fa0/24
  20    00e0.f758.1e83    DYNAMIC     Fa0/2
```

Summary

In this chapter, we took a deeper look into what Ethernet is, and how it plays a vital role in networking. Both the LLC and the MAC sublayers were discussed, giving an overview of the responsibilities they each have within the network.

In the next chapter, we will be covering IPv4 and IPv6 in detail with subnetting.

Questions

1. How many bits are there in a MAC address?
    1. 8
    2. 16
    3. 32
    4. 48

2. Which sublayer is responsible for assigning layer 2 addressing?
    1. The Data Link Layer
    2. The Logical Layer Control
    3. The Media Access Control
    4. The Network

3. Which layer is considered to be the NIC device driver?
    1. The Data Link Layer
    2. The Logical Layer Control
    3. The Media Access Control
    4. The Network

4. Where are MAC addresses stored on a switch?
    1. The MAC address table
    2. The CAM table
    3. HDD
    4. A memory card

5. What is the name of the PDU at the Data Link Layer?
    1. Frame
    2. Segment
    3. Packet
    4. Bit

6. The trailer of an Ethernet message contains which of the following?
    1. The MAC address
    2. The IP address
    3. Data
    4. A file check sequence

4
Understanding IPv4 and IPv6

In any network, **Internet Protocol** (**IP**) addressing is needed to ensure that data is sent to the correct recipient or device. Imagine you're writing a letter (data) to a friend. When you've finished writing, you decide to enclose it in an envelope (encapsulation) with your friend's mailing address (addressing information). This is the typical procedure for sending a letter before dropping it off at the local postal office (network). Most importantly, the addressing information you've written on the envelope must be put into a particular format to ensure that the postal service company (network devices) are able to deliver it to the appropriate destination.

On a TCP/IP network, the process is similar. Each device on a network has a unique IP address (compared to a mailing address). In this chapter, we will be covering the following topics:

- Converting binary to decimal and vice versa
- Understanding IPv4 and IPv6 protocol structure
- Classes of IP addresses
- Types of transmissions in IPv4 and IPv6
- Special IP addresses
- Subnetting
- Configuring an IP address on various devices

Let's begin!

One of the many questions you may have is, who created the IP addressing scheme and *how is it regulated?* To provide a better insight and help you understand this, we will discuss a few governing bodies with their functions and responsibilities on the internet.

Both IP versions 4 and 6 address schemes are managed by the **Internet Assigned Numbers Authority (IANA)**. They governed the uses of the **Domain Name System (DNS)** root directory services, IP versions 4 and 6, and many other internet protocols (some of which were mentioned in `Chapter 2`, *Network Ports, Protocols, and Topologies*). The IPv4 scheme was deployed on January 1, 1983. Most of the internet that we know today is based on the IPv4 addressing scheme and is still the predominant method of communication on both the internet and private networks. IPv6 was deployed not too long after; this occurred in 1999.

IANA has developed two separate address spaces for IPv4, and these are known as the public and the private address spaces. The public IPv4 address space, defined as **RFC 1466**, has approximately 4 billion public IPv4 addresses. At the time of development, 4 billion was a huge number, but with the advancement of technology, networks are growing exponentially to accommodate smart devices and other appliances that require internet access. It soon exhausted the IPv4 public address space in almost every region globally.

Whenever an **Internet Service Provider (ISP)** needs to obtain an address block, the ISP goes to a **Regional Internet Registry (RIR)**. There are five RIRs globally, and each manages the IP address schemes for a different region of the world. The following are the five RIR of the world:

- **African Network Information Centre (AFRINIC)**: Covers the continent of Africa
- **Asia Pacific Network Information Centre (APNIC)**: Covers the regions of Asia and the Pacific
- **American Registry for Internet Numbers (ARIN)**: Covers Canada, USA, and part of the Caribbean
- **Latin American and Caribbean Internet Addresses Registry (LACNIC)**: Covers Latin America and part of the Caribbean
- **Réseaux IP Européens Network Coordination Centre (RIPE NCC)**: Covers Europe, the Middle East, and Central Asia

Each RIR is assigned blocks of IP addresses for distribution to ISPs or other large organizations.

To get further information on the assignments of IPv4 address allocation, you can visit `https://www.iana.org/assignments/ipv4-address-space/ipv4-address-space.xhtml`.

Later in this chapter, we'll dive further into the characteristics and features of IP version 6, such as its structure in comparison to an IPv4 packet, and the types of IPv6 transmissions and addresses with its subnet masks.

IPv4 concepts

In this section, we will focus on IP version 4. As mentioned earlier, electronic devices are able to send and receive electrical signals. The operating systems on network devices and components are able to interrupt these signals, whether it's a high voltage such as a 1 or a low voltage such as a 0. So, *why do we need to understand this piece of information?* We need to understand how devices communicate on the physical layer. As we've already mentioned, it does this in the form of electrical signals. Computers and other network-related components reassemble these electrical signals into data and process them so that they create information. This information is represented as ones (1s) and zeros (0s) to the computer system, but to we humans, we may see a file such as a document, music file, video file, and so on.

These electrical signals can further be represented as an IP address. As defined by the IANA, an IPv4 address is made of 32-bits. These bits are either a 1 or a 0. For every 8-bits of numbers, there is a period or dot (.) to separate it. These 8-bits are known as an **octet**. Therefore, there are four octets in a single IPv4 address.

Converting binary into decimal

Let's take a further look into the orientation of the IPv4 address, with its binary format as well. Since an IPv4 address is 32-bits in length with four octets, the following is an example of an IPv4 address in the binary notation:

```
11000000.10101000.00000001.10000001
```

We have been presented with a binary number, so the challenge now is converting binary into decimal. To better understand how the conversion process works, we must first understand the purpose of a base system or radix in mathematics. The radix (base) is a unique number that's used in a positioning system. Since binary is base 2, the radix is 2. Using the positioning system, the first position value (starting from the right) is 0.

In basic mathematics, $A^0 = 1$. This can be further expressed as $A \times 0 = 1$. To further express the remaining positions with the radix of 2, we get the following:

```
2^0 = 2 x 0 = 1
2^1 = 2 x 1 = 2
2^2 = 2 x 2 = 4
2^3 = 2 x 2 x 2 = 8
2^4 = 2 x 2 x 2 x 2 = 16
2^5 = 2 x 2 x 2 x 2 x 2 = 32
2^6 = 2 x 2 x 2 x 2 x 2 x 2 = 64
2^7 = 2 x 2 x 2 x 2 x 2 x 2 x 2 = 128
```

From the preceding expressions, the following table can be used to assist with calculating base (radix) 2 with its positioning values:

Radix	2^7	2^6	2^5	2^4	2^3	2^2	2^1	2^0
Decimal	128	64	32	16	8	4	2	1

Why did we use the range from 0 to 7 as our positioning values? We need to remember that the number zero (0) is the first of the natural numbers and an integer on the numerical table, and hence the reason we started with 2^0 as our first position. Another highlight regarding the table is that the last position is 2^7. This position represents the eighth position on the table. As mentioned earlier in this chapter, there are 8-bits in an octet; whenever we are converting an IP address from binary to decimal notation, we must convert one octet at a time. This means that each bit in an octet is also positioned on the table as well.

To further express a bit that is in the **ON** state, we use a one. Combining this information with the positioning system, we get the following expressions:

```
2^0 = 00000001
2^1 = 00000010
2^2 = 00000100
2^3 = 00001000
2^4 = 00010000
2^5 = 00100000
2^6 = 01000000
2^7 = 10000000
```

Let's use an example by representing 2^7 in the table:

Radix	2^7	2^6	2^5	2^4	2^3	2^2	2^1	2^0
Decimal	128	64	32	16	8	4	2	1
Binary	1	0	0	0	0	0	0	0

We know from the previous expressions that $2^7 = 2 \ x \ 2 \ x \ 2 \ x \ 2 \ x \ 2 \ x \ 2 \ x \ 2 = 128$. As we can see from the previous table, the bit in the column that has the radix of 2^7 is turned ON with a 1 in the third row. *What if we wanted to represent an entire binary octet such as* 10101000? This can simply be substituted in the binary row of the table:

Radix	2^7	2^6	2^5	2^4	2^3	2^2	2^1	2^0
Decimal	128	64	32	16	8	4	2	1
Binary	1	0	1	0	1	0	0	0

Since we substituted the binary number into our time, let's add the columns that are ON (those that contain the 1s):

$2^7 + 2^5 + 2^3 = 168$

A further breakdown is as follows:

$128 + 32 + 8 = 168$

We can conclude from this example that the binary equivalent of 10101000 to decimal is *168*. To get an even a better understanding, some practice is recommended. Let's convert the following binary numbers into decimal notation:

- Converting 11100101 to decimal:

Radix	2^7	2^6	2^5	2^4	2^3	2^2	2^1	2^0
Decimal	128	64	32	16	8	4	2	1
Binary	1	1	1	0	0	1	0	1

$128 + 64 + 32 + 4 + 1 = 229$

- Converting 10000100 to decimal:

Radix	2^7	2^6	2^5	2^4	2^3	2^2	2^1	2^0
Decimal	128	64	32	16	8	4	2	1
Binary	1	0	0	0	0	1	0	0

128 + 4 = 132

- Converting 11111111 to decimal:

Radix	2^7	2^6	2^5	2^4	2^3	2^2	2^1	2^0
Decimal	128	64	32	16	8	4	2	1
Binary	1	1	1	1	1	1	1	1

128 + 64 + 32 + 16 + 8 + 4 + 2 + 1 = 255

- Converting 01010101 to decimal:

Radix	2^7	2^6	2^5	2^4	2^3	2^2	2^1	2^0
Decimal	128	64	32	16	8	4	2	1
Binary	0	1	0	1	0	1	0	1

64 + 16 + 4 + 1 = 85

- Converting 10101010 to decimal:

Radix	2^7	2^6	2^5	2^4	2^3	2^2	2^1	2^0
Decimal	128	64	32	16	8	4	2	1
Binary	1	0	1	0	1	0	1	0

128 + 32 + 8 + 2 = 170

Converting decimal into binary

So far, we have learned how to convert binary into a decimal. Now it's time to do the opposite and convert a decimal number into binary format. There are many different techniques for converting decimal to binary and vice versa. Here, I will show you a very simple step-by-step method that will make the conversion process seamless. We must remember the following:

- Convert one octet at a time
- The maximum value an octet can have is 255

 If an octet in an IPv4 address is greater than 255, it's an invalid address.

First, we will convert the IPv4 address, `172.20.10.48`, into a binary value. We shall begin with the first octet, then move onto the second, and so on. Our process regarding conversion includes the utilization of the radix 2 with its positioning values. We will start by subtracting the highest power of 2, which is $2^7 = 128$, then $2^6 = 64$, and so on. If our decimal value is able to be subtracted from a power of 2, we will place a *1* to indicate YES or a *0* to indicate NO:

1. Let's begin by converting 172 into binary:
    1. *Could 172 minus 128 (2^7)?* Yes, with a remainder of *44*. We get a *1*.
    2. *Could 44 minus 64 (26)?* No, therefore we carry the *44* forward to try with another lesser power of 2. We get a *0*.
    3. *Could 44 minus 32 (25)?* Yes, with a remainder of *12*. We get a *1*.
    4. *Could 12 minus 16 (24)?* No, therefore we will carry the *12* forward to try with a lesser power of 2. We get a *0*.
    5. *Could 12 minus 8 (23)?* Yes, with a remainder of *4*. We get a *1*.
    6. *Could 4 minus 4 (22)?* Yes, with a remainder of *0*. We get a *1*.
    7. *Could 0 minus 2 (21)?* No, we get a *0*.
    8. *Could 0 minus 1 (20)?* No, we get our final value, *0*. Since there are no more powers of 2, we stop here.

For a better visualization, the following is a diagram demonstrating how this works:

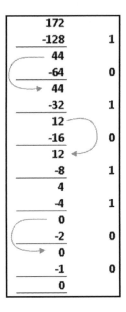

To arrange our binary value, starting from the top to the bottom with the values of 1s and 0s, we get *10101100* as the binary equivalent of *172*.

2. Next, we'll convert the second octet, 20, into binary:

1. *Could 20 minus 128 (2⁷)? No, therefore we will carry the 20 forward to try to minus a lesser power of 2. We get a 0.*
2. *Could 20 minus 64 (2⁶)? No, therefore we will carry the 20 forward to try to minus a lesser power of 2. We get a 0.*
3. *Could 20 minus 32 (2⁵)? No, therefore we will carry the 20 forward to try to minus a lesser power of 2. We get a 0.*
4. *Could 20 minus 16 (2⁴)? Yes, with a reminder of 4. Now, we have a 1.*
5. *Could 4 minus 8 (2³)? No, therefore we will carry the 8 forward to try to minus a lesser power of 2. We get a 0.*
6. *Could 4 minus 4 (2²)? Yes, with a remainder of 0. We get another 1.*
7. *Could 0 minus 2 (2¹)? No, therefore we get a 0.*
8. *Could 0 minus 1 (2⁰)? No, we got our final value, 0. Since there are no more powers of 2, we stop here.*

For a better visualization, the following is a diagram demonstrating how this works:

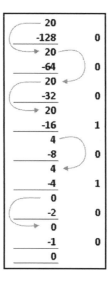

Starting from the top to the bottom with the values of 1s and 0s, we get `00010100` as the binary equivalent of *20*.

3. Now, it's time to convert *10* into its binary format:
    1. *Could 10 minus 128 (2^7)?* No, therefore we get a *0*.
    2. *Could 10 minus 64 (26)?* No, therefore we get a *0*.
    3. *Could 10 minus 32 (25)?* No, therefore we get a *0*.
    4. *Could 10 minus 16 (24)?* No, therefore we get a *0*.
    5. *Could 10 minus 8 (23)?* Yes, with a remainder of 2. We get a *1*.
    6. *Could 2 minus 4 (22)?* No, therefore we get a *0*.
    7. *Could 2 minus 2 (21)?* Yes, with a remainder of 0. We get a *1*.
    8. *Could 0 minus 1 (20)?* No, we got our final value, *0*. Since there are no more powers of 2, we stop here.

For a better visualization, the following is a diagram demonstrating how this works:

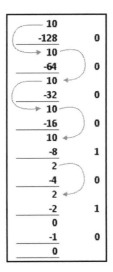

Starting from the top to the bottom with the values of 1s and 0s, we get `00001010` as the binary equivalent of 10.

4. Now, for our last octet, we will be converting *48* into binary:

    1. *Could 48 minus 128 (27)?* No, therefore we get a *0*.

    2. *Could 48 minus 64 (26)?* No, therefore we get a *0*.

    3. *Could 48 minus 32 (25)?* Yes, with a remainder of *16*. We get a *1*.

    4. *Could 16 minus 16 (24)?* Yes, with a remainder of *0*. We get a *1*.

    5. *Could 0 minus 8 (23)?* No, therefore we get a *0*.

    6. *Could 0 minus 4 (22)?* No, therefore we get a *0*.

    7. *Could 0 minus 2 (21)?* No, therefore we get a *0*.

    8. *Could 0 minus 1 (20)?* No, we got our final value, *0*. Since there are no more powers of 2, we stop here.

For a better visualization, the following is a diagram demonstrating how this works:

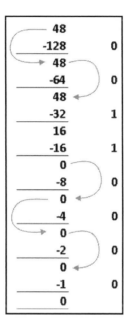

48	
-128	0
48	
-64	0
48	
-32	1
16	
-16	1
0	
-8	0
0	
-4	0
0	
-2	0
0	
-1	0
0	

Starting from the top to the bottom, with the values of 1s and 0s, we get `00110000` as the binary equivalent of *48*.

Now, let's put everything together to see the binary equivalent of `172.20.10.48`. We get the following:

172	20	10	48
10101100	00010100	00001010	00110000

Therefore, `172.20.11.48 = 10101100.00010100.00001010.00110000`.

 Always include all of the zeros, regardless of whether they have a value. This is to ensure the proper positioning of digits in the binary system and to display an octet (8 bits).

The format of an IPv4 packet

We've been talking about IPv4 and packets for quite some time, so let's take a look at the fields that make up an IPv4 packet and their purpose. The following diagram displays the fields of an IPv4 packet:

32 bits in length					
Version	Internet Header Length	Differentiated Services (DS)		Total Length	
		DSCP	ECN		
Identification				Flag	Fragment Offset
Time-to-Live (TTL)		Protocol		Header Checksum	
Source IP Address					
Destination IP Address					
Options					

As shown in the preceding diagram, there are many fields. As an upcoming network professional, it's important to understand the purpose of these fields and how they play a vital role in the composition of the IPv4 packet. The following is a description of each field:

- **Version**: This field identifies whether the packet is version 4 or version 6. This field is 4 bits in length.
- **Internet Header Length (IHL)**: This is used to indicate the beginning of data that is 4 bits in length.
- **Differentiated Services (DS)**: This field was originally named **Type of Service (ToS)**. It is used to determine the priority of a packet. This field is 8 bits in length.
- **Total Length**: This field allows a datagram to be up to 65,535 octets in size. This field is 16 bits in length.
- **Identification**: As mentioned previously, a sender usually assigns a value to each bit as they are placed on the physical layer. The value that's assigned is placed in this field to assist the receiver in the reassembly process. This field is 16 bits in length.

- **Flags**: This is used to enable various flag options in the IP packet. This field is 3 bits in length.
- **Fragment Offset**: This field is used to indicate where in the datagram this fragment belongs. It is 13 bits in length.
- **Time to Live (TTL)**: This field can only be found in packets. It is used to set the maximum time a packet is allowed to remain in a network. When each hop passes, the TTL value decreases by 1. If the TTL reaches 0, the last hop to set it to 0 discards the packet from the network. The TTL field has a size of 8 bits.
- **Protocol**: This field indicates the network protocol that is being used in the packet. It is 8 bits in length.
- **Header Checksum**: This field contains a checksum (hash) value of the header only. It is 16 bits in length.
- **Source IP address**: This field contains the sender's IP address. It is 32 bits in length.
- **Destination IP address**: This field contains the destination's IP address. It is 32 bits in length.
- **Options**: This field is a variable field.

These fields may look a bit overwhelming on the theoretical side of networking, but if you use a network protocol analyzer tool such as **Wireshark** (www.wireshark.org), you would be able to see the fields of a packet that we just described.

The following is a **Wireshark** capture of an IPv4 packet. This capture (challenge 14 – Weird Python) was taken from **The Honeynet Project** (www.honeynet.org), which is a non-profit security organization that promotes internet security globally.

Let's take a look at packet 682. We can see all of the fields with their corresponding values:

```
 conference.pcapng
File  Edit  View  Go  Capture  Analyze  Statistics  Telephony  Wireless  Tools  Help

 http2

No.         Time        Source            Destination       Protocol  Length  Info
       646 6.758506  a.thumbs.redditmedia…  172.16.254.128        HTTP     195 HTTP/1.1 200 OK  (PNG)
       648 6.760432  172.16.254.128         a.thumbs.redditmedia…  HTTP     514 GET /9FkUjylHkmm-P0jauxAc2Qvl56nz1CfXK023PGWB5mA.jpg HTTP/1.1
       682 6.825246  a.thumbs.redditmedia…  172.16.254.128        HTTP    1388 HTTP/1.1 200 OK  (JPEG JFIF image)
       702 6.839142  172.16.254.128         a.thumbs.redditmedia…  HTTP     514 GET /fTMgRASiBOAIHNGuCVuGxX8GpnGta4d5DaI6vGgkKPg.jpg HTTP/1.1

> Frame 682: 1388 bytes on wire (11104 bits), 1388 bytes captured (11104 bits) on interface 0
> Ethernet II, Src: Vmware_f3:f2:f6 (00:50:56:f3:f2:f6), Dst: Vmware_b6:b5:48 (00:0c:29:b6:b5:48)
v Internet Protocol Version 4, Src: a.thumbs.redditmedia.com (198.41.208.145), Dst: 172.16.254.128 (172.16.254.128)
      0100 .... = Version: 4
      .... 0101 = Header Length: 20 bytes (5)
    v Differentiated Services Field: 0x00 (DSCP: CS0, ECN: Not-ECT)
        0000 00.. = Differentiated Services Codepoint: Default (0)
        .... ..00 = Explicit Congestion Notification: Not ECN-Capable Transport (0)
      Total Length: 1374
      Identification: 0xe925 (59685)
    v Flags: 0x0000
        0... .... .... .... = Reserved bit: Not set
        .0.. .... .... .... = Don't fragment: Not set
        ..0. .... .... .... = More fragments: Not set
        ...0 0000 0000 0000 = Fragment offset: 0
      Time to live: 128
      Protocol: TCP (6)
      Header checksum: 0x0b28 [validation disabled]
      [Header checksum status: Unverified]
      Source: a.thumbs.redditmedia.com (198.41.208.145)
      Destination: 172.16.254.128 (172.16.254.128)
> Transmission Control Protocol, Src Port: http (80), Dst Port: 52147 (52147), Seq: 8902, Ack: 921, Len: 1334
> [5 Reassembled TCP Segments (7174 bytes): #673(1460), #674(1460), #676(1460), #681(1460), #682(1334)]
> Hypertext Transfer Protocol
> JPEG File Interchange Format
```

If you're interested in learning about packet analysis and network forensics, The Honeynet Project (`www.honeynet.org`) is a good place to start. Their challenges will broaden your analytical skills as a network professional.

Public IPv4 addresses

We spoke about IPv4 addresses in a few discussions previously. In this section, we'll go even further and discuss the actual grouping of the addresses.

There are two main IPv4 address spaces—the public address space and the private address space. The primary difference between both address spaces is that the public IPv4 addresses are routable on the internet, which means that any device that requires communication to other devices on the internet will need to be assigned a public IPv4 address on its interface, which is connected to the internet.

The public address space is divided into five classes:

Class A	0.0.0.0 – 126.255.255.255
Class B	128.0.0.0 – 191.255.255.255
Class C	192.0.0.0 – 223.255.255.255
Class D	224.0.0.0 – 239.255.255.255
Class E	240.0.0.0 – 255.255.255.255

 Class D addresses are used for multicast traffic. These addresses are not assignable. Class E addresses are reserved for experimental usage and are not assignable.

On the internet, classes A, B, and C are commonly used on devices that are directly connected to the internet, such as layer 3 switches, routers, firewalls, servers, and any other network-related device. As mentioned earlier, there are approximately four billion public IPv4 addresses. However, in a lot of organizations and homes, only one public IPv4 address is assigned to the router or modem's publicly facing interface. The following diagram shows how a public IP address is seen by internet users:

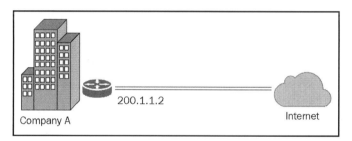

So, *what about the devices that require internet access from within the organization or home?* There may be a few devices to hundreds or even thousands of devices that require an internet connection and an IP address to communication to the internet from within a company. If ISPs give their customers a single public IPv4 address on their modem or router, *how can this single public IPv4 address serve more than one device from within the organization or home?*

The internet gateway or router is usually configured with **Network Addresses Translation** (**NAT**), which is the method of mapping either a group of IP addresses or a single IP address on the internet-facing interface to the **local area network** (**LAN**). For any devices that are behind the internet gateway that want to communicate with another device on the internet, NAT will translate the sender's source IP address to the public IPv4 address. Therefore, all of the devices on the internet will see the public IPv4 address and not the sender's actual IP address.

Private IPv4 addresses

As defined by **RFC 1918**, there are three classes of private IPv4 address that are allocated for private use only. This means within a private network such as LAN. The benefit of using the private address space (RFC 1918) is that the classes are not unique to any particular organization or group. They can be used within an organization or a private network. However, on the internet, the public IPv4 address is unique to a device. This means that if a device is directly connected to the internet with a private IPv4 address, there will be no network connectivity to devices on the internet. Most ISPs usually have a filter to prevent any private addresses (RFC 1918) from entering their network.

The private address space is divided into three classes:

Class A—10.0.0.0/8 network block	10.0.0.0-010.255.255.255
Class B—172.16.0.0/12 network block	172.16.0.0-172.31.255.255
Class C—192.168.0.0/16 network block	192.168.0.0-192.168.255.255

Subnet mask

For every IP address, there's an accompanying subnet (work) mask. This address is used to define the following:

- The subnet mask is used to indicate the network and host portion of an IP address
- The subnet mask is used to determine the number of available IP addresses on a network
- If two or more devices, such as computers, are communicating over multiple networks, the subnet mask of each device determines whether a computer should send the packet to the default gateway/router

There are three default classes of the subnet mask:

- Class A: 255.0.0.0
- Class B: 255.255.0.0
- Class C: 255.255.255.0

Each IPv4 address class has their own default subnet mask. An IP address such as 10.10.10.1, which is a private Class A address, will use the subnet mask of 255.0.0.0. Another example we can use is the address 191.5.4.6, which is a public Class B address. This address will use a default subnet mask of 255.255.0.0 and so on.

In some of the earlier sections of this chapter, you will have noticed after some IPv4 addresses that there's a forward slash (/) with a number next to it such as /8, /16, and /24. This is a shorthand method of representing a subnet mask. This is known as a **network prefix**. How does /8, /16 or even /24 represent an entire subnet mask? To explain this further, I'll use some examples:

1. First, let's convert a Class A subnet mask:
   - Decimal: 255.0.0.0
   - Binary: 11111111.00000000.00000000.00000000

   Here, we can see that there are eight 1s in the subnet mask. From this denotation, we get /8.

2. Second, we'll convert a Class B subnet mask:
   - Decimal: 255.255.0.0
   - Binary: 11111111.11111111.00000000.00000000

   Here, we can see that there are sixteen 1s in the subnet mask. From this denotation, we get /16.

3. Finally, we'll convert a Class C subnet mask:
   - Decimal: 255.255.255.0
   - Binary: 11111111.11111111.11111111.00000000

   Now, we have twenty-four 1s, which means that we have a /24 subnet mask.

Furthermore, an IP address can have a custom subnet mask apart from the default address classes. Let's assume that we have an address of 192.168.100.1 with a customized subnet mask of 255.255.255.224.

Converting this subnet mask is much simpler than you think. First, we know that when all 8-bits are all 1s within an octet, we get the maximum value of 255. Therefore, the first three octets are 24-bits. Now we need to convert the last octet into binary:

```
224
-128    1
 96
-64     1
 32
-32     1
  0
-16     0
  0
 -8     0
  0
 -4     0
  0
 -2     0
  0
 -1     0
  0
```

The following is another graphical representation:

Radix	2^7	2^6	2^5	2^4	2^3	2^2	2^1	2^0
Decimal	128	64	32	16	8	4	2	1
Binary	1	1	1	0	0	0	0	0

The last octet is `11100000`. Now, putting it all together, we get `11111111.11111111.11111111.11100000`, which is the binary equivalent of `255.255.255.224`. As we can see, there are twenty-seven 1s in binary notation, and so we get a `/27` network prefix. The new representation of the IP address is `192.168.100.1/27`.

Within a subnet mask, there's always a continuous stream of 1s. There are never any 0s between the 1s.

Determining the Network ID

The subnet mask helps determine which network (subnet) an IP address belongs to. The process of determining the network or subnetwork is done by **ANDing** the IP address and the subnet mask together. The result will provide the Network ID. Let's take a look at the following diagram:

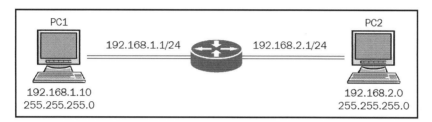

We would like to determine which network **PC1** belongs to. To do this, we need to AND both the IP address: 192.168.1.0 against the subnet mask, which is 255.255.255.0. To proceed further, we'll convert both the IP address and subnet mask into binary and use the laws of ANDing.

The laws of ANDing

The following are the laws of ANDing:

```
0 AND 1 = 0
0 AND 0 = 0
1 AND 0 = 0
1 AND 1 = 1
```

IP	11000000.10101000.00000001.00001010
Subnet mask	11111111.11111111.11111111.00000000
Network ID	11000000.10101000.00000001.00000000

By converting the Network ID from binary to decimal, we get 192.168.1.0/24. **PC1** belongs to this network.

If we look carefully, we can see that the first 24-bits are the same, and that the subnet mask is also used to indicate the portion of the address which represents the network portion (purple) and the host portion (green). All devices within the same subnet or network will have the same network portion as part of their IP address, and the host portion will be unique to the end device/host.

Let's assume that we have a network connectivity issue between two devices. In this scenario, we are going to use a customized subnet mask and apply the ANDing process to have a better understanding of why **PC2** is unable to communicate with the router:

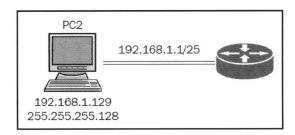

Looking at the preceding network diagram, the /25 network prefix is 255.255.255.128 when it's converted into decimal notation. Therefore, both the subnet masks of **PC2** and the router are the same. However, this makes us wonder, *how come there will be no connectivity between each device?* To solve this issue, let's check whether these two devices are on the same logical IP subnet/network.

First, we'll begin by ANDing **PC2**'s IP address and subnet mask:

IP	11000000.10101000.00000001.10000001
Subnet mask	11111111.11111111.11111111.10000000
Network ID	11000000.10101000.00000001.10000000

PC2 belongs to the 192.168.1.128/25 network.

Now, let's apply the ANDing process to the router:

IP	11000000.10101000.00000001.00000001
Subnet mask	11111111.11111111.11111111.10000000
Network ID	11000000.10101000.00000001.00000000

The router belongs to the 192.168.1.0/25 network.

As we can see, the Network IDs for both the PCs and the router are different, both in binary and in decimal notation. This is because they are on separate logical IP networks, and so they will not be able to communicate.

To resolve this issue, the IP address of the PC2 must exist within the same subnet as the router or vice versa. Later in this chapter, we will be covering subnetting, and you'll be able to identify the ranges of a subnet.

Special IPv4 addresses

Unique addresses which have special purposes, either on the internet or the private network, exist. In this section, we'll provide a list of these special addresses, along with their purposes.

Loopback addresses

The loopback address is used by a host to send traffic to itself. The loopback address ranges from `127.0.0.1 /8 to 127.255.255.254/8`. A simple example of using the loopback address is to check whether the TCP/IP stack is working properly on a local system. Network professionals usually ping the address, that is, `127.0.0.1`:

```
C:\>ping 127.0.0.1

Pinging 127.0.0.1 with 32 bytes of data:
Reply from 127.0.0.1: bytes=32 time<1ms TTL=128
Reply from 127.0.0.1: bytes=32 time<1ms TTL=128
Reply from 127.0.0.1: bytes=32 time<1ms TTL=128
Reply from 127.0.0.1: bytes=32 time<1ms TTL=128

Ping statistics for 127.0.0.1:
 Packets: Sent = 4, Received = 4, Lost = 0 (0% loss),
Approximate round trip times in milliseconds:
 Minimum = 0ms, Maximum = 0ms, Average = 0ms
```

 If you ping any address within the `127.0.0.0/8` network block, the local host will respond.

Link-local

In most cases, our computers are set to receive an IP address automatically once connected to a network. This is assuming that there is a **Dynamic Host Configuration Protocol (DHCP)** server on the network as well as an available pool of addresses for distribution:

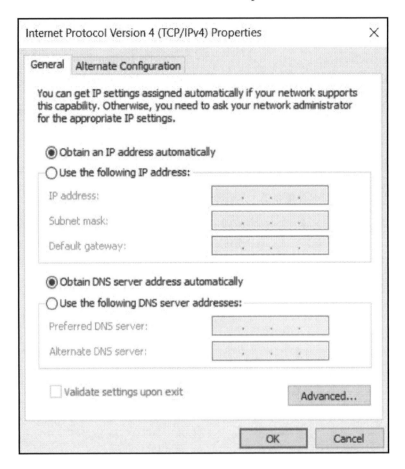

What if the DHCP server is not available, or down from the network? How would the operating system, such as Windows, compensate for the lack of a DHCP server? **Automatic Private IP Addressing (APIPA)** is a feature that Windows DHCP clients use to self-assign an automatic private IPv4 address to themselves on a network to ensure basic connectivity.

APIPA scheme uses a network block of 169.254.0.0/16, with a range of 169.254.0.1/16 to 169.254.255.254/16.

TestNet

TestNet uses the network block of 192.0.2.0/24 with an address range of 192.0.2.0/24 to 192.0.2.255/24. According to **RFC 3330**, these addresses are to be used with domain names within vendor and protocol documentation, and should not appear on the internet. To put this simply, they can only be used for teaching and learning purposes.

 The Class E range of addresses, 240.0.0.0 to 255.255.255.254, are known as the **experimental addresses**, and they are reserved for future use. For further information, please visit https://tools.ietf.org/html/rfc3330.

IPv4 transmission types

On an IPv4 network, a host can communicate with other devices on the network by using the following transmission types:

- **Unicast:** The unicast transmission type is where one host communicates with another host directly, such as a client and server, or what is better referred to as a **peer-to-peer** network. This is a one-to-one transmission:

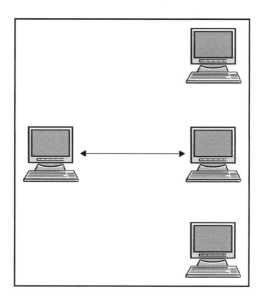

- **Multicast:** In a multicast transmission, a single host communicates with many other hosts on the network, but not all of them. This reduces the traffic on the network by sending the message to only those who need it. The devices that participate in multicast transmissions are called **multicast groups**. As mentioned earlier, the IPv4 Class D network range represents the multicast addresses 224.0.0.0 to 239.255.255.255:

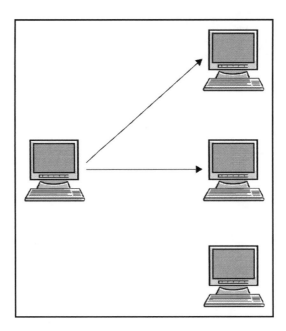

- **Broadcast:** In a broadcast transmission, a message is sent to all of the devices on the same network. Here's a simple analogy—let's assume that there's a group of people within a single room for a conference. The speaker will be addressing the audience while sending a single uniform message by using the microphone system, and each person within the room will receive a copy of the message. This is how broadcasting works, and its application is the same on an IP network:

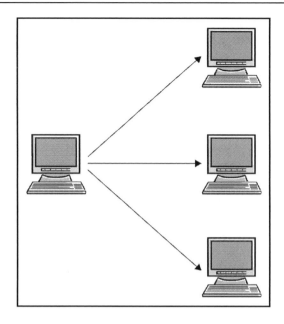

Subnetting

What is subnetting and why do we need to subnet a network? First, **subnetting** is the process of breaking down a single IP address block into smaller subnetworks (subnets). Second, the reason we need to subnet is to efficiently distribute IP addresses with the result of less wastage. This brings us to other questions, such as why do we need to break down a single IP address block, and *why is least wastage so important? Could we simply assign a Class A, B, or C address block to a network of any size?* To answer these questions, we will go more in depth with this topic by using practical examples and scenarios.

Let's assume that you are a network administrator at a local company and one day the IT manager assigns a new task to you. The task is to redesign the IP scheme of the company. He has also told you to use an address class that is suitable for the company's size and to ensure that there is minimal wastage of IP addresses.

The first thing you decided to do was draw a high-level network diagram indicating each branch, which shows the number of hosts per branch office and the **Wide Area Network** (**WAN**) links between each branch router:

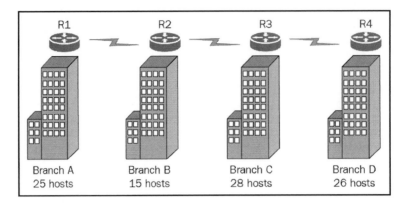

Network diagram

As we can see from the preceding diagram, each building has a branch router, and each router is connected to another using a WAN link. Each branch location has a different number of host devices that requires an IP address for network communication.

Step 1 – determining an appropriate class of address and why

The subnet mask can tell us a lot about a network, such as the following:

- The network and host portion of an IP address
- The number of hosts within a network

If we use a network block from either of the address classes, we will get the following available hosts:

Class A – 255.0.0.0	11111111.00000000.00000000.00000000
Class B – 255.255.0.0	11111111.11111111.00000000.00000000
Class C – 255.255.255.0	11111111.11111111.11111111.00000000

As you may remember, the network portion of an address is represented by 1s in the subnet mask, while the 0s represent the host portion. We can use the following formula to calculate the total number of IP addresses within a subnet by the known the amount of host bits in the subnet mask.

Using the formula 2^H, where H represents the host bit, we get the following results:

- Class A = 2^{24} = 16,777,216 total IPs
- Class B = 2^{16} = 65,536 total IPs
- Class C = 2^8 = 256 total IPs

In IPv4, there are two IPs that cannot be assigned to any devices. These are the **Network ID** and the **Broadcast IP address**. Therefore, you need to subtract two addresses from the total IP formula.

Using the formula 2^H-2 to calculate usable IPs, we get the following:

- Class A = $2^{24} - 2$ = 16,777,214 total IPs
- Class B = $2^{16} - 2$ = 65,534 total IPs
- Class C = $2^8 - 2$ = 254 total IPs

Looking back at *Network diagram*, we can identify the following seven networks:

- **Branch A LAN**: 25 hosts
- **Branch B LAN**: 15 hosts
- **Branch C LAN**: 28 hosts
- **Branch D LAN**: 26 hosts
- **WAN R1-R2**: 2 IPs are needed
- **WAN R2-R3**: 2 IPs are needed
- **WAN R3-R4**: 2 IPs are needed

Determining the appropriate address class depends on the largest network and the number of networks needed. Currently, the largest network is **Branch C**, which has 28 host devices that needs an IP address. We can use the smallest available class, which is any Class C address because it will be able to support the largest network we have. However, to do this, we need to choose a Class C address block. Let's use the 192.168.1.0/24 block.

Remember, the subnet mask is used to identify the network portion of the address. This also means that we are unable to modify the network portion of the IP address when we are subnetting, but we can modify the host portion:

Network	11000000.10101000.00000001.00000000
Subnet mask	11111111.11111111.11111111.00000000

The first 24-bits represent the network portion and the remaining 8-bits represent the host portion. Using the formula $2^H - 2$ to calculate the number of usable host IPs, we get the following:

```
2^H - 2
2^8 - 2 = 256 - 2 = 254 usable IP addresses
```

Assigning this single network block to either of the seven networks, there will be a lot of IP addresses being wasted. Therefore, we need to apply our subnetting techniques to this Class C address block.

Step 2 – creating subnets (subnetworks)

To create more subnets or subnetworks, we need to borrow bits on the host portion of the network. The formula 2^N is used to calculate the number of subnets, where N is the number of bits borrowed on the host portion. Once these bits are borrowed, they will become part of the network portion and a new subnet mask will be presented.

So far, we have a Network ID of 192.168.1.0/24. We need to get seven subnets, and each subnet should be able to fit our largest network (which is **Branch C**—28 hosts).

Let's create our subnets. Remember that we need to borrow bits on the host portion, starting where the 1s end in the subnet mask. Let's borrow two host bits and apply them to our formula to determine whether we are able to get the seven subnets:

Network	11000000.10101000.00000001.00000000
Subnet mask	11111111.11111111.11111111.11000000

When bits are borrowed on the host portion, the bits are changed to 1s in the subnet mask. This produces a new subnet mask for all of the subnets that have been created.

Let's use our formula for calculating the number of networks:

```
Number of Networks = 2^N
2^2 = 2 x 2 = 4 networks
```

As we can see, two host bits are not enough as we need at least seven networks. Let's borrow one more host bit:

Network	11000000.10101000.00000001.00000000
Subnet mask	11111111.11111111.11111111.11100000

Once again, let's use our formula for calculating the number of networks:

```
Number of Networks = 2^N
2^3 = 2 x 2 x 2 = 8 networks
```

Using 3 host bits, we are able to get a total of 8 subnets. In this situation, we have one additional network, and this additional network can be placed aside for future use if there's an additional branch in the future.

Since we borrowed 3 bits, we have 5 host bits remaining. Let's use our formula for calculating usable IP addresses:

```
Usable IP addresses = 2^H - 2
2^5 - 2 = 32 - 2 = 30 usable IPs
```

This means that each of the 8 subnets will have a total of 32 IP addresses, with 30 usable IP addresses inclusive. Now we have a perfect match. Let's work out our 8 new subnets.

The guidelines we must follow at this point are as follows:

- We cannot modify the network portion of the address (red)
- We cannot modify the host portion of the address (black)
- We can only modify the bits that we borrowed (green)

Starting with the Network ID, we get the following eight subnets:

Subnet 1	11000000.10101000.00000001.00000000 = 192.168.1.0
Subnet 2	11000000.10101000.00000001.00100000 = 192.168.1.32
Subnet 3	11000000.10101000.00000001.01000000 = 192.168.1.64
Subnet 4	11000000.10101000.00000001.01100000 = 192.168.1.96
Subnet 5	11000000.10101000.00000001.10000000 = 192.168.1.128
Subnet 6	11000000.10101000.00000001.10100000 = 192.168.1.160
Subnet 7	11000000.10101000.00000001.11000000 = 192.168.1.192
Subnet 8	11000000.10101000.00000001.11100000 = 192.168.1.224

We can't forget about the subnet mask:

Subnet mask	11111111.11111111.11111111.11100000

As we can see, there are twenty-seven 1s in the subnet mask, which gives us `255.255.255.224` or `/27` as the new subnet mask for all eight subnets we've just created.

Take a look at each of the subnets. They all have a fixed increment of 32. A quick method to calculate the incremental size is to use the formula 2^x. This assists in working out the decimal notation of each subnet much easier than calculating the binary. The last network in any subnet always ends with the customized ending of the new subnet mask. From our example, the new subnet mask `255.255.255.224` ends with `224`, and the last subnet also ends with the same value, `192.168.1.224`.

Step 3 – assigning each network an appropriate subnet and calculating the ranges

To determine the first usable IP address within a subnet, the first bit from the right must be **1**. To determine the last usable IP address within a subnet all of the host bits except the first bit from the right should all be 1s. The broadcast IP of any subnet is when all of the host bits are 1s.

Let's take a look at the first subnet. We will assign subnet 1 to the Branch A LAN:

Network ID:	11000000.10101000.00000001.00000000	= 192.168.1.0/27
1st usable IP:	11000000.10101000.00000001.00000001	= 192.168.1.1/27
Last usable IP:	11000000.10101000.00000001.00011110	= 192.168.1.30/27
Broadcast IP:	11000000.10101000.00000001.00011111	= 192.168.1.31/27

The second subnet will be allocated to the Branch B LAN:

Network ID:	11000000.10101000.00000001.00100000	= 192.168.1.32/27
1st usable IP:	11000000.10101000.00000001.00100001	= 192.168.1.33/27
Last usable IP:	11000000.10101000.00000001.00111110	= 192.168.1.62/27
Broadcast IP:	11000000.10101000.00000001.00111111	= 192.168.1.63/27

The third subnet will be allocated to the Branch C LAN:

Network ID:	11000000.10101000.00000001.01000000 = 192.168.1.64/27
1st usable IP:	11000000.10101000.00000001.01000001 = 192.168.1.65/27
Last usable IP:	11000000.10101000.00000001.01011110 = 192.168.1.94/27
Broadcast:	11000000.10101000.00000001.01011111 = 192.168.1.95/27

The fourth subnet will be allocated to Branch D LAN:

Network ID	11000000.10101000.00000001.01100000 = 192.168.1.96/27
1st usable IP:	11000000.10101000.00000001.01100001 = 192.168.1.97/27
Last usable IP:	11000000.10101000.00000001.01111110 = 192.168.1.126/27
Broadcast IP:	11000000.10101000.00000001.01111111 = 192.168.1.127/27

At this point, we have successfully allocated subnets 1 to 4 to each of the branch's LANs. During our initial calculation for determining the size of each subnet, we saw that each of the eight subnets are equal, and that we have 32 total IPs with 30 usable IP addresses. Currently, we have subnets 5 to 8 for allocation, but if we allocate subnet 5, 6 and 7 to the WAN links between the branches R1-R2, R2-R3 and R3-R4, we would be wasting 28 IP addresses since each WAN link (point-to-point) only requires 2 IP addresses.

What if we can take one of our existing subnets and create even more but smaller networks to fit each WAN (point-to-point) link? We can do this with a process known as **Variable Length Subnet Masking (VLSM)**. By using this process, we are subnetting a subnet.

For now, we will place aside subnets 5, 6, and 7 as future reservation for any future branches:

Subnet 5	11000000.10101000.00000001.10000000 = 192.168.1.128 – Reserved
Subnet 6	11000000.10101000.00000001.10100000 = 192.168.1.160 – Reserved
Subnet 7	11000000.10101000.00000001.11000000 = 192.168.1.192 – Reserved

Step 4 – VLSM and subnetting a subnet

For the WAN links, we need at least three subnets. Each must have a minimum of two usable IP addresses. To get started, let's use the following formula to determine the number of host bits that are needed so that we have at least two usable IP addresses: $2^H - 2$, where H is the number of host bits.

We are going to use one bit, $2^1 - 2 = 2 - 2 = 0$ usable IP addresses. Let's add an extra host bit in our formula, that is, $2^2 - 2 = 4 - 2 = 2$ usable IP addresses. At this point, we have a perfect match, and we know that only two host bits are needed to give us our WAN (point-to-point) links.

We are going to use the following guidelines:

- We cannot modify the network portion of the address (red)
- Since we know that the two host bits are needed to represent two usable IP addresses, we can lock it into place (purple)
- The bit between the network portion (red) and the locked-in host bits (purple) will be the new network bits (black)

| Network ID | 11000000.10101000.00000001.11100000 = 192.168.1.224 |
| Subnet mask | 11111111.11111111.11111111.11111100 = 255.255.255.252 |

- To calculate the number of networks, we can use $2^N = 2^3 = 8$ networks. Even though we got a lot more networks than we actually needed, the remainder of the networks can be set aside for future use.
- To calculate the total IPs and increment, we can use $2^H = 2^2 = 4$ total IP addresses (inclusive of the Network ID and Broadcast IP addresses).
- To calculate the number of usable IP addresses, we can use $2^H - 2 = 2^2 - 2 = 2$ usable IP addresses per network.

Let's work out our eight new subnets for any existing and future WAN (point-to-point) links:

Subnet 1	11000000.10101000.00000001.11100000 = 192.168.1.224/30
Subnet 2	11000000.10101000.00000001.11100100 = 192.168.1.228/30
Subnet 3	11000000.10101000.00000001.11101000 = 192.168.1.232/30
Subnet 4	11000000.10101000.00000001.11101100 = 192.168.1.236/30
Subnet 5	11000000.10101000.00000001.11110000 = 192.168.1.240/30
Subnet 6	11000000.10101000.00000001.11110100 = 192.168.1.244/30
Subnet 7	11000000.10101000.00000001.11111000 = 192.168.1.248/30
Subnet 8	11000000.10101000.00000001.11111100 = 192.168.1.252/30

Now that we have eight new subnets, let's allocate them accordingly.

The first subnet will be allocated to WAN 1, R1-R2:

Network ID:	11000000.10101000.00000001.11100000 = 192.168.1.224/30
1st usable IP:	11000000.10101000.00000001.11100001 = 192.168.1.225/30
Last usable IP:	11000000.10101000.00000001.11100010 = 192.168.1.226/30
Broadcast IP:	11000000.10101000.00000001.11100011 = 192.168.1.227/30

The second subnet will be allocated to WAN 2, R2-R3:

Network ID:	11000000.10101000.00000001.11100100 = 192.168.1.228/30
1st usable IP:	11000000.10101000.00000001.11100101 = 192.168.1.229/30
Last usable IP:	11000000.10101000.00000001.11100110 = 192.168.1.230/30
Broadcast IP:	11000000.10101000.00000001.11100111 = 192.168.1.231/30

The third subnet will be allocated to WAN 3, R3-R4:

Network ID:	11000000.10101000.00000001.11101000 = 192.168.1.232/30
1st usable IP:	11000000.10101000.00000001.11101001 = 192.168.1.233/30
Last usable IP:	11000000.10101000.00000001.11101010 = 192.168.1.234/30
Broadcast IP:	11000000.10101000.00000001.11101011 = 192.168.1.235/30

Now that we have allocated the first three subnets to each of the WAN links, the following remaining subnets can be set aside for any future branches which may need another WAN link. These will be assigned for future reservation:

Subnet 4	11000000.10101000.00000001.11101100 = 192.168.1.236/30
Subnet 5	11000000.10101000.00000001.11110000 = 192.168.1.240/30
Subnet 6	11000000.10101000.00000001.11110100 = 192.168.1.244/30
Subnet 7	11000000.10101000.00000001.11111000 = 192.168.1.248/30
Subnet 8	11000000.10101000.00000001.11111100 = 192.168.1.252/30

 Another benefit of subnetting is being able to reduce the broadcast domain of a domain.

IP version 6 concepts

When IPv4 was created, we knew that it would one day be exhausted. With the increase of **Internet of Things (IoT)** devices and with the internet expanding each day, the IPv4 public space became exhausted a bit faster than expected. Most RIRs have already exhausted their IPv4 blocks of addresses:

- **APNIC**: IPv4 exhausted in April 2011
- **RIPE NCC**: Exhausted in September 2012
- **LACNIC**: Exhausted in June 2014
- **ARIN**: Exhausted in July 2015
- **AFRINIC**: Expected to be exhausted in 2019

Therefore, a new IP addressing scheme was needed. This was IP version 6. There are approximately one undecillion (10^{36}) IPv6 addresses compared to IPv4, which is approximately one billion (10^{9}) addresses. Since the internet is currently in the IoT stage, where smart devices such as phones, tablets, and even computers are all accessing the internet, eventually sensor-equipped, internet-ready devices will be of the future, such as automobiles, household appliances, and so on. This will create the **Internet of Everything (IoE)** era, where everything is connected.

According to RFC 1881, IPv6 was formally entrusted to the IANA in December 1995. This means that a few other protocols were developed to works with IPv4, a few of which are **Internet Control Message Protocol (ICMP)** version 6, NAT64, and DHCPv6.

The format of an IPv6 packet

Earlier in this chapter, we described the fields within an IPv4 packet. In this section, we'll describe the fields which make up an IPv6 packet. However, the IPv6 packet is a bit simpler and has less fields than an IPv4 packet. The following diagram is the IPv6's packet orientation, along with its fields:

Version	Traffic Class	Flow Control	
Payload Length		Next Header	Hop Limit
Source IP Address			
Destination IP Address			

Let's break down each field and explain their purpose and functionality:

- **Version**: This field is used to identify the packet as IP version 6.
- **Traffic Class**: This field provides the same details as the **Differentiated Services** (**DS**) field of an IPv4 packet.
- **Flow Control**: This field informs the receiving routers to process all of the packets with the same flow label exactly the same.
- **Payload Length**: This field simply indicates the length of the data portion of the packet.
- **Next Header**: This field the same purpose as the protocol field in an IPv4 packet.
- **Hop Limit**: This field replaces the TTL field from the IPv4 packet. However, it has the same functionality as the TTL field.
- **Source IPv6 Address**: This field is used to identify the sender's IPv6 address.
- **Destination IPv6 Address**: This field is used to identify the destination's IPv6 address.

We have spoken about the composition of an IPv6 packet. Now, let's take a look a real packet flow using Wireshark:

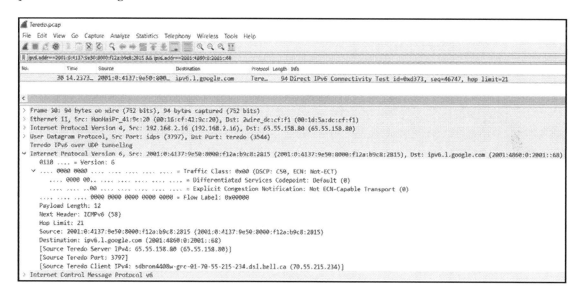

As we can see in the preceding screenshot, all of the fields we have discussed are all presented by the Wireshark output.

The sample capture was taken from Wireshark's official sample repository at `https://wiki.wireshark.org/SampleCaptures`.

IPv6 coexistence on a network

As we have learned, both IPv4 and IPv6 address spaces exist on the internet. An important question is, *how do they both coexist on the same network, such as the internet?* We will discuss three main techniques that are used to aid with the communication between an IPv4 and an IPv6 network:

- **Dual stack**: On most routers, both an IPv4 and an IPv6 address can be assigned to the same internet/port without creating an issues. This allows the IPv4 address to communicate with an IPv4 network and the IPv6 address to communicate seamlessly with an IPv6 network. This allows for the coexistence of both addresses on a single interface.
- **Tunneling**: This enables the transportation of the IPv6 packet across an IPv4 network. This is known as **6to4** tunneling. The router encapsulates the IPv6 packet within an IPv4 packet for transportation across the IPv4 network:

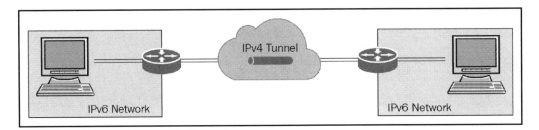

- **Translation (NAT64)**: This allows an IPv6 device to communicate with an IPv4 network. **Network Address Translation 64** (**NAT64**) translates the IPv6 header of an address into an IPv4 header and vice versa, enabling communication between address spaces.

IPv6 address representation

Like IPv4, this new address has a format of its own. As you may recall, an IPv4 address consist of 32-bits in length, and can be written in decimal notation for easier interpretation. An IPv6 address consist of 128-bits in length and is written in hexadecimal notation. With 128 bits, this allows IPv6 to scale to approximately one undecillion (10^{36}) addresses. An IPv6 address is made up of eight hextets, each comprised of 16 bits, which means that it is *8 x 16 = 128* bits in length.

Since hexadecimal numbers are *0 1 2 3 4 5 6 7 8 9 A B C D E F (0 - F)*, each hextet ranges from *0000–FFFF*.

Let's take a look at a few IPv6 addresses:

```
2001:0DB8:0000:1111:0000:0000:0000:0200
```

As we have noticed with the address, each hextet is separated with a colon (:) in IPv6. Whenever we write an IPv6 address, it is not necessary to write in all capital letters as the operating system is able to detect the character value. Regardless of whether your letters are uppercase or lowercase, it will be accepted.

We can write the same IPv6 address in a short format. The leading 0s can be removed, and where a hextet is 0000, it can be substituted with a single 0, thus giving us the following:

```
2001:DB8:0:1111:0:0:0:200
```

Furthermore, whenever there are two or hextets with a continuous length of 0s, we can substitute it with a double colon (::):

```
2001:DB8:0:1111::200
```

This final value is the shortest version of the original IPv6 address we had previously.

The double colon (::) can only be used once in an IPv6 address.

Prefix length

As with all IPv4 addresses, there is usually a subnet mask to accompany it. The same also applies to IPv6. The default subnet mask or prefix length of an IPv6 address is /64. This means that the first 64-bits of the address will represent the network portion and the second, which is known as the **Interface ID**, is 64-bits and will be unique to the host. To further elaborate this, take a look at the following diagram:

Prefix	Interface ID
2001:0DB8:0000:1111	0000:0000:0000:0200

Types of IPv6 addresses

There are different types of addresses in IPv6, each of which has a unique purpose. In this section, we will discuss each, along with their characteristics:

- **Global unicast**: In IPv4, we called an internet assigned address a public address. In IPv6, we have a public address as well, however this time it's known as a **global unicast address**. This address has the same functionality as a public IP address.

 More information about the allocation of IPv6 addresses can be found at https://www.iana.org/assignments/ipv6-unicast-address-assignments/ipv6-unicast-address-assignments.xhtml.

- **Link-local**: An IPv6 link-local address can be found in the FE80::/10 network block. The link-local address is used for local network communication only. This means that there are two IPv6 addresses on an interface—one global unicast address for communication outside the local network and one link-local address communication with devices within a local network. Just as devices use **Media Access Control** (**MAC**) addresses to communicate within a LAN, in an IPv6 network, the link-local address functions the same way. Once communication is beyond the local network, the global unicast address is used.

- **Loopback**: The link-local address has the same functionality as the link-local address in the IPv4 address space. However, in the IPv6 space, the link-local address is : :1/128. This means that only the first bit is 1 in the entire address. Unlike IPv4, the IPv6 link-local address is a single address.

IPv6 transmission types

The following are the three different types of transmissions that can occur on an IPv6 network:

- **Unicast**: The unicast transmission type is where one host communicates with another host directly, such as a client and server, or what is better referred to as a peer-to-peer network. This is a one-to-one transmission.
- **Multicast**: In a multicast transmission, a single host communicates with many other hosts on the network, but not all. This reduces the traffic on the network by sending the message to only those who need it. The devices that participate in multicast transmissions are called a multicast group.
- **Anycast**: An IPv6 anycast address, which is a single IPv6 address, can be assigned to multiple devices. Whenever a packet is sent to the IPv6 anycast address, it is sent to the closest device that shares the anycast address.

Configuring an IP address on a Windows system

Go through the following steps to configure an IP address on a Windows system:

1. Open the **Control Panel** and click on the **Network and Sharing Center** icon:

2. Click on **Change adapter settings**:

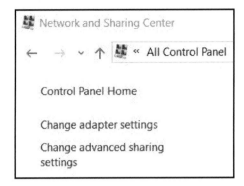

3. Right-click on the network adapter that you would like to configure the IP address settings for and select the **Properties** option:

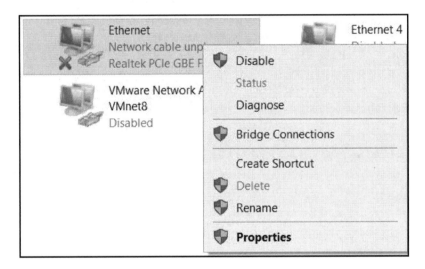

4. Select **Internet Protocol Version 4 (TCP/IPv4)** and click on **Properties** as shown in the following screenshot:

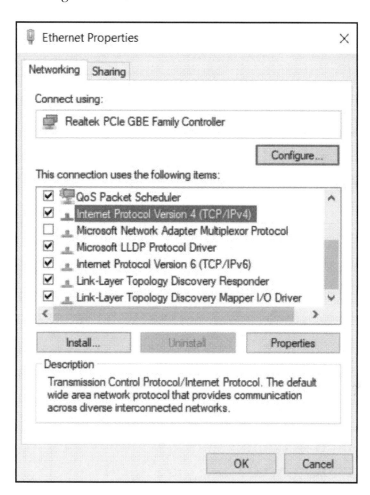

The following window will allow you to choose whether this network adapter automatically receives both an IP address and DNS server setting. Alternatively, you can manually configure the addressing information:

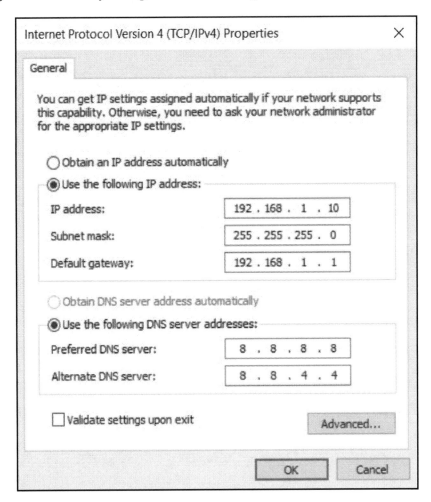

However, if you want to configure IPv6 addressing information, simply click on **Internet Protocol Version 6 (TCP/IPv6)** and click on **Properties**:

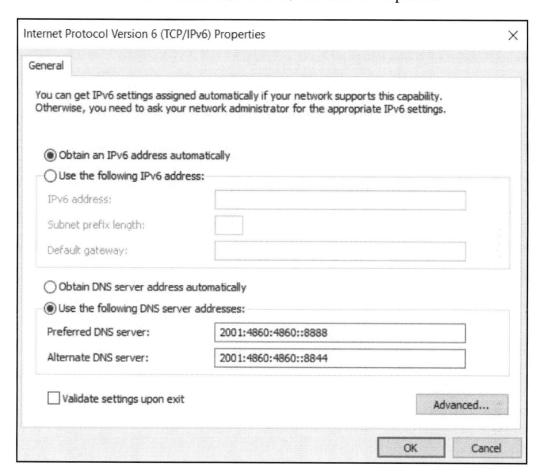

Configuring an IP address on a Linux system

Go through the following steps to configure IP addressing on a Linux system (Debian):

1. In the top-right corner, click on the drop-down arrow and select the gear icon:

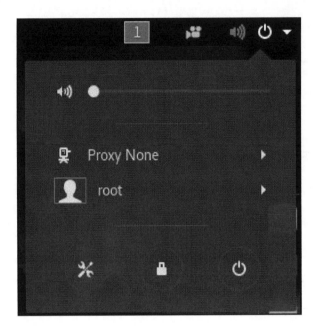

2. Select **Network** and click the gear icon under the **Wired** section:

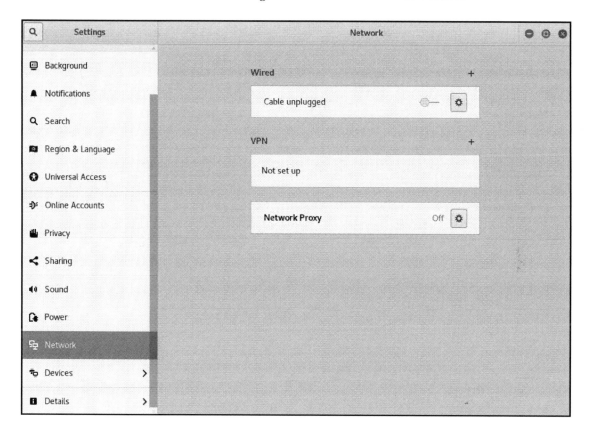

3. Similar to Windows, the adapter settings will open. Click on the **IPv4** tab to adjust the IPv4 settings. Use the **Automatic (DHCP)** option to allow the adapter to receive IP addressing information automatically:

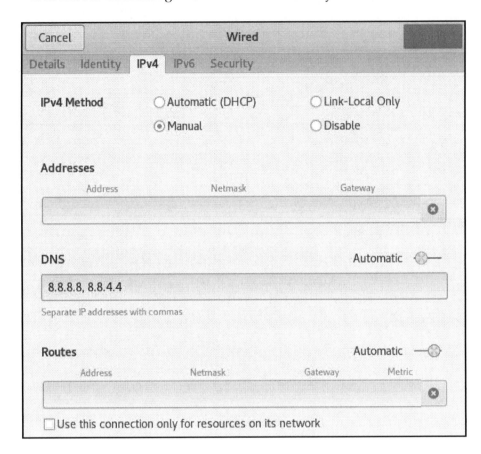

If you click on the **IPv6** tab, you'll have options available so that you can configure the adapter to work with an IPv6 network:

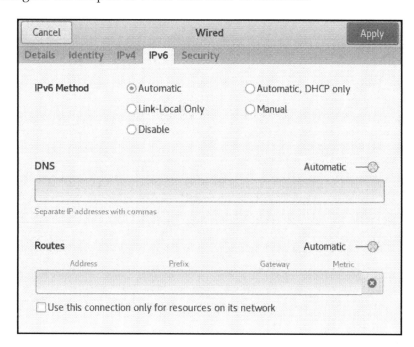

Configuring an IP address on a Cisco IOS router

To configure an IPv4 address on a Cisco IOS router, use the following commands:

```
Router>enable
Router#configure terminal
Router(config)#interface gigabitEthernet 0/1
Router(config-if)#ip address 192.168.1.1 255.255.255.0
Router(config-if)#no shutdown
```

To configure an IPv6 address on a Cisco IOS router, use the following commands:

```
Router>enable
Router#configure terminal
Router(config)#ipv6 unicast-routing
Router(config)#interface gigabitEthernet 0/1
Router(config-if)#ipv6 address 2001:1234:4567:89AB::1/64
Router(config-if)#no shutdown
```

Summary

Understanding IP communication is a very important part of beginning your journey in the field of networking. In this chapter, we covered the fundamentals of IP, and we dove into the concepts and characteristics of both IPv4 and IPv6. We saw the differences in both versions, their advantages and disadvantages, their usage situations, their various types of addresses, the transmission types of both IPv4 and IPv6, and we covered subnetting and VLSM.

In the next chapter, we'll cover routing and switching concepts, such as understanding network traffic and segmentation, how routers and switches function, and their benefits in increasing the performance of the network.

Questions

1. How many bits are there in an **Internet Protocol (IP)** version 4 address?
    1. 48
    2. 128
    3. 64
    4. 32

2. How many usable IP addresses are there in a Class C address?
    1. 256
    2. 200
    3. 254
    4. 255

3. What is the default subnet mask of `172.18.1.1`?
    1. `255.0.0.0`
    2. `255.255.0.0`
    3. `255.255.255.0`
    4. `255.224.0.0`

4. How many usable IPv4 addresses are there in a `/29` network?
    1. 6
    2. 8
    3. 10
    4. 12

5. Which of the following is a Public IPv4 address?
    1. `172.16.56.89`
    2. `192.168.47.96`
    3. `10.11.12.48`
    4. `172.15.58.5`

6. Which of the following is a Private IPv4 address?
    1. `172.33.5.98`
    2. `172.19.5.63`
    3. `12.52.69.41`
    4. `192.167.59.21`

7. How many bits are there in an IP version 6 address?
    1. 32
    2. 48
    3. 128
    4. 127

8. Which of the following is the binary equivalent of 235?
    1. 11101011
    2. 10101010
    3. 11100101
    4. 00101011

9. What is 10101010 in decimal?

   1. 179
   2. 200
   3. 185
   4. 170

10. If a device is communicating with another device, what type of transmission is taking place?

    1. Anycast
    2. Multicast
    3. Broadcast
    4. Unicast

Further reading

To get more information on the allocation of address spaces, visit the Internet Assigned Numbers Authority's Number Resources at `https://www.iana.org/numbers`.

5

Routing and Switching Concepts

As a network professional, we usually engage in the implementation and configuration of various networking appliances, either to build or extend a network. As an upcoming networking professional, it is important to understand the various properties of network traffic and how to design a network to ensure it is performing at an optimal level.

In this chapter, we will cover the following topics:

- Properties of network traffic
- Network segmentation
- Switching concepts
- Routing concepts
- **Network Address Translation (NAT)**

Let's begin!

Properties of network traffic

In this section, we will outline and discuss the properties of network traffic.

Collision domain

In a collision domain, all end devices, such as computers, compete with each other to use the medium for transmitting a message over the network. An example of a collision domain is a **hub-based network**. A hub operates on half duplex, which means only one device can transmit data at any point in time, and each connected device on the hub has to share the same bandwidth with the other devices.

Switches were invented to be smarter devices than hubs. In a switch, bandwidth is not shared but rather dedicated on each port; however, if the switch port is operating on half-duplex, the port is said to be a collision domain. Switch ports usually default to auto negotiate the duplex settings on each interface, such as half, full, or auto. It is recommended to hard set the duplex mode on all devices to ensure you achieve a desired outcome. If you devices are set to be on auto mode, when connected, they both will negotiate to a mutual duplex mode.

Broadcast domain

A broadcast domain is a logically segmentation on the network. It allows nodes to be reachable by a broadcast message. This means if a single computer sends a message to a destination MAC address of FF-FF-FF-FF-FF-FF, all devices in the same network segment will receive a copy of the message.

 When switches are interconnected, the broadcast domains increase in size.

Imagine you're attending classroom-based training for the CompTIA Network+ certification at a training institute where there are multiple training sessions for various courses happening simultaneously, each in a separate classroom. In each room, there are the students for a unique training course with their instructor, such as in your classroom, where the topic is CompTIA Network+. All conversation (verbal dialog) during the classroom session stays in the room and does not penetrate the classroom walls or partitions. If the instructor or a student is speaking, everyone in the room will most likely hear the message at the same time. This is an example of a broadcast domain.

 A broadcast is isolated by a layer 3 device such as a router.

Contention-based communication

In this section, we will discuss various contention-based mechanisms on both wired and wireless networks.

Carrier Sense Multiple Access/Collision Detection (CSMA/CD)

All devices which are connected to a Hub network, all uses CSMA/CD to prevent collision and there operates at half duplex. In CSMA, only a single device can transmit a message on a network at a time; therefore, each device on the network segment must check the medium to determine whether another device is transmitting data. If the medium is busy, the computer waits for a period of time, then checks the medium again and if the medium is free/clear, then it transmits the message over the network.

CD is the ability to recognize that a collision has occurred on the network. A network collision happens when two or more devices transmit at the same time. Whenever a collision happens, a jam signal is sent out to notify devices in the segment. The devices that were transmitting will try again later, until the transmission is successful.

Carrier Sense Multiple Access/Collision Avoidance (CSMA/CA)

CSMA/CA was designed for wireless networks using the IEEE 802.11 standard. CSMA/CA functions a bit similarly to the previously mentioned CSMA/CD. However, there are additional techniques in CSMA/CA to prevent a collision from occurring on a wireless network; this means that CSMA/CA does not detect any collisions, but rather avoids them. On an IEEE 802.11 network (wireless LAN), the sender device inserts a time duration that it needs for the transmission of the message on the medium. The time duration is then sent to all other devices on the wireless network, indicating the unavailability of the medium. When the IEEE 802.11 frame is received on the **Access Point** (**AP**) or wireless router, a notification (acknowledgement) is provided to the sender.

 Switch networks do not use contention-based mechanisms as their ports operate on full duplex, which allows simultaneous communication.

Maximum Transmission Unit (MTU)

As the name says, it is the maximum transmission unit or the largest packet that can be sent over a network. The Ethernet protocol specifies the largest packet is 1,500 bytes in size. Usually, the upper layers, such as the Application Layer, create datagrams or **Protocol Data Units** (**PDUs**) of greater sizes. Since most networks won't allow any packet or frame greater than 1,500 bytes in size, to circumvent this situation, the Network Layer (layer 3) is responsible for fragmenting the packets into smaller, manageable sizes for transmission over the network.

Network segmentation

To ensure our network performs at its optimal capacity, network design and configuration is critical. Network segmentation allows for scalability, improved security, and efficiency in the network. In this section, we will be discussing various switching and network segmentation techniques.

Virtual Local Area Network (VLAN)

In most networks, there are a lot of different traffic types, such as voice traffic generated from IP phones, video traffic from surveillance systems and tele-presence equipment, and data traffic from end devices such as computers, servers, printers, and so on. Imagine an organization segmenting these traffic types by implementing separate and dedicated network equipment for each type of traffic. This would result in having three separately isolated physical networks. The largest downfall of this idea is the high cost for each physically dedicated network.

The evolution of networks has brought us what we have today, that is, a converged network. This allows for the creation of a single, well-designed physical network for voice, video, and data traffic. You may be wondering whether there would be any sort of interference between these traffic types over the same physical network. To further help you understand the logical segmentation in the switches, we'll begin our discussion with the concept of VLANs.

A VLAN allows for the segmentation of physically connected components on switches to be logically organized. Implementing VLANs has the benefits of improving network performance and management, reducing the size of a broadcast domain, and increasing security.

Types of VLANs

The different types of VLANs are as follows:

- **Data VLAN**: The data VLAN is usually configured to transport traffic generated by end devices such as computers, servers, printers, access points, and so on.
- **Default VLAN**: The default VLAN is the primary VLAN, which is loaded onto a managed switch after booting up. A new, out-of-the -box switch normally has all it ports assigned to VLAN 1 by default. This means that if you connect multiple devices on any number of physical ports on the switch, by default, all devices will be able to communicate with each other.
- **Native VLAN**: The native VLAN is used for carrying untagged traffic on an IEEE 802.1Q trunk link. Whenever an end device such as a computer sends traffic to a switch, the receiving switch port inserts an IEEE 802.1Q tag VLAN ID into the frame; this is known as tagged traffic. Untagged traffic does not originate from a VLAN, so *where does it come from?* An example of untagged traffic is self-generated traffic from the switch itself, such as **Cisco Discovery Protocol** (**CDP**) messages.
- **Management VLAN**: The management VLAN is used to remotely access the switch over a network for management purposes. To put it simply, it is the **Switch Virtual Interface** (**SVI**), which is configured with an IP address and subnet mask. A network administrator can HTTP, HTTPS, Telnet or SSH to remotely manage a device. An SVI is a logical interface on a switch.
- **Voice VLAN**: Voice traffic uses the **User Datagram Protocol** (**UDP**), which does not provide any reliability for the delivery of each packet. Since a converged network is the most highly recommended type of network infrastructure, having a dedicated network for all voice traffic is recommended. Using a dedicated VLAN for voice traffic will ensure that all traffic is kept separated from the other traffic types on the physical network.

 Only one VLAN can be assigned to a switch port; this type of assignment will create an access port on the switch. Two VLANs can be assigned to an access port, but only if the other is a voice VLAN; therefore, only one data and one voice VLAN are allowed on a single access port.

Trunks

Trunk links are point-to-point connections from switch-to-switch or switch-to-router. Trunks allow multiple VLANs to carry their traffic between switches and routers. Unlike access ports, which allow only one statically assigned VLAN on the interface, a trunk link allows many VLANs at the same time.

To provide a more practical example of the function of trunk links, we'll the topology, as shown in the following diagram:

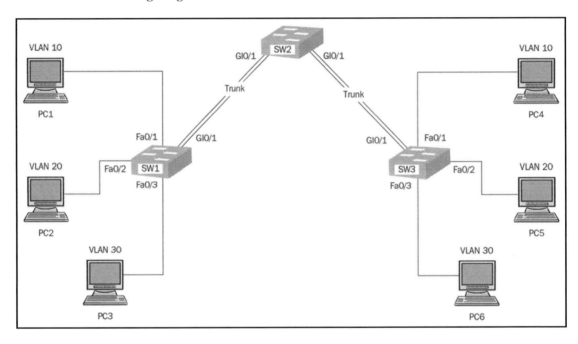

Imagine the link between **SW1** and **SW2** wasn't a Trunk, but rather an access port assigned to **VLAN 10**. If **PC1** is sending a message to **PC4** and at the time same time **PC2** is attempting to communicate with **PC5**, only VLAN 10 traffic will be sent across, while **VLAN 20** and **VLAN 30** will be denied. By converting the ports between **SW1** and **SW2** to a trunk link, **VLAN 10**, **VLAN 20**, and **VLAN 30** will all be allowed between the switches.

Port mirroring

For network and security professionals to conduct packet analysis properly, they need to receive a copy of the traffic flowing through a switch or a VLAN. Port mirroring allows a network switch to send a copy of all Ethernet frames from either a specific port or VLAN to a destination port that has a network protocol analyzer such as Wireshark connected to it.

Spanning Tree Protocol (STP)

Imagine that there's only one available path between your place of residence and the city; if, for some unforeseen reason, the path is obstructed, you won't be able to visit the city by any means. However, if there are multiple paths, should one path be obstructed, another is available, and this does not impact you travel too greatly. Redundancy ensures that a network can continue to operate efficiently, even if a path has failed. Network redundancy allows for the sharing of network traffic, such as by load balancing, and increases the capacity.

Let's take a look at the following topology to observe any issues in layer 2 (Data Link Layer) communication:

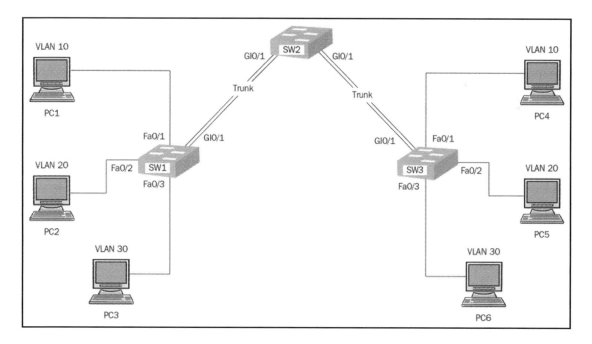

Let's imagine **PC1** wants to send a message to the server. Since the communication is on the same **local area network (LAN)**, **PC1** would send its message to the layer 2 address (MAC address) of the server and not the logical IP address. Therefore, **PC1** will send the frame to **SW1**, then **SW1** will forward the frame to both **SW2** on **Trunk 1** and **SW3** on **Trunk 2**, because there are multiple open paths on the network. **SW3** will forward the frame to the server; let's call this message 1. Let's not forget about the frame that was received on **SW2** from **SW1**; now, **SW2** will forward it to **SW3** and then forward it to the server as message 2. At this point, the server has received two copies of the same message from **PC1**.

The following diagram is the result of the traffic returning from the server to **PC1**:

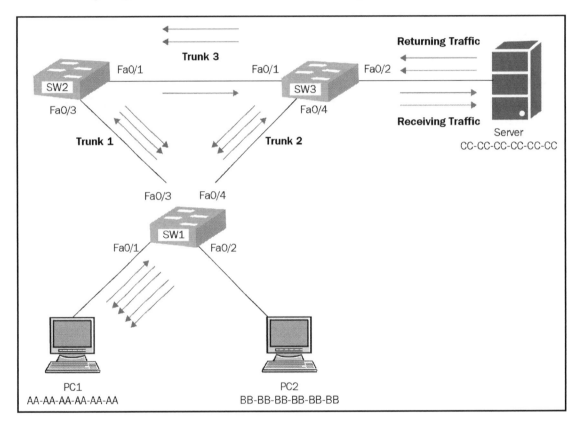

This is a layer 2 loop on the network. It's not too bad, but imagine a larger network in an organization; this can be critical to the performance of the network. As a switch or layer 2 network grows, so does the increase in traffic duplication and loops on the network. STP was developed to prevent and mitigate this issue on layer 2 networks.

STP, as defined by **IEEE 802.1D**, ensures that there's only one logical path to all destinations of the network. It does this by logically blocking other redundant paths that may cause the layer 2 loop on the network. A block path is an interface that prevents any traffic from entering the interface, with the exception of a special frame known as a **Bridge Protocol Data Unit (BPDU)**.

 Switches simply extend a LAN.

Port roles

The following are the different port states on a switch using the STP:

- **Root ports**: These are the ports closest to the root bridge.
- **Designated ports**: These are the non-root ports that allow traffic to flow.
- **Alternate and backup ports**: These are the ports that are logically blocked by the STP. If the primary path has failed, an alternate and backup port may be opened automatically by STP to provide redundancy on the network.
- **Disable ports**: These are the ports that are in a shutdown or administratively down state on the switch.

The following diagram is an example of role assignment using STP:

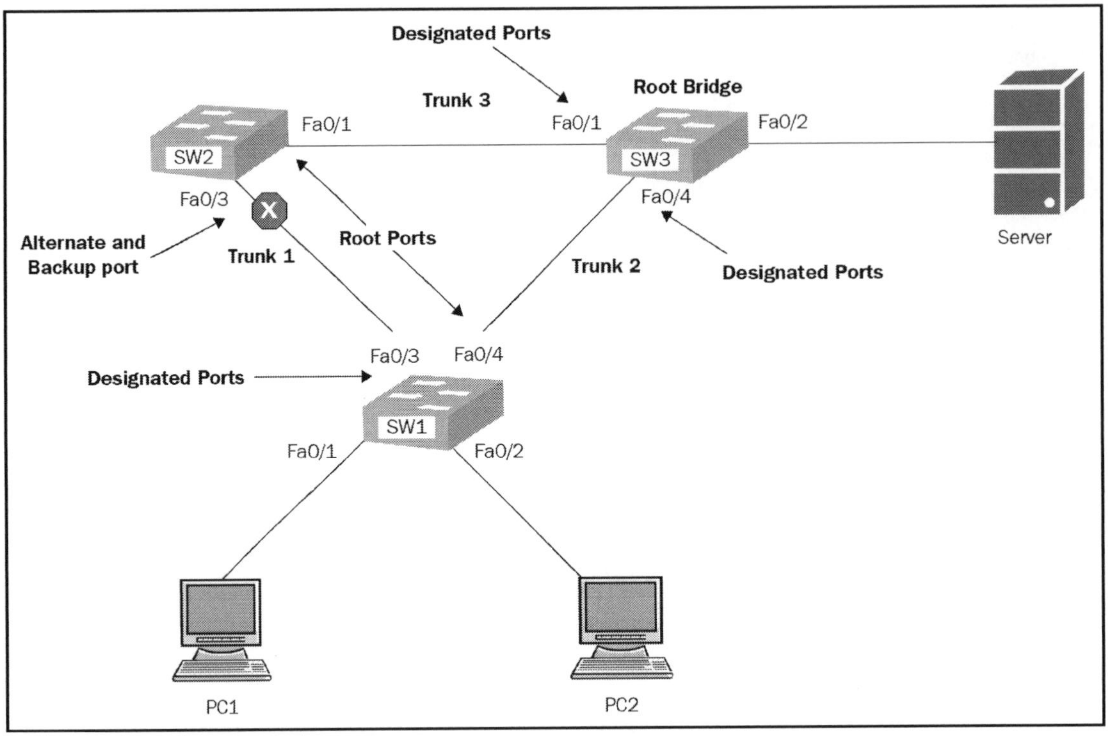

The **Root Bridge** is elected, and then the assignment of the ports occurs. The Root Bridge is the switch that controls the path for traffic flowing over the network. All network traffic passes through the Root Bridge before going to its destination.

Routing protocols

In this section, we will cover the characteristics and features of various routing protocols in the networking world.

Communicating between various networks will not be possible without the use of a router to determine the best path to ensure that the message is delivered to the intended recipient. Imagine you are traveling to a foreign country for the first time; most likely you won't know how to move around the country or the city with getting some directions. Let's imagine you want to visit a famous tourist site, but walking would take too long or the distance is quite far, so you decide to hire a local taxi service. The country or city would be the various networks, you would be the network traffic, and the taxi driver would be the router who is making the decision on the best path to reach your destination.

 Routers are used to interconnect networks and choose the best path to send packets.

Routing types

Whenever a router is powered on, it knows about its directly connected networks, and no other remote networks. A router can learn about remote networks in one of two ways, manually and dynamically.

Static routing

In static routing, the network administrator or engineer can manually install static routes in the routing table of a router. Static routes always take precedence over dynamically learned routes. The reason for this is that the router trusts a static route more than a dynamically learned one because the router trusts the decision of the network administrator or engineer.

Implementing static routes on an entire network topology is not the most feasible course of action for many reasons—a network administrator may accidentally misconfigure a static route and doing so will cause an interruption in network traffic for the intended destination. Another reason, as the network grows more routes will be needed. This also means, the network administrator will be required to manually install a static route for each new network per router within the topology. The biggest disadvantage of using static routing is that if a path goes down due to a network failure, the routers won't be able to re-route any traffic and won't be able to detect the failure.

The following is the command format used for configuring a static route on a Cisco IOS router:

```
ip route destination-network subnet-mask {next-hop-ip- address or exit-
interface}
```

Here is an example of creating a static route to the network, `192.168.1.128/25`, using the next hop IP address of `172.16.1.1`:

```
ip route 192.168.1.128 255.255.255.128 172.16.1.1
```

Dynamic routing

Dynamic routing ensures that the routers discover remote networks automatically, choose the best path to a destination network, and always maintain an updated routing table. If a network path should fail, the dynamic routing protocol can detect the failure in a few seconds and make the decision to re-route traffic to the same destination network using another available path.

Dynamic routing is implemented using a dynamic routing protocol to exchange routing messages with each router on the network. The routing protocols each use a unique algorithm for making a choice in the selection of the best path.

Dynamic routing protocols fall into two main categories:

- Distance vector routing protocols
- Link-state routing protocols

Default route

A default route is used to send all packets that do not match any other routes in the routing table of a local router. These are also known as **default gateways**. Imagine working in a large building; there are many floors and people that you can visit and interact with there, but the people in the building all work for the same company. If you wanted to interact with other people, such as the employees of a local coffee shop, then you would uses the main doorways to exit the building to visit the coffee shop. The main doorways of the building are like the default gateway, and your choice in using this path to go outside the building is like a default route that has been implemented in your mind.

Default routes can be learned either statically or dynamically, and are also known as the gateways of last resort. A default route always points to a way out of LAN, such as toward the internet.

The following is the command format used to create a default route on a Cisco IOS router:

```
ip route 0.0.0.0 0.0.0.0 {next-hop-ip- address or exit-interface}
```

Distance-vector routing protocols

In distance-vector routing, the protocol identifies how far away the destination network is using a metric system. The metric is considered to be a cost value, which can be the number of hops, the average bandwidth, or the latency, such as the delay between the local router and the destination network. This type of routing protocol also determines the direction to send the packet, either using the next hop (the IP address of the next router) or the exit interface of the local router.

Routing Information Protocol (RIP)

RIP is the first generation of routing protocols, and is widely available for anyone to use. RIP uses the Bellman-Ford algorithm in determining the best path when forwarding packets to a destination network. This algorithm uses a metric (cost) of hop counts, which is the number of hops between the source and destination of the packet. A network topology may have multiple paths to the same network, but the Bellman-Ford algorithm chooses the path with the least number of hops as the best path.

However, the RIP has a few disadvantages in its design. The Bellman-Ford algorithm uses a maximum hop count of 15. Any network or route that is greater than 15 hops is considered to be an infinite route. Another disadvantage of using the RIP is that every 15 seconds, each router broadcasts its routing table to each other router in the network topology; it does this regardless of whether a change has happened in the topology or not. This creates an inefficient use of network bandwidth.

Enhanced Interior Gateway Routing Protocol (EIGRP)

EIGRP was created for Cisco devices only, but in 2013, EIGRP was made an open standard by the **Internet Engineering Task Force (IETF)**. Just like other routing protocols, EIGRP uses the **Diffusing Update Algorithm (DUAL)** routing algorithm for determining the best path. DUAL uses a combination of the following: minimum bandwidth, delay, load, reliability, and MTU on the path between the source of the message and the destination.

EIGRP sends an update only if a change has occurred in the topology, and sends it only to the routers that need it (bounded updates). The EIGRP routing messages are sent to the multicast address of 224.0.0.10. EIGRP supports the routing of networks that use **Variable Length Subnet Masking (VLSM)**.

Link-state routing protocols

Unlike distance-vector, link-state routing protocols create a complete view of the network topology on each router. By creating a complete map, a router can choose the best path to all destination networks in the topology.

Open Shortest Path First (OSPF)

The OSPF routing protocol exists in two versions—OSPFv2 for IPv4 networks and OSPFv3 for IPv6 networks. OSPF was designed to be efficient, have fast convergence, and be scalable. Similarly to EIGRP, OSPF uses the **Shortest Path First** (**SPF**) algorithm to makes its choice in forwarding packets using the best path. The OSPF routing messages are sent to the multicast address of either 224.0.0.5 or 224.0.0.6.

The **International Organization for Standardization** (**ISO**) worked on developing their own link-state routing protocol known as **Intermediate System-to-Intermediate System** (**IS-IS**).

Path vector routing protocol

Unlike other dynamic routing protocols, which use bandwidth, delay, distance, and so on, a path-vector routing protocol uses many more attributes to determine the best path to forward packets. It usually maintains the path's information, which is dynamically shared among other **Internet Service Providers** (**ISPs**).

Border Gateway Protocol (BGP)

BGP is currently the only **Exterior Gateway Protocol** (**EGP**) used for exchanging routing information between internet service protocols, and is the only path-vector routing protocol at the time of writing this certification guide. Each service provider has a unique **Autonomous System** (**AS**) number, which is used as an identifier in BGP routing. The AS value is usually 16 or 32 bits in length. BGP is the protocol that routes all internet traffic between ISPs; however, the biggest disadvantage of using BGP is its extremely slow convergence for a network and the time it takes to send an update to another AS.

BGP is only used on the internet. Imagine an internet route goes down in North America; the routers immediately send an update to the rest of the world (wave 1). Before all internet routers are able to make the changes in their local routing table, the down network has been restored and another update is sent out (wave 2). Imagine the impact on the performance of routers that are constantly updating their routing tables; this would be very bad. Using BGP, the protocol waits for a long time to determine whether the failed network will be restored before telling everyone in the world.

There are two types of BGP—Internal BGP (**IBGP**), which is used in an organization, and **External BGP** (**EBGP**), which is used on the internet and is commonly referred to as the BGP we know today.

Network Address Translation (NAT)

As we learned in Chapter 4, *Understanding IPv4 and IPv6*, there are a finite number of IPv4 addresses that can be publicly assigned to devices that are connected directly to the internet. Imagine if each device, both in a LAN (computers, servers, printers, and so on) and the internet, all had a unique public IPv4 address. The pool of public IPv4 addresses would have been exhausted many years ago, probably before the creation of smartphone and **Internet of Things** (**IoT**) devices.

The private IPv4 address space, defined by RFC 1918, was designed for IP networks within an organization and not on the internet. As we learned in the previous chapter, the private IPv4 address space is not unique per organization. The following is the private IPv4 address range:

Private IPv4 Address Space		
Class	**Address Range**	**Network Prefix**
A	10.0.0.0 - 10.255.255.255	10.0.0.0/8
B	172.16.0.0 - 172.31.255.255	172.16.0.0/12
C	192.168.0.0 - 192.168.255.255	192.168.0.0/16

Now, the following questions arise—*how can organizations communicate on the internet with a private IPv4 address, which is non-routable on the internet?*, and if two or more organizations use the same scheme of IPv4 addresses, *how can they communication properly without have duplication or conflicts in network traffic?*

NAT was created to allow an organization to allow their internal IPv4 networks, containing private IPv4 addresses, to be translated into a public IP address that can be routable over the internet. A simple example of NAT operations is your internet connection at home. Your internet network uses a private IPv4 addressing scheme, but on your ISP router (modem), there's a public IPv4 address on the internet-facing interface. When you send traffic to the internet, the IPv4 address on the packets is translated to a public IPv4 address on your ISP router (modem):

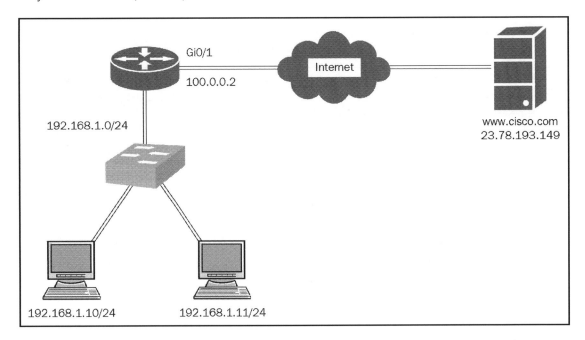

There are three types of NATs:

- Static NAT
- Dynamic NAT
- **Port Address Translation (PAT)**

Static NAT

This is a one-to-one mapping between an internal and external IP address. A static NAT is used when access to an internal device is required over the internet. Whenever a company hosts their own internal web server, they can either obtain a public IP address from their local ISP or assign a private IPv4 address and use static NAT to allow users from the internet to access the private internal server. Internet users would simply use the public IP address; when the incoming traffic reaches the company's internet router, the router checks for any NAT maps for a valid entry. Once an entry is found, the traffic is sent to the private internal server. The internet user would think that the server has a public address and not realize an NAT translation is taking place.

Dynamic NAT

This is a many-to-many type of mapping where multiple internal addresses are mapped to multiple external addresses. In dynamic NAT, a pool of public IP addresses is assigned to the private IPv4 addresses on a first come, first served basis. If there are six public IP addresses on the internet-facing port, and on the LAN interface there are 50 devices, only a maximum of six devices can use the available public IP addresses. If a seventh device wants to communicate over the internet while the pool is exhausted, the seventh device will need to wait until one of the public IP addresses is made available by the router.

PAT

PAT is a many-to-one type of mapping, and is commonly used to translate multiple private IPv4 addresses to a single public IP address. These are commonly found residential internet connections and small businesses. ISPs usually assign one public IP address to their customer; using PAT allows all devices on a LAN to simultaneously access the internet.

If you recall, there are 65,535 logical port numbers. PAT takes advantage of assigning a unique source port for each new conversation that needs to be translated into a public IP address:

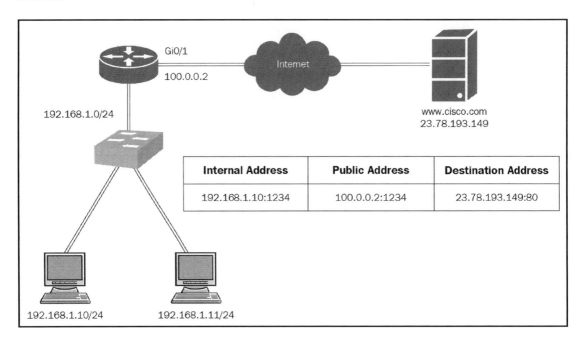

Internal Address	Public Address	Destination Address
192.168.1.10:1234	100.0.0.2:1234	23.78.193.149:80

Summary

Let's recap, in this chapter, we saw the benefits of creating smaller broadcast domains and how VLANs help improve overall network performance. Furthermore, we discussed various routing and switching concepts, and completed this chapter with an overview of network address translation.

In the next chapter, we will discuss wireless and cloud technologies.

Questions

1. What is the largest packet that can traverse a modern network?
    1. 1492
    2. 1493
    3. 1499
    4. 1500

2. Which of the following methods can be used to a segment a layer 2 network?
    1. VLAN
    2. Collision domain
    3. Broadcast domain
    4. STP

3. Which IEEE standard defines loop prevention in a layer 2 network?
    1. IEEE 802.11
    2. IEEE 802.3
    3. IEEE 802.1D
    4. IEEE 802.1Q

4. What type of port exists on a root bridge?
    1. Root ports
    2. Designated ports
    3. Alternate and backup ports
    4. Fast Ethernet ports

5. Which type of route is used to send traffic to the internet?
    1. Static
    2. Default
    3. Dynamic
    4. RIP

6. Which routing protocol uses hop count as its metric?
    1. EIGRP
    2. OSPF
    3. BGP
    4. RIP

7. Which protocol is used on the internet?
    1. EIGRP
    2. OSPF
    3. BGP
    4. RIP

6
Wireless and Cloud Technologies

Networks have evolved a lot since the **Advanced Research Projects Agency Network** (**ARPANET**). Now there are so many devices with wireless capabilities existing. Long ago, smartphones and tablets were not in existence, and a cellular phone was simply a mobile phone that could fit in a person's pocket and its main function was simply for sending and receiving a call with **Short Message Service** (**SMS**) features. Since the launch of Apple's first smartphone back in June 2007, many mobile phone companies such as Motorola, Sony, and Nokia begin manufacturing smartphones and other smart devices such tablets and smart watches.

The need for more efficient methods of communication and the development of various technologies and devices has grown over the past years. In today's world, a person may not have only a mobile device but sometimes a few wireless devices that are all connected to the internet for a specific purpose. Some of these devices are connected to cellular networks and even personal area networks, such as fitness and health monitors.

This chapter focuses on understanding the various wireless and cloud computing technologies and their concepts. The following topics will be covered:

- Various wireless technologies
- Mobile technologies
- IEEE 802.11 standards
- Wireless LAN topologies
- Cloud computing concepts
- Types of cloud services
- Cloud delivery models

Let's begin!

Wireless technologies

The use of wireless technologies has been around for quite some time, from cellular towers to Walkie Talkie, Wi-Fi, LTE, and 4G networks. Wireless technologies can always make a convenience for us; whether at home, at work, or even when operating an organization, wireless makes portability of a computer system or mobile device possible.

Let's imagine a world without any sort of wireless technologies, a world without a portable phone, a world where radar technology does not exist, and a world without computers that are portable such as laptops; everything requires a physical network cable to be connected to a network, whether the network is a computer network, a telecommunication network, or even an aviation system with radar systems for tracking airplanes while they are in flight. One of the many benefits of using wireless technology is that it has reduced the need for physical wiring and increased portability of mobile devices while still allowing devices to exchange information among themselves.

In this section, we will take a look at various wireless technologies and some common **Institute of Electrical and Electronics Engineers** (**IEEE**) standards.

Let's get started!

Z-Wave

Over recent years, with the evolution of networks and the internet, there are a lot of technology companies that are focusing on producing **Internet of Things** (**IoT**) devices and appliances for both home and industrial consumers. From home automation products such as lighting controllers and security systems to industrial plant sensors, the world is dynamically growing toward automation with the IoT-ready devices. Many new wireless standards and technologies were created, one of which was the Z-Wave technology.

Z-Wave was first introduced in 2001 as a wireless communication protocol for compatible devices. Like many other standards and protocols, Z-Wave operates between the **800–900 Megahertz** (**MHz**) radio frequency range, which makes it better for home automation devices as they would not experience any interference with devices that operate on the 2.4 GHz and 5 GHz radio frequency band. Since it is operating on a different frequency rather than on the Wi-Fi spectrum (2.4 GHz and 5 GHz), Z-Wave reduces the possibility of any sort of interference from other electronic devices, making it suitable for the IoT devices within a household.

According to the Z-Wave Alliance (`www.z-wavealliance.org`), the Z-Wave protocol has the following features:

- Low powered, **Radio Frequency (RF)** based technology
- It was designed for the home automation industry
- Operating in a mesh type topology
- Data rates up to 100 KBps and supports data encryption using AES-128

This technology allows the creation of smart homes where each device, such as home control systems, home entertainment systems, and even home security systems, can communicate with each other seamlessly using Z-Wave.

 For further details on Z-Wave, you can visit the Z-Wave Alliance at `www.z-wavealliance.org` and Silicon Laboratories at `www.z-wave.com`.

ANT+

Since the smart technology era began, we have been seeing an increasing amount of health and fitness monitoring devices from smartphones to smart watches and apps. Usually, there is a sensor device that is placed on your body, such as the Nike fitness tracker, which is a wristband. Some fitness trackers are capable of monitoring a person's heart rate, number of steps per day, their sleep patterns, and many others. The sensor band would need to send its recorded data to a smart device, which can then interpret it and provide information to us humans, and this is where ANT+ comes into the picture.

ANT+ is a wireless technology that allows health and fitness monitoring devices to exchange data between a sensor and another device. This wireless technology allows interconnectivity between various vendor devices.

Some areas of use are as follows:

- Cycling
- Geriatric care
- Gym fitness
- Tennis
- Activity monitoring

The following are some of the characteristics of ANT+:

- Operates on the 2.4 GHz wireless frequency band
- Uses low power
- Provides scalability
- Uses peer to peer, star, and even mesh topologies

For further information on the ANT+ technology, you can visit the ANT+ Alliance at www.thisisant.com.

Bluetooth

The main feature of Bluetooth is to pair with another Bluetooth-compatible device for the purpose of creating a **Personal Area Network (PAN)**. Just as with any type of network, a PAN is used to share a resource. Bluetooth radio frequencies operate over a short distance. This wireless technology is mostly found in cellular phones, headphones, health and fitness monitors, smart watches, external speakers that are Bluetooth-compatible, and even modern automobiles.

Characteristics of Bluetooth include the following:

- Bluetooth is designed for low power operation
- It utilizes the 2.4 GHz frequency band for wireless communication
- Data transfer rates ranging from 125 KBps to 2 MBps
- It uses a PAN topology

Some examples of the usage of Bluetooth are as follows:

- Pairing a mobile phone to an automobile's audio system for hands-free support while driving
- Exchanging files between two mobile devices such as music, video, and pictures
- Two smartphones can be paired to exchange notifications and messages

Further information on Bluetooth can be found at the official website: www.bluetooth.com.

IEEE 802.15

Bluetooth utilizes the IEEE 802.15 standard, which outlines the specification for Wireless PAN.

Near Field Communication (NFC)

NFC is a type of radio frequency technology that allows a two-way wireless communication between compatible devices. NFC is widely used in payment systems, such as Google Wallet and MasterCard partnership. So *how can someone make a payment using NFC?* The Google Wallet app allows a person to store their credit card details on their Google account; this can be used as a payment option either when making online or in-store purchases wherever it is accepted. For an in-store purchase, the customer (which is yourself) would enable the NFC feature on their smartphone and simply touch it against the NFC transceiver at the checkout counter. This would allow the transfer of the currency from their credit card through the Google Wallet to the store by using NFC technology.

The characteristics of NFC include the following:

- Short range—works when 10 cm apart
- Two-way communication
- Allows easy sharing of resources between two or more devices

As with most digital and wireless technologies, NFC has its fair share of security concerns such as the following:

- Eavesdropping
- Interception
- Data corruption and manipulation
- Theft

 Further information about NFC can be found at
www.nearfieldcommunication.org.

Infrared

Infrared uses a line-of-sight, electromagnetic radiation that is not always visible to the human eye. Infrared technology is mostly used in entertainment controllers for your television, cable box, and so on. The benefit of using infrared is its long wavelength, which means it can travel further than previously mentioned wireless technologies.

Some of the earlier generations of cellular phones were manufactured with Infrared transceivers. This allowed two infrared-compatible devices such as two phones to exchange pictures, videos, music files, and even contact cards. The only downside of using infrared as a wireless technology is dependency on a line-of-sight for operation.

Infrared use cases include the following:

- Communication
- Meteorology
- Astronomy
- Night vision

Radio-Frequency Identification (RFID)

RFID has been around for quite some time; it can be found almost everywhere. RFID can be commonly found in a lot of corporate organizations—each employee is given a staff ID badge, which is sometimes an RFID card. This RFID card can be used to allow and deny access to areas within a building. A simple example is access control to restricted areas in a building such as a data center or a company's vault.

RFID uses a radar technology which uses radio energy; this radio energy is transmitted from an RFID reader to the RFID tag, and the radio frequency from the reader powers the RFID tag and transmits an identification back to the reader. This communication is bidirectional between the RFID reader and the RFID tag.

RFID use cases are as follows:

- Access badges for employees
- Animal identification
- Item tracking

There are many security vulnerabilities with RFID technology, and the following are some of them:

- **RFID sniffing**: This vulnerability exists when a malicious person uses an RFID reader to send a signal (request) to a victim's RFID card; the victim's RFID card will reply with its identification back to the malicious person's reader.
- **RFID spoofing**: Once a malicious user has obtained the identity from a legitimate user's RFID card (through RFID sniffing), it's quite simple for the attacker to make a clone of the RFID card. This fake RFID card can be used to access secure areas at the victim's workplace.
- **Electromagnetic attack**: Electromagnetic interference can disrupt the communication between an RFID reader and the RFID card/tag.

IEEE 802.16

Another notable wireless technology that is used in various countries is known as **Worldwide Interoperability for Microwave Access** (**WiMAX**). WiMAX is defined by IEEE 802.16, which outlines the specification for wireless broadband.

802.11 wireless standards

In 1997, the IEEE introduced the 802.11 standard for **Wireless Local Area Network** (**WLAN**), which allowed any device with a **Wireless Interface Card** (**WIC**) to connect and communicate over an IEEE 802.11 network. Today, most consumers may not know what IEEE 802.11 is, but what they do know is the term—Wi-Fi.

Wi-Fi is another type of wireless technology that uses radio waves/frequencies to provide communication between devices. Wi-Fi is based on the IEEE 802.11 standards for wireless networking. Most portable devices such as laptops, smartphones, tablet computers, and even entertainment systems, such as gaming consoles, for example, the Sony PlayStation and Microsoft Xbox, each has a built-in Wi-Fi card or a WIC, which is used to communicate on an IEEE 802.11 network or what is better known as a Wi-Fi network.

Since 1997, there have been many updates to the IEEE 802.11 standard and newer variations are currently available. Later in this chapter, we will discuss the more recent updates to this standard, with their comparisons and contrasts. You can always check the IEEE website at www.ieee.org for more information on any of their standardizations.

In this section, we will discuss the various 802.11 standards that outline their similarities and differences.

 Wi-Fi is managed by the Wi-Fi Alliance; further information can be found at www.wi-fi.org.

802.11a

In October 1999, IEEE created the 802.11a standard, which defines how wireless communication can occur on compatible devices. This was one of the first generations of the 802.11 standard. The IEEE 802.11a standard operates on the 5 GHz frequency band and is able to transmit up to 54 MBps of data at any point in time.

The advantages of using the IEEE 802.11a standard are as follows:

- Less susceptible to interference from out Wi-Fi bands such as the 2.4 GHz band. This improves the performance of the wireless network.
- Supports high bandwidth of 54 Mbps.

The disadvantages of using the IEEE 802.11a standard are as follows:

- Since this standard uses the 5 GHz frequency band, higher frequencies are weakened, as there are objects between the wireless router and the client devices. The 5 GHz band also produces short distances unlike the 2.4 GHz frequency, which provides longer distances.
- In modern networks, the IEEE 802.11a is not seen too often but is used in special cases.

802.11b

The second official standard was the IEEE 802.11b standard. This version allows all wireless-compliant devices to operate on the 2.4 GHz frequency band rather than the previous 802.11a standard, which operates on the 5 GHz band. Unlike the 802.11a, which has a bandwidth up to 54 MBps, the IEEE 802.11b standard has a capacity of up to 11 MBps.

Advantages of using the IEEE 802.11b standard include the following:

- Most modern-day Wi-Fi compatible devices have a 2.4 GHz wireless transceiver and are able to communicate with most Wi-Fi networks
- The 2.4 GHz band provides greater distance than the 5 GHz band and therefore a better range in signal

Disadvantages of using the IEEE 802.11b standard are as follows:

- Since most modern-day Wi-Fi networks operate on the 2.4 GHz band, the possibility for interference is much higher.
- There are other appliances that can cause interference on the 2.4 GHz band such as some cordless phones, Bluetooth technology, baby monitors, and microwave ovens as all these emit and work on the 2.4 GHz band as well.
- Since the 802.11b standard does provide low bandwidth capacity of 11 MBps, this can be an issue if there is need to support more devices and application streaming across multiple wireless devices simultaneously. The bandwidth of the 802.11b standard can cause a bottleneck in the network.
- It's not backward compatible with IEEE 802.11a devices.

802.11g

After some years, in June 2003, IEEE later created the 802.11g standard. This was the golden child of the 802.11 standard; it defines 802.11g-compatible devices that can operate on the 2.4 GHz band and provide a bandwidth up to 54 Mbps. 802.11g, providing longer range since it is using the 2.4 GHz band and higher bandwidth than the previous 802.11b standard. Another benefit of the 802.11g standard is its backward compatibility with devices that operate on the 802.11b standard.

The only downside to using the 802.11g standard is that almost all wireless router and access points that were manufactured between 2003 and 2009 supported the 802.11g standard, which means they all operated on the 2.4 GHz band. This would cause nearby wireless routers to experience channel overlapping and interference with other wireless-compatible routers.

The benefits of using the IEEE 802.11g standard are as follows:

- Support for backward compatible for IEEE 802.11b
- Farther distance due to the 2.4 GHz band
- High bandwidth support of 54 Mbps
- Has an average range of 70 m

The disadvantage of using the IEEE 802.11g standard is that, since there are a lot of wireless routers and access points that use the 2.4 GHz band, the possibility for interference is much higher. The interference can cause packet drop on the wireless network.

802.11n

IEEE continuously develops newer standards, some of which are updated versions of an original standard with fixes and improvement with increased performance. Six years after of the release of the 802.11g standard, the IEEE released a newer and more advanced version of 802.11; this is known as the IEEE 802.11n standard.

The IEEE 802.11n standard operates on both the 2.4 GHz and 5 GHz band. This allows Wi-Fi-compatible devices to connect to the 802.11n wireless router/access point despite its wireless interface card type. Earlier generations of the wireless routers that supported the 802.11n standard only used the 2.4 GHz band but later they eventually supported both bands. This means that, if a device has an 802.11n network adapter that operates on the 5 GHz band, it will connect to the radio antenna that utilizes the 5 GHz frequency on the wireless router or access point accordingly. Since more of the wireless networks are using the 2.4 GHz band, this frequency will be very saturated with the number of devices are using at any point in time; with the 5 GHz band available, it provides a less saturated channel for network traffic and communication.

The 802.11n standard has the capacity of transferring 600 MBps using a 40 MHz channel width using four antennas. This allows for higher bandwidth capacity on the 802.11n-compatible wireless routers and access points. Unlike traditional wireless routers and access points, which use either a single radio antenna for sending and receiving bits or a wireless router that has multiple antennas but each individual antenna is used for both sending and receiving data, 802.11n takes advantage of technology known as **Multiple-Input Multiple-Output (MIMO)**.

MIMO uses multiple radio antennas for transmitting and receiving, however, MIMO handles the radio communication a bit differently from traditional wireless routers/access points. In most modern-day wireless routers, there are usually 3–6 external radio antennas; one such wireless router is the NETGEAR Nighthawk series. Let's imagine a wireless router has a total of four antennas; MIMO would use two antennas for transmitting and the remaining two antennas would be for receiving. MIMO ensures each antenna has a particular role in communication and is not overworked like older wireless routers where each antenna handles both transmitting and receiving functions.

Benefits of using the IEEE 802.11n standard are as follows:

- Operates on both the 2.4 GHz and 5 GHz band
- Supports bandwidth of up to 600 MBps
- Has an average range of 70 m
- Uses the 20 MHz and 40 MHz channels
- Backward compatible with 802.11a, 802.11b, and 802.11g devices

Disadvantages of using the IEEE 802.11n standard are as follows:

- Since 802.11n provides better features and performance, the 802.11n wireless routers/access points are usually at a higher cost than the older devices that support the 802.11a/b standards
- Even though 802.11n operates on both the 2.4 GHz and the 5 GHz band, since most devices still utilize the 2.4 GHz band, there will be interference on this particular band rather than on the 5 GHz frequency band

802.11ac

One of the most recent wireless standards is the IEEE 802.11ac standard for wireless networks. This standard was released back in January, 2014 and contains a lot of improvements from its predecessors.

The IEEE 802.11ac standard outlines the use of the 5 GHz band only; this allows less interference on this radio frequency, however, not all devices are 802.11ac-compatible and are able to communicate on the 5 GHz band.

A notable improvement is its capability to operate on wider channels of up to 160 MHz, allowing for data to flow, hence providing a maximum bandwidth of 7 GBps, which is a huge jump from its predecessor, IEEE 802.11n. Furthermore, the IEEE 802.11ac standard uses an improved version of MIMO, which is known as **Multiuser MIMO (MU-MIMO)**.

Traditional wireless routers/access points can communicate to only one device at time even though there are many connected. A simple example is within a household—there are many devices that may be using Wi-Fi such as smart TVs, tablet computer, laptops, and smartphones. When all of these are connected to the wireless network, the wireless router/access can serve only one device at time. A result would be receiving poor stream performance if you're watching a video on YouTube or Netflix. MU-MIMO solves this issue by improving performance and user experience on the wireless network. Even though there are multiple devices connected and simultaneously using the wireless network, MU-MIMO ensures each device has less waiting time to be served.

Benefits of using IEEE 802.11ac include the following:

- Supports bandwidth of up to 7 GBps
- Has less interference
- Uses MU-MIMO, which improves the wireless network experience for the user

Disadvantages of using IEEE 802.11ac are as follows:

- Not all devices are compatible with the 5 GHz frequency band
- Shorter range due to the operating frequency

802.11 comparison table

The following table shows a comparison between each of the IEEE 802.11 standards:

IEEE Standard	Frequency	Maximum Bandwidth	Backward Compatiblity
802.11a	5 Ghz	54 Mb/s	n/a
802.11b	2.4 Ghz	11 Mb/s	n/a
802.11g	2.4 Ghz	54 Mb/s	802.11b
802.11n	2.4 Ghz & 5 Ghz	600 Mb/s	802.11a/b/g
802.11ac	5 Ghz	7 Gb/s	802.11a/n

Frequencies

As you probably have noticed already, during all of our discussions of 802.11 and Wi-Fi, the only two frequency bands that are currently in use are the 2.4 GHz and 5 GHz ranges. The IEEE 802.11 standard outlines the use of particular frequencies within the 2.4 GHz and 5 GHz ranges. Since the frequencies are a bit challenging to remember all of the time, the IEEE put these frequencies into groups, which are known as channels.

A frequency of 20 MHz is like a small water line; if we increased the size of the water line to 40 MHz, there would be an increased in the capacity of water supported by the line. In the 802.11 standard, an access point either can use a single 20 MHz frequency for transmitting data or can combine multiple 20 MHz frequencies to achieve a higher data rate.

2.4 GHz

The IEEE 802.11 has outlined the use of the 20 MHz frequency with the 2.4 GHz range. Within the 2.4 GHz range, there are multiple channels; each operates on a 20 MHz frequency ranging from 2,412 MHz to 2,482 MHz. There are a total of 11 channels, which are channels 1–11. Since each channel is close by, the recommended channels to use are channels 1, 6, and 11. These three channels do not overlap with each other and therefore do not cause any interference:

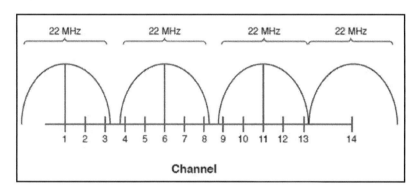

5 GHz

Unlike the 2.4 GHz band, which uses a frequency of 20 MHz, the 5 GHz band uses channel sizes of 20 MHz, 40 MHz, 80 MHz, and 160 MHz; this allows the more recent 802.11 standard to transport a much higher capacity of data over its channels, allowing data rates of up to 7 GBps when using the 802.11ac standard.

Cellular technologies

Original phones required a physical copper cable connecting each landline phone to the local telecommunication company. This made it difficult for anyone to be contacted if they were not at home. The creation of cellular phones and cellular towers made it possible for each person to have a mobile phone with a direct telephone number attached to it; this made for easier reachability and improved communication.

Cellular technology comprises the mobile device that is known as a cellular phone. Within each cellular phone, there's a tiny antenna that operates on certain cellular type frequencies, which are known as **Global System for Mobile Communication (GSM)**, **Time Division Multiple Access (TDMA)**, **Code Division Multiple Access (CDMA)**, and **Long Term Evolution (LTE)**. The cellular phone connects automatically to the closest cellular tower, which then connects to the telecommunication service provider internal network. The telecommunication service provider is responsible for the routing of calls, messages, and any other types of communication between cellular phones, landlines, messaging, and interconnecting other service providers' network to have interoperability between various telecommunication companies.

These large cellular towers are large antennas that point in a 360° direction to ensure coverage surrounding the tower; since a wireless signal deteriorates over distance, the telecommunication provider strategically places multiple cellular towers to provide almost maximum coverage of their cellular network within their operating territory such as an island, country, or state.

GSM

GSM is a mobile network standard that is adopted around the world by many telecommunication providers. In a GSM network, the telecommunication provider uses a **Subscriber Identity Module (SIM)** card, which is inserted into a SIM module slot in a GSM-compatible phone. In older cellular phones, the SIM slot was usually found on the back the phone, sometimes under the battery. In newer smartphones, the SIM slot is sometimes found on the side of the phone.

Once the SIM card has been inserted and the phone is powered on, the SIM card will register to the telecommunication service provider network and to the closest available cellular tower. If a person with a GSM phone is travelling, the GSM phone will automatically connect to a cellular tower with a stronger GSM signal reception.

The following is a image of a SIM card:

GSM has been one of the most widely used cellular technologies in the mobile market; one of the benefits of using GSM is its ability to move a SIM card from one cellular phone to another. However, some telecommunication providers sometimes lock the phones they sold to only their cellular network, which means that if you try to use a SIM card from another provider, it will not work.

TDMA

TDMA is another mobile carrier standard. Each device on a TDMA network for a single service provider uses a single stream within the provider network. There is a multiplexer device where all of the individual streams from cellular phones meet and are combined into a single stream over the TDMA network. At the receiving end, the single stream is split apart and is transported to the receiving cellular device. This process is known as **muxing**.

CDMA

The CDMA standard uses a unique code during a conversation between two cellular devices on the CDMA network. Let's imagine there are two people who would like to have a telephone conversation over a CDMA network; these people are Bob and Alice. When Bob initiates a call to Alice, the cell traffic is tagged with a unique code while in the telecommunication provider CDMA network—this ensures the identification and filtering of each call on the receiving end.

The disadvantage of using a CDMA is that it is not widely used globally as compare to GSM.

4G and LTE

One of the most recent mobile technologies is the LTE standard, which is based on 4G technology on the mobile market. LTE merges the GSM and CDMA standards to create a converged standard. With LTE, telecommunication providers are able to deliver both **second generation** (2G) and newer services over a single network. LTE is able to carry data rates of up to 150 MBps.

There's another version of LTE, which is known as **LTE-Advanced (LTE-A)**, which has the capability of carrying data rates up to 300 MBps.

 Both GSM and CDMA are 2G mobile technologies.

Antenna and power requirements

So far, we've discussed various wireless technologies and we've realized that, to communicate, each device requires some sort of antenna and power to emit a radio frequency signal to receiving devices such as cellular phones and laptops. One of the most important things to consider when setting up any sort of wireless network, whether it's a GSM, Wi-Fi, or Z-Wave, is the power levels on the antennas. If the power level is too low, mobile devices further away may not receive a signal and this would be a major issue. If the signal is too weak between the transmitting antenna and the mobile device, the mobile device may experience attenuation. Attenuation is a loss of signal such as an electrical current due to distance; when this happens on a network, the loss of signal will result in data loss during transmission.

Another important factor is the type of antenna and the direction it is facing:

- **Omnidirectional antenna**: This is the most commonly found type of antenna. The omnidirectional antenna is mostly found on wireless routers and access points; the antenna itself emits its signal in all directions at the same time, hence the name, omni, *which means all*. This is a good choice if your goal is to cover all directions at once. The downside of using an omnidirectional antenna is its inability to focus its signal—without focus, the signal is limited to a shorter distance:

- **Yagi antenna**: The Yagi antenna is a directional and high gain antenna. This type of antenna is able to focus its signal in a single direction, and this allows to increase the range even further but only in the direction it is pointing toward.
- **Parabolic antenna**: The parabolic antenna focuses its signal towards a single point. This type of antenna provides even greater range than the Yagi antenna. Most of us would have known this by another name—satellite dish. An example of a use case of parabolic antennas is the DIRECTV antennas on the rooftops of houses, which point to a satellite in the sky.

Site surveys

Before and after a wireless network deployment, a wireless network engineer should always conduct a wireless site survey to determine the number of cell towers, access points, and wireless routers and even signal repeaters needed and their placements. This will help in determining and ensuring proper signal coverage over the area and any sort of potential interference that may be causing any issues.

Some notable tools that can assist in a Wi-Fi site survey are **Netstumbler** (www.netstumbler.com) and **inSSIDer** (www.metageek.com).

Types of wireless LAN topologies

The different types of wireless LAN topologies are as follows:

- **Independent Basic Service Set (IBSS)**: In this topology, Wi-Fi-compatible devices connect to each other without a wireless router or an access point:

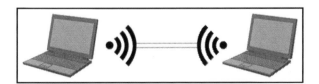

- **Basic Service Set (BSS)**: In a BSS configuration, also known as infrastructure mode, the end devices such as laptops connect to a wireless network through a wireless router or an access point. This is the method type for most WLAN setups:

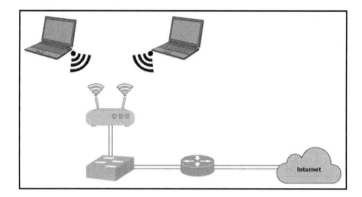

- **Extended Service Set (ESS)**: This configuration also uses the infrastructure mode, however, in this network layout, there are several wireless router/access points connected to the same LAN:

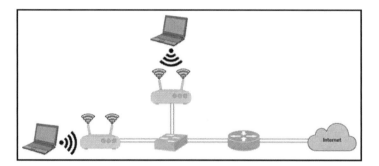

Wireless router configurations

Most vendors' wireless routers setups are very similar. Behind the wireless router there are typically five Ethernet ports; one connects to the internet (WAN) and the remaining four are switch ports, which are for the LAN.

The main components needed for a Wi-Fi router are as follows:

- Wireless router or **Access Point (AP)**
- A wireless-compatible device such as a laptop
- A wireless NIC (only if the device does not have a wireless network interface card)

Once your wireless router is powered on, connect your laptop to the default **service set identifier (SSID)**. The SSID is the name of the wireless network. If you aren't sure, simply connect an Ethernet cable between the computer and the wireless router and ensure the cable is connected to one of the LAN ports on the wireless router.

Once connected, ensure you are receiving an IP address and subnet mask on your local network interface card by opening Windows Command Prompt and using the `ipconfig` command. To do this, simply press the Windows key on your keyboard and *R* at the same time. You'll see the **Run** dialog box appear. Type `cmd` and click on the **OK** button:

Next, type `ipconfig` and hit the *Enter* key on your keyboard. Then, look under the Ethernet adapter and you should see an IP address and subnet mask from IPv4 private Scheme. In most cases, the wireless router IP address is `192.168.1.1`.

Simply open your web browser and enter the wireless router's IP address in the address bar and hit *Enter*. If you get a prompt asking for a username and password combination, use the defaults that are provided within the packaging of the device. During your initial setup of the device, make sure to change the default settings to ensure any unauthorized persons do not have access to your device.

Once you're on the main, you should see a tab named internet or WAN. Ensure the configuration within this section is correct. If you're unsure about the IP address for the internet port, select the DHCP option.

You may want to manually configure your DNS settings by adjusting the DNS servers. DNS is responsible for resolving hostname to IP address. If you're planning on changing your DNS settings, consider using Google DNS, CloudFlare DNS, or Cisco OpenDNS settings.

Please note that, during this exercise, a NETGEAR Nighthawk x4 wireless router was used, however, any brand of wireless router can be used as the configuration windows are very similar:

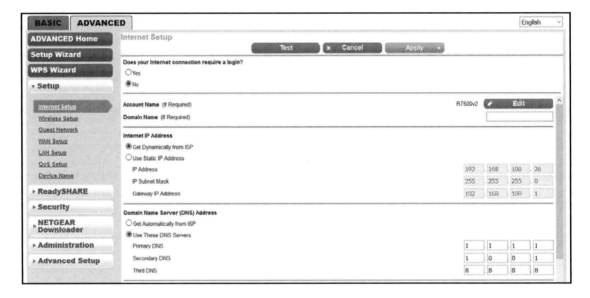

 Further information on DNS performance can be found at www.dnsperf.com.

Another tab would be the **Wireless Setup** section. In this section, you would be able to configure the SSID, the password, and operating channels and frequencies:

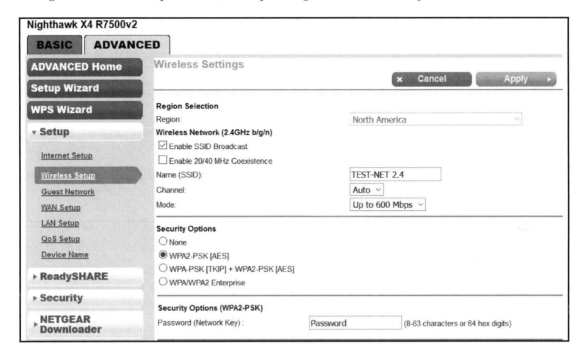

 Disabling the SSID Broadcast prevents mobile devices such as laptops, tablets, and smartphones from seeing an available wireless network. Furthermore, it is recommended to use WPA2 encryption over a wireless network.

Some wireless routers have the **Guest Network** feature, which allows you, the administrator, to create a temporary wireless network for temporary users while limiting their access to only the internet and not any local resources on the LAN:

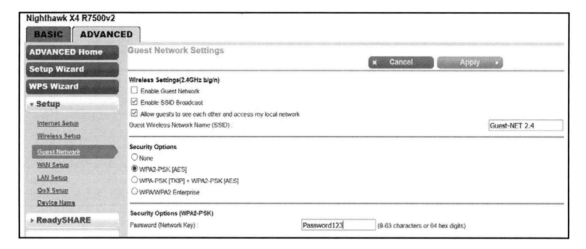

Another important tab is **LAN Setup**. In this section, the DHCP server setting can be applied, indicating the DHCP pool (ranges) and any other relevant settings:

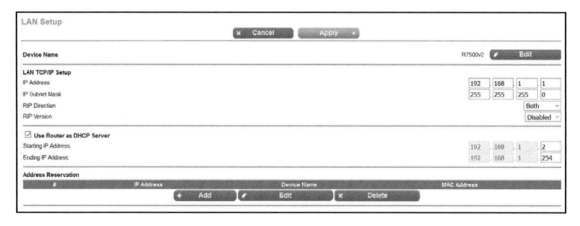

Some of the higher-end wireless routers have an advanced section, which would allow the creation of schedules of when the SSID would be visible, the selection of wireless frequencies, and the power levels on the antenna:

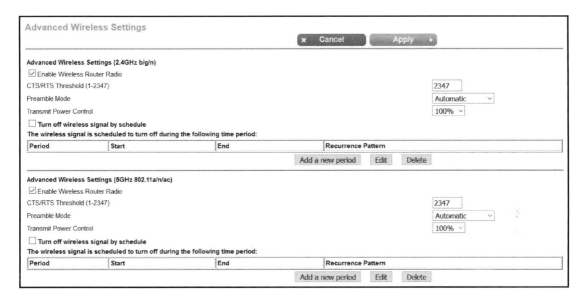

Cloud computing

Cloud computing is typically access resources on another server within a data center on the internet. Cloud computing has been a growing factor in the field of IT. A lot of businesses are using this type of technology to improve their daily functions and to reduce their annual expenditure.

Let's imagine you are starting up a local business within your community. Within your company, there are a few IT services that are essential for almost every company and organization—this is **Email**. Having a dedicated email server within the company would mean regular maintenance, paying IT personnel for their work, and, if there is a power outage within the community or building, the server would be offline. Furthermore, a company expands and so does the storage requirements for each user on the email server; the storage space is used to store messages and, as more employees join the organization, there would be a need for a dedicated IT department together with more hardware appliances and servers.

Cloud computing allows consumers to pay for the service they needed only, creating a pay-as-you-go model. If a company requires email services within their organization, senior management can purchase either an Office 365 or G Suite email product. This would allow the purchaser to pay per user per storage unit. This ensure the purchaser only pays for exactly what they want or are using. Some email providers start at $5 per user per month for an email account with the company's domain name.

Using cloud computing provides many benefits, such as the following:

- The resources on a cloud computing system can be accessible from anywhere and at any time
- It reduces the need for physical appliances and equipment at a location
- It reduces the maintenance of the online platform as most are automatically done by the Cloud solution provider
- It reduces the need for a dedicated IT team within an organization
- It allows organizations to only pay for the resources they use and nothing more
- Typical access to the cloud resource is usually done through a web browser, thereby reducing the need for any specialized software/application on the client's end

Disadvantages of using cloud computing include the following:

- Data security and privacy is a concern as you may not be aware of persons or monitoring applications that are looking at your data on the cloud servers
- An internet connection is mandatory from the consumer end to access the resources through the internet
- The limited control over the backend technology on the server

Some examples of cloud computing providers are the following:

- Microsoft
- Google Cloud
- **Amazon Web Services** (**AWS**)
- GoDaddy
- DigitalOcean

Types of cloud services

In cloud computing, there are three main types of services that are typically offered by cloud solution providers. In this section, we will briefly discuss each and take a look at their use cases.

Software as a Service (SaaS)

SaaS deployment model is where the cloud solution provider offers access to only the interface of an application. A simple example is using either Microsoft's Office 365 solution or Google's G Suite of applications. This allows the end user, such as yourself, to access their email inbox and other collaboration applications using simply a web browser. This solution eliminates the need for locally installed programs on a computer.

Platform as a Service (PaaS)

In a PaaS model, the cloud solution provider offers the operating systems, programming frameworks such as a programming language environment, for example, a developer environment. Some examples are Microsoft's Windows Azure, AWS Elastic Beanstalk, and Google's App Engine.

Infrastructure as a Service (IaaS)

IaaS are the actual physical hardware and software resources that are used for storage and networking. These devices are firewalls, **virtual machines** (**VMs**), databases, and storage clusters. Some example of IaaS services/platforms are Microsoft's Azure, **Google Cloud Platform** (**GCP**), and Amazon AWS.

Cloud delivery models

In the cloud environment, there are many deployments or what is better known as cloud delivery models. Each model has its own advantages and disadvantages based on their architecture. In this section, we will discuss the following cloud models—**private**, **public**, **hybrid**, and **community**.

Private

In the private cloud model, the organization owns the data center and the infrastructure is managed locally. The data center would contain SaaS, PaaS, and even IaaS solutions, all virtualized and accessible by the employees within the organization only. This is an on-premise solution.

Public

Unlike the private model, the public deployment model is available to everyone on the internet. This includes Google Drive and Dropbox.

Hybrid

The hybrid model is a mixture between the private and the public cloud deployment model. An organization may have their data locally backed up on the private data center but have it replicated to an online public cloud solution provider. Another example is an organization can have their local **Active Directory** (**AD**) server replicate to the cloud-based Microsoft Azure platform as a redundant **Domain Controller** (**DC**).

Community

The community is where several organizations share the resources on a cloud platform. This can be a group of companies with similar interest or partnerships all accessing and sharing resources among each other.

Summary

In this chapter, we've covered both wireless technologies and cloud computing concepts. We opened the chapter by discussing the various wireless technologies and standards that are in the world that surround us each day. We've discussed, compared, and contrasted various IEEE 802.11 standards, taking a look at the characteristics and benefits of each and not forgetting various mobile wireless technologies such as GSM, TDMA, CDMA, and LTE.

We took a look at how each technology can be used to improve IT efficiency for both business and individual consumers. The growth of cloud computing has exponentially increased as businesses see the need to outsource either part of or their entire IT infrastructure for many reasons such as cost, human resources, and storage for physical devices.

In the next chapter, we will be covering networking components such as network cable types, networking devices and their deployment models, and advanced networking appliances.

Questions

1. Which IEEE standard has a bandwidth capacity of 11 MBps?
    1. 802.11a
    2. 802.11g
    3. 802.11ac
    4. 802.11b

2. Which 802.11 standard uses MIMO technology?
    1. 802.1b
    2. 802.11n
    3. 802.11g
    4. 802.11a

3. Which wireless technology is best suited for interconnected IoT devices?
    1. Wi-Fi
    2. Bluetooth
    3. Z-Wave
    4. ANT+

4. Health and fitness monitoring systems usually use which of the following?
    1. ANT+
    2. Bluetooth
    3. Wi-Fi
    4. 802.16

5. Which type of cloud services provides the user with access to the application only?
    1. PaaS
    2. SaaS
    3. IaaS
    4. HaaS

6. What is an example of SaaS?
    1. Microsoft Azure
    2. Gmail
    3. Amazon AWS
    4. Google Cloud

7. Which cloud model is shared between multiple organizations?
    1. Private
    2. Public
    3. Hybrid
    4. Community

Further reading

To get more information on wireless communications, you can visit the IEEE Xplore Digital Library at `https://ieeexplore.ieee.org/xpl/RecentIssue.jsp?punumber=7742`.

7
Network Components

Modern networks are constructed from a myriad of fascinating and functional infrastructures. At the core of the network, we find an assortment of devices that control the movement of data through both wired and wireless media, all pushing data through a vast array of cables and connectors at incredible speeds. In this chapter, we will describe some of the most common cabling and connector types that you are likely to come across in your professional career, as well as some of the most common networking devices that are deployed in networks today.

In this chapter, we will cover the following topics:

- Networking cables
- Connector types
- Networking devices

By the end of this chapter, you'll be able to properly determine and justify which types of cables, connectors, and devices are most appropriate for which situations, thereby saving yourself and your company a lot of wasted time, effort, and money, and ensuring that your network is efficient, scalable, reliable, and secure.

Let's get started!

Networking cables and connector types

Physical cables form the backbone of virtually every network in existence. While wireless links may be more appropriate for certain situations (for example, establishing communication between ground stations and satellites), wired media typically constitutes the vast majority of links in a network. This wired media can be broadly categorized into two main groups—**copper cables** and **fiber cables**.

In the following subsections, we will discuss both of these broad categories of cables, the termination points and connectors that each of them use, and the various standards and transceivers associated with each category.

Copper cables

Copper cables typically consist of one or more cores of solid or stranded copper metal, surrounded by a jacket of insulating material. The copper wires in the core provide high electrical conductivity, allowing electrical signals carrying data to travel through the core with little impedance.

Unshielded Twisted Pair (UTP) copper cables

The most common type of copper cable found in indoor network installations is called an UTP cable. This type of cable consists of an outer **Polyvinyl Chloride** (**PVC**) jacket, encircling a set of individually insulated copper wires, each of which is twisted into a pair. Some UTP cables may also have a plastic spline separating the twisted pairs:

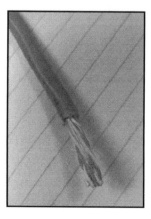

The outer jacket provides physical protection to the cable. The individual copper conductors carry electrical signals (either for communications between equipment or to provide power to equipment). These individual copper conductors are insulated to prevent electrical conduction between themselves, and are twisted throughout the entire length of the cable to minimize cross-talk (interference created in one pair of wires due to a signal being passed through another pair) and electromagnetic interference (unwanted time-varying electrical signals in a system). The insulation on the cables is color coded to help distinguish them and arrange them according to wiring standards. The spline separating the cables helps to reduce cross-talk between the pairs.

It is common to find UTP cables in all indoor network installations where significant external interference does not exist, such as in enterprises, data centers, or home networks. Cost and space are the predominant factors in these installations, as UTP cables are usually the thinnest and cheapest copper cables available.

Shielded Twisted Pair (STP) copper cables

The second type of twisted pair copper cable is called STP. This type of twisted pair media adds either a layer of aluminum foil or a braided copper jacket around the copper conductors. This extra layer of metal may be added either below the outer jacket or around each of the twisted pairs in the copper wires:

This foil jacket serves to further reduce cross-talk and **electromagnetic interference** (EMI) for signals through the cable, making it ideal for high-interference locations such as near airports or high voltage transmission lines. Due to its common use in these types of industrial locations, many manufacturers also reinforce the outer PVC jacket.

These additions make this type of cable thicker, costlier, and more difficult to work with. Engineers, therefore, have to consider the situation and determine whether or not STP cables would be beneficial over UTP cables.

Coaxial copper cables

A third type of copper cable that's commonly used in networking infrastructure is the coaxial cable. Coaxial cables are so named because they are composed of two metallic conductors that follow the same axis:

This type of cable transmits its electrical signals through an inner core of either solid or stranded copper, or copper-clad steel. This inner conductor is surrounded by a layer of insulating material (usually plastic), which is itself surrounded by braided copper cable. This outer braided copper cable (which is usually grounded) serves to protect the inner core from EMI (keeping noise in the radio frequency domain out of the core) and signal leakage (keeping signals through the core inside of the coaxial cable). The inner insulating material (sometimes called a dielectric material) serves to separate the two conductors in the cable, while the outermost insulating sheath serves to cover and protect the outer braided jacket, and the entire cable by extension.

Coaxial cables can often be found in cable operator networks, carrying both **audiovisual** (**AV**) signals as well as data signals (packets to and from the internet) as the last part of **Hybrid Fiber Coaxial** (**HFC**) networks. Two main classes of coaxial cables are used today—RG-6 and RG-59 cables. RG-6 cables typically have an 18 **American Wire Gauge** (**AWG**) copper core, while RG-59 cables usually have a 20 AWG core. This larger core of RG-6 cables, combined with their thicker insulation and better shielding, means that they are more suited to higher frequency applications (frequencies above 50 MHz). Thus, RG-6 cables are typically used in **community access television** (**CATV**) or satellite applications, while RG-59 cables are used in analog CCTV and base-band video transmissions.

Copper cable and termination standards

In addition to these broad categories of UTP, STP, and coaxial copper cables, further subdivisions exist between different classes or standards of copper cables. In this subsection, we will examine some of the common standards of copper cables that you are likely to come across. We will also examine the different Ethernet standards that each category supports and the two main termination standards in use today. Note that Ethernet over coaxial cables is not commonplace:

Cable standard	Twisted-pair/coaxial	Maximum supported frequency	Ethernet standards commonly used	Additional notes/comments
Cat 3	Twisted-pair	16 MHz	10Base-T	This was popular for data networks at one point in time, but is now mainly used for voice networks, since they are not rated for speeds above 16 Mbps.
Cat 5	Twisted-pair	100 MHz	100Base-T, 1000Base-T	This is still fairly popular for data networks. The maximum rated distance is 100 m. These cables, when run and terminated properly and operated in low-noise environments, can run 1000Base-T Ethernet (Gigabit Ethernet).
Cat 5e	Twisted- pair	100 MHz	100Base-X, 1000Base-T	This has replaced Cat 5 cables for many installations. It stipulates better testing and introduces a specification to reduce cross-talk between wire pairs, allowing more reliable Gigabit Ethernet.
Cat 6	Twisted- pair	250 MHz	1000Base-T, 10GBase-T	This further reduces cross-talk and noise in cables, allowing for 10 Gigabit Ethernet. Limited to 55 m at 10 G speeds. It is replacing Cat 5 and Cat 5e cables in newer installations.
Cat 6a	Twisted- pair	500 MHz	1000Base-T, 10GBase-T	This further improves standards to allow for a full 100 m at 10GBase-T standards.
Cat 7	Twisted- pair	600 MHz	10GBase-T	This is a fully shielded cable. It is not recognized by the EIA/TIA.

It is important to note how Ethernet standards are named. The first part of the name indicates the capacity (the maximum speed, in megabits per second) supported by the standard; the second part indicates whether the Ethernet protocol transmits using base-band (digital signaling) or broadband (analog signaling), and the last part of the name differs between Ethernet standards for copper and fiber cables. For copper cables, the last part is commonly **T**, for twisted-pair, while for fiber cables, the last part may be **SX**, for short wavelengths (850 nm), or **LX**, for long wavelengths (1310 nm).

Fiber cables

Although copper cables are still used in the vast majority of networks, fiber optic cables continue to replace copper cables in many sections of modern networks. These cables transmit data using pulses of light, sending these pulses down a thin core of plastic or glass, which is surrounded by a material called cladding. This combination of core and cladding allows for the light to be transmitted through the process of either total internal reflection or continuous refraction of the light. The core and cladding are coated and protected by buffers and jackets to reinforce the cable:

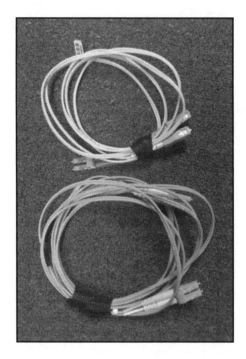

Fiber optic cables offer a significant number of advantages over their copper counterparts, including the following:

- Data is transferred over the cable faster, since data is transferred over fiber cables using light rather than electrical signals. Also, photons travel at a higher speed than electrons, meaning that bits of data are delivered across the ends of fiber cables faster than in copper cables.
- Cables can be run for longer lengths since attenuation over fiber optic cables is lower than that of copper cables. Copper cables are typically rated for a maximum length of 100 m, while fiber optic cables can run for many kilometers before needing a repeater.

There are two major categories of fiber cables—**single-mode** and **multimode**. In the following subsections, we will discuss the difference between these categories and explain which category is suitable for which situations.

Single-mode fiber (SMF) cables

In the context of fiber optic cables, a mode defines the method in which a wave travels through space. A SMF optic cable is constructed to transmit only one mode of light through the fiber (in a direction parallel to the fiber). Thus, these cables consist of a core with a diameter that is quite small in relation to the diameter of the cladding, since it only needs to accommodate a single mode of light. For example, one type of SMF cable is called **9/125** fiber, which means that the core is 9 µm in diameter, while the cladding is 125 µm. Light through SMF can consist of multiple frequencies, but all of these frequencies follow a single path through the fiber.

SMF is usually used for fibers that need to span several kilometers. Since all light waves follow a single mode, concepts such as modal dispersion (the spreading of light due to different modes) are not applicable, meaning that the attenuation of the light through the fiber is low and allows these links to span several kilometers without the need for an optical repeater. The light sources for SMF are usually lasers. Due to this requirement for laser light that can align well with the small diameter of SMF, transceivers (transmitters and receivers at either end of the fibers) are often costlier than their **multimode fiber** (**MMF**) counterparts. SMF often operates using wavelengths of 1310 nm or 1550 nm, and is often colored yellow. Common Ethernet standards for SMF include 1000Base-LX, 10GBase-LR, and 10GBase-ER.

MMF cables

MMF cables are constructed with much larger diameters than their SMF counterparts. For example, one common type of MMF is 62.5/125, meaning that the cable has a diameter of 62.5 µm, compared to the 9 µm of some SMF cables.

This wider core allows multiple modes of light to propagate through the fiber, giving rise to additional losses due to phenomenon such as modal dispersion, and limiting the maximum link length to much lower distances than SMF. However, because of the wider core diameter, less precise transceivers can be used, allowing the cost of MMF systems to be generally lower than equivalent SMF systems. For example, MMF transceivers may be constructed using cheaper LEDs instead of lasers as light sources. Therefore, engineers need to weigh the cost of their fiber systems with their expected link distances appropriately, and determine whether the extra cost of SMF systems are necessary for the links that they require, or whether MMF would suffice for their situation. Common Ethernet standards for MMF include 1000Base-SX and 10GBase-SR. MMF is often colored orange, aqua, or lime green.

Before we move on to the next section to discuss the different connector types for the cables we have explored, we must discuss a critical safety consideration that is applicable to all cable types.

Plenum-rated cables

Throughout this section, we've discussed how most of the cables that we use in our networks possess an outer sheath of protective PVC. This PVC material works well for a number of cases, but there are particular applications that require a special type of cable called a **plenum-rated** cable. This type of cable is manufactured from special components that are flame-resistant and non-toxic. The cable gets its name from plenum spaces, which are spaces in a building that are designed to circulate air. Since these places often have no objects present to curtail the spread of fire, it is important that the cables themselves do not contribute to the fire. Additionally, in these spaces, it is important that the cables do not produce toxic fumes when they burn, as these fumes would be quickly distributed to people throughout the building. Plenum-rated cables therefore satisfy both of these requirements of non-toxicity and flame-resistance. However, these cables are also significantly more expensive than their PVC counterparts. Plenum-rated cable is therefore usually only used in places where it is required, such as in hospitals and schools.

In the next section, we will now describe some of the common connectors that are used with all of the cables that we have discussed.

Connector types

All cables require some type of connector to properly attach to equipment on either side of the link. In this section, we will first describe the most common connectors used with copper cables, after which we will delve into the fiber optic cable connectors and the transceivers that may be required to connect different types of cabling and connectors.

Copper cable connector types

The copper cable connector types are as follows.

Registered Jack (RJ)-45

RJ-45 jacks are the connectors that you are most likely to come across when dealing with twisted pair copper cables in modern-day networks. Although they are not the *true* keyed RJ-45 S jacks that were once used for modems and telephone systems, most professionals in the industry refer to the **8 position 8 contact** (**8P8C**) connector that we use at the ends of twisted pair cables as RJ-45 connectors or jacks:

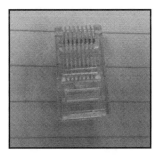

Both the male and female versions of this connector contain eight equally spaced copper conductors that connect electrically when a male jack (with a cable attached) is inserted into a female port (on networking and computing equipment). When a twisted-pair cable is crimped, each of the eight conductors is pressed down onto each of the conductors of the wire, thereby providing electrical connectivity to each wire, while the plastic hammer presses down onto the outer sheath of the cable and locks the cable into the jack. The large plastic clip on the outer part of the connector locks the jack in place when it is inserted into a port on equipment.

RJ-11

The most common types of RJ-11 jacks are **6 position 4 conductor** (**6P4C**) jacks, which are most frequently used for telephone wires. These telephone cables usually consist of two pairs of twisted-pair cabling, which are connected to the four conductors of the jack. The remaining two positions (or contacts) on the 6P4C jack remains unused. It is physically smaller than the 8P8C connector, but contains similar mechanisms for crimping cables and locking the connector into ports.

Bayonet Neill-Concelman (BNC)

BNC, named after both its locking mechanism type and its creators, are connectors that are commonly used at the end of coaxial cables to transmit RF signals for equipment such as televisions and radios. BNC connectors are primarily made in 75 ohm and 50 ohm variants so that they can be used in cables with similar impedance. Mismatches between the connector and the cable results in attenuation of the RF signals across the link. BNC connectors are attached to coaxial cables with the aid of a crimper, while male and female connectors are attached by mating them and turning them in a quarter rotation:

F-type

F-type connectors (or simply **F** connectors) are another type of connector thats's used with coaxial cables. Male connectors (most often used for terminating cables) can be attached to their coaxial cables using crimpers or by simply twisting them onto the coaxial, depending on the type of connector. These male connector ends are then simply screwed on to the female connector for connectivity. They are commonly available in 50 ohm and 75 ohm variants. F-type connectors are commonly used for transmitting RF signals in over-the-air video and cable television.

DB-9 and DB-25

D-Subminiature (**D-Sub**) connectors (so named because they were some of the smallest connectors available at their time of launch) are a family of connectors constructed from D-shaped shells (or shields) and several rows of pins (for male connectors) or sockets (for female connectors). The outer shells provide mechanical support, and are D-shaped to ensure the correct orientation. DB-25 connectors (which contain 25 pins) were (once) popular connectors that were used with parallel and RS-232 serial port communications in computers. They consist of 13 pins on the top row and 12 pins on the bottom row:

These DB-25 ports on computers were eventually succeeded by DB-9 ports (also known as DE-9 ports because of their shell sizes). DB-9 connectors consist of nine pins (for male connectors) or nine sockets (for female connectors), with five pins/sockets in the top row and four pins/sockets in the bottom row. They are among the smallest D-Sub connectors available.

Many modern-day computers, however, do not include either of these ports, so USB-to-Serial adapters are often required for RS-232 applications.

Fiber cable connector types

The fiber cable connector types are as follows:

Little Connector (LC)

LC also known as the **Lucent Connector**, is a type of fiber connector that was created by the Lucent Corporation. The connectors consist of a small plastic latch, similar to an RJ-45 jack, which helps secure the fiber connector to the port, and a 1.25 mm ferrule, which is used to align the fiber optic cable with the connector. Because of this small ferrule size, the LC connector is a small form factor connector, making it suitable for high density fiber deployments such as in data centers.

Straight Tip (ST)

ST, or bayonet connectors, are a type of fiber connector that was created by AT&T. These types of connectors were popular in the late 1980s and 1990s, and consist of a larger ferrule (2.5 mm) and a twist-type, spring-loaded, cylindrical, nickel-plated or stainless steel bayonet connector for locking. Its use has declined in the last few years because other connectors (such as LC connectors) are cheaper and easier to connect/disconnect.

Subscriber Connector (SC)

SC, also known as **Square Connectors** or **Standard Connectors**, are connectors that were developed by **Nippon Telegraph and Telephone** (**NTT**). They are push-pull square-shaped connectors with 2.5 mm, spring-loaded, ceramic ferrule and snap-in connector latches. They are easy to disconnect/reconnect and can be found in many network installations.

Mechanical Transfer Registered Jack (MT-RJ)

MT-RJs, also known as **Media Termination Recommended Jack**, are small, duplex fiber connectors, with both fibers terminating on a single 2.45 x 4.4 mm ferrule. They are roughly half the size of SC connectors and are easy to connect/disconnect from their ports using plastic latches, similar to RJ-45 connectors. Two pins, located on transceivers, allow for easy alignment of the connector.

Angled Physical Connector (APC) versus Ultra Polished Connector (UPC)

All of the previous fiber connector types are available as either APC or UPC. The difference between these connector types stems from the fiber end face or ferrule. UPC connectors are polished and possess a mostly flat face with some curvature only toward the outer edges of the connector. UPC connectors are polished more than their **Polished Connector** (PC) counterparts, bringing return losses down to the range of approximately—50 dB. APC connectors are polished with the face angled at an 8-degree angle, bringing the return losses even lower to the range of 60 dB, since the reflected light is now directed into the cladding of the fiber as opposed to being reflected back into the source. APC connectors are usually colored green, while UPC connectors are colored blue.

Transceivers

A transceiver is a device that is required to be inserted into a cage or slot on certain pieces of networking equipment to provide an interface for certain types of copper or fiber cable to connect. In this subsection, we will examine some common transceivers.

Gigabit Interface Converter (GBIC)

GBICs are hot-swappable (can be removed and reinserted while equipment is powered on) transceivers that introduced the concept of removable transceivers, as opposed to fixed physical ports on networking devices, allowing for more flexibility in network links. Due to the appeal of these GBICs, modern networking equipment requires transceivers (combined transmitter/receiver devices) on many ports to provide interfaces for different types of copper and fiber optic connectors, and cables to connect to the equipment.

Small Form-Factor Pluggable (SFP), Enhanced Small Form-Factor Pluggable (SFP+), and Quad Small Form-Factor Pluggable (QSFP)

SFP devices are compact, hot-swappable devices that are extremely common in modern networks, facilitating data rates of 1-2.5 Gbps through LC connectors (using both MMF and SMF) and data rates of 1 Gbps for twisted pair copper cables (using RJ-45 connectors). SFPs have largely replaced GBICs because of their smaller size. For fiber SFPs, transceivers exist to facilitate link lengths from several hundred meters to several kilometers, while copper SFPs are usually rated for a maximum of 100 m.

For higher data rates, some equipment supports SFP+ transceivers, which are commonly used for 10 Gbps links using SMF or MMF cables. Copper SFP+ modules, which provide 10 Gbps speeds over twisted pair cables, also exist, but they are less common and more expensive.

Lastly, for even higher data rates, some equipment supports QSFP or **Enhanced Quad Small Form-Factor Pluggable (QSFP+)**, which provide capacities of 4 Gbps and 40 Gbps respectively. As the names imply, they are constructed from four individual SFP or SFP+ channels, which are aggregated to provide four times the speed with significant space savings on devices, allowing for more dense deployments.

Duplex and bidirectional transceivers

Many transceivers in modern networks require two strands of fiber cable (duplex fiber) for operation. These transceivers use one strand to transmit data to a device, and the other strand to receive data from a device. However, there may be situations where only a single strand of fiber is available, or where additional strands are difficult or expensive to run. In these types of situations, it is beneficial to utilize **bidirectional (BiDi)** transceivers, which utilize different frequencies on a single (simplex) fiber strand for the transmission and reception of data. The disadvantages of BiDi transceivers is that they are often more expensive than their regular (duplex) counterparts, and that they are often not available at higher capacities (such as 40 Gbps):

Termination points

There may exist a plethora of termination points in the context of networking. Cables from different uplink providers often terminate at a particular location in a network, while cables on downlinks to customers or staff may terminate at a different location. In this subsection, we will examine two popular types of termination points found in networks today:

- 66 and 110 blocks
- Patch panels

66 and 110 blocks

66 and 110 blocks are two types of punch-down blocks that are commonly used to connect copper wires in networking systems. In a punch-down block, individual copper wires are pressed down into open-ended slots using a punch-down tool, causing two sharp metal blades in the slot to cut into the insulation of the wire, thus achieving electrical connectivity. The 66 block is so named because of its model number, but it actually provides slots to accommodate 25 pairs, or 50 split pairs of copper wire. 66 blocks are often used for voice/telephone cabling. 110 blocks are an upgraded version of the 66 block, providing increased slot density and meeting newer standards of twisted-pair copper cables, thus allowing these blocks to accommodate higher bandwidth links. 110 blocks can often accommodate hundreds of copper cables.

Patch panels

In the context of networking, patch panels are pieces of equipment that facilitate Physical Layer (L1) connections between links. Different patch panel types allow connections to be made between different types of cables. For example, fiber optic patch panels (or fiber distribution panels) provide ports for different types of fiber connectors (LC, SC, and so on), allowing connectivity to and between different strands of fiber cables. These panels are frequently used at locations where trunk cables (cables containing many individual copper or fiber cables) enter premises, allowing these individual cables to be terminated in a manner that is easy to manage on premises. Patch (or jumper) cables are usually used to connect equipment to the ports of these patch panels, or to connect between ports on the panels.

Copper termination standards

For twisted-pair copper cables, the ends of the cables are commonly terminated according to one of two standards—TIA/EIA 568A and TIA/EIA 568B. In this subsection, we will examine how cables are arranged in both of these standards, and how different types of cables can be made by different combinations of these standards at either end.

TIA/EIA 568A versus TIA/EIA 568B

The following diagram illustrates the two common pin-to-pair assignments for each of the eight cables in a four-pair twisted-pair cable, according to the ANSI/TIA-568 standard. Although it is not mandatory, most network engineers follow these standards when terminating their copper cabling so that other engineers can easily understand and maintain their cabling work. Note that the only difference between these assignments is that the orange and green pairs are swapped:

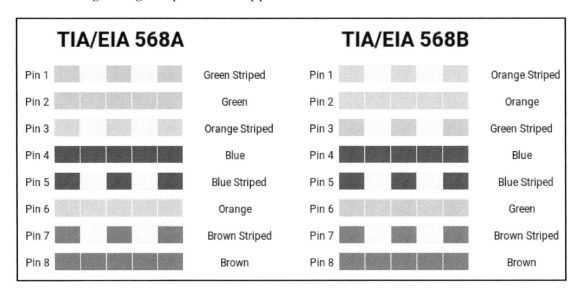

Crossover versus straight-through

A straight-through cable is formed by terminating a twisted-pair cable run with the same pin-to-pair assignments on both ends. For example, if the TIA-568B standard is used on one end of a cable, the same TIA-568B standard is used to terminate the other end. In this manner, each pin in a connector on one end of the cable corresponds to the same pin on the other end of the cable. A crossover cable, on the other hand, is formed by swapping the pair going to pins 1 and 2 with the pair to pins 3 and 6. This is equivalent to terminating one end according to the T568A standard, and the other end according to the T568B standard. This mixture of standards is significant because it swaps the pins used for transmission and reception on equipment, allowing two similar devices to communicate. Therefore, **straight through** cables (also called patch cables) are used to connect computers to switches or switches to routers, whereas crossover cables are used to connect switches to other switches, routers to other routers, or computers to routers. However, modern equipment often possesses a feature called **Auto-MDIX**, which automatically detects that a crossover cable is required on a link and swaps the pins used for transmission or reception accordingly.

Networking devices and their deployment

In this section, we will discuss some of the most common devices that constitute network infrastructure. We will categorize the devices according to the main OSI layer at which they operate (you remember your OSI layers from Chapter 1, *The OSI Reference Model and the TCP/IP Stack, right?*) and discuss the main functions and features that each device provides.

Layer 1 devices

Layer 1 (Physical Layer) devices are responsible for manipulating the electromagnetic and optical signals that carry the bits of data through both wired and wireless media.

Hubs

A hub is one such device. Hubs provide a number of ports, interconnecting devices on a LAN. Hubs do not perform at any time of processing of data. Rather, every frame received on one port is broadcast to all other ports on the hub (excluding the port that the frame was received on). This method ensures that the frame gets to its intended destination on the LAN, but it also leads to a lot of congestion on the LAN as more and more devices are added.

Modulators/Demodulators (Modems)

Modems also operate at layer 1. Modems are responsible for both modulating digital data (from computers) into a signal that can be transmitted over telephone cables, cable networks, and fiber infrastructure, and demodulating signals received from these WAN networks into digital signals for computers.

Media converters

Media converters are devices that are often used to connect networks with two dissimilar physical media types. The most popular type of media converter is one that converts electrical signals in twisted-pair copper cables to optical signals in fiber optic cables.

Wireless Access Points (WAPs) and Wireless Repeaters

WAPs or APs are devices that create **Wireless Local Area Networks** (**WLANs**). WAPs connect to switches or routers using cables (usually twisted-pair copper cables), and broadcast **electromagnetic** (**EM**) radio waves over the air. End user devices (such as laptops and mobile phones) then connect to this WLAN, establishing communication to other devices on the WLAN or the wired LAN. Wireless range extenders (also called wireless repeaters) forgo the cables entirely, instead connecting to existing WLANs and rebroadcasting those wireless signals over the air to extend the coverage area of their WLANs. Wireless range extenders are therefore easier to set up, because they don't require a cable to the device, but they also offer lower speeds than their wired equivalents (WAPs).

In a small network, these WAPs (and wireless repeaters, by extension) can be managed individually with relatively little hassle. When configured in this management mode, these devices are called fat APs. However, as WLANs grow larger, it becomes exponentially more difficult to configure, troubleshoot, monitor, and maintain these WAPs individually. Instead, these WAPs may be configured as thin APs, moving all of their management plane functions to a centralized wireless controller. This method of managing WAPs from a centralized controller becomes invaluable as WLANs scale to the order of hundreds or thousands of WAPs across an enterprise or service provider network.

Layer 2 devices

Layer 2 devices work by grouping bits of data into frames, and using the destination MAC addresses on these frames to selectively forward them on specific interfaces of the device, toward their intended destinations only. This process greatly improves the performance of LANs compared to utilizing layer 1 devices, as network devices now mostly only have to process frames that are intended for them.

Bridges and switches

Unlike layer 1 devices (such as hubs), which do not keep track of which hosts are communicating on the network, layer 2 devices track which MAC addresses are seen on which interface/port and keep a table of this relationship (called a MAC or CAM table) to perform this selective forwarding. Bridges utilize a lot of software to perform this lookup of the CAM table and the subsequent forwarding process. Switches replace many of these software functions and calls with specialized hardware called **Application-Specific Integrated Circuits** (**ASICs**), resulting in improvements to the performance and efficiency of the layer 2 forwarding process. Due to the drop-in prices of switches over the last few decades, switches have largely replaced both hubs and bridges in modern networks.

In addition to the regular switching functions that layer 2 switches provide, contemporary networks also feature **multilayer switches** (**MLSes**) that provide features such as the creation of VLANs and gateways for VLANs on the switch, and the forwarding of packets/frames based on higher-layer information such as IP addresses and port numbers. Many of these MLSes can provide these functions just as quickly as regular switching due to the additional ASICs included in them. They can therefore be used to relieve routers from these functions (to allow routers to focus on other more complex tasks that MLSes can't perform) or to free valuable ports on routers for other uses.

Layer 3 and higher devices

The layer 3 and higher devices are as follows.

Routers

While switches are largely responsible for moving frames at layer 2, routers are the devices that are responsible for moving packets at layer 3. Routers interconnect networks and sub-networks. Since IP has become the most popular layer 3 protocol that's used today, routers mostly handle IP addresses (both IPv4 and IPv6) and IP routes, moving packets selectively out through their interfaces by reading their destination IP addresses. Routers decide which packets go out through which interfaces by consulting their routing table. This routing table matches particular destination routes to particular outgoing interfaces, similar to the function of CAM tables in switches. However, routers usually possess a lot more complexity and functionality than switches, and as such, routers are usually a lot larger, heavier, and more expensive than switches. Routers also typically include less ports than switches:

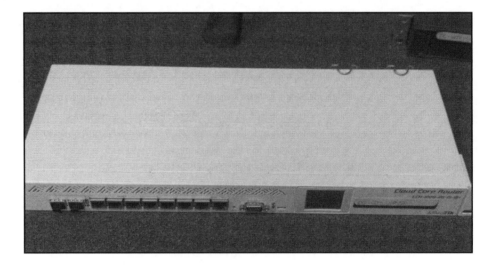

Security appliances

Firewalls facilitate security in the network, allowing or denying both incoming and outgoing data through the network according to a set of configured security policies. These policies typically examine source and destination IP addresses, transport layer ports, physical device ports, and even protocols at different layers. In recent years, firewalls have evolved significantly and now offer a plethora of additional features and security policies. **Next-Generation Firewalls** (**NGFWs**) or layer 7 firewalls add significantly more *intelligence* to firewall appliances, allowing administrators to implement security policies governing applications themselves. For example, in order to control web traffic, rather than simply blocking port 80, these advanced firewalls may be able to block specific malicious web applications communicating over this port, while allowing other regular traffic freely through the port.

In addition to implementing and enforcing security policies using a firewall, security administrators may implement additional appliances such as content filters, which allow the administrators to build filters that block users from accessing or serving certain web content. For example, a content filter may be implemented in a business to prevent staff from accessing social media websites during work hours.

Administrators may also implement an **Intrusion Detection System** (**IDS**) and an **Intrusion Prevention System** (**IPS**). IDSes monitor network traffic or host systems, searching for suspected malicious traffic (using heuristics or stored signatures) or preconfigured security rule violations. On detection of the suspected breaches, IDSes generate and deliver reports to security engineers individually or to a central collection system such as **Security Information and Event Management** (**SIEM**) system. An IDS in a network may also be called a **Network-Based Intrusion Detection System** (**NIDS**). IPSes, on the other hand, provide additional capabilities, giving the security appliance the ability to stop malicious traffic from propagating through the appliance and potentially causing damage to the network.

In a network where multiple users are concurrently connected through **Virtual Private Network** (**VPN**) connections, administrators may also install a VPN concentrator, which is a device that allows for the creation and management of a large number of VPN tunnels, providing services such as authenticating users to the VPN and providing encryption/decryption of data across each tunnel.

A **Unified Threat Management** (**UTM**) appliance may also be implemented in a network, as it provides many of the security features that we discussed here in a single appliance. This may allow security administrators to save on costs and rack space and simplify configuration, but it may also provide a single point of failure for all of these functions.

Voice over Internet Protocol (VoIP) devices

Before the advent of IP networking, network administrators created and maintained separate networks for separate services. For example, administrators would maintain data networks for internet traffic, telephone networks for voice traffic, and cable networks for video traffic. However, many administrators have begun to run integrated services over IP networks, forgoing these independent networks and allowing for the simplified management of a single, converged network. VoIP aims to provide telephone services over IP networks.

VoIP endpoints are the devices that users interact with to make calls across the VoIP network. These endpoints may be hardware-based VoIP phones that resemble traditional telephones, or they may be entirely software-based phones, allowing users to make and receive calls on their computers.

A VoIP **Private Branch Exchange (PBX)** or IP PBX is the equivalent of a traditional PBX, providing services such as establishing, maintaining, and tearing down calls when users hang up, as well as services for switching or routing calls between VoIP users on the LAN, or between VoIP users and external users on the **Plain Old Telephone Service (POTS)** by utilizing a trunk of external telephone lines.

A VoIP gateway is a device that connects the POTS and VoIP network, allowing VoIP users to place calls to users on the traditional telephone network, or allowing users on the POTS to call users on the VoIP network.

Servers

Servers in data centers or enterprise networks are simply computers mounted in chassis of a different form. These servers are general purpose, and allow for software to be installed onto them to provide various functions in contemporary networks.

One such function is as a **proxy**. Proxy servers may operate in one of two ways. Forward proxy servers (or simply proxy servers) act as mediators for requests on the network. Therefore, instead of an end user device requesting data from a content server directly, end user devices place the request to the proxy server, and the proxy forwards the request to the content server on behalf of the user device. Most proxies in modern networks are web proxies, fetching web pages on behalf of user devices. Reverse proxies work at the other end, receiving requests from end user devices and forwarding these requests to internal servers on their network. Reverse proxies may also be configured as load balancers, receiving requests from clients and distributing them to a cluster of internal servers according to a particular load balancing algorithm.

Proxies may also be categorized as transparent (the client devices are not aware that their data is being redirected by a proxy) or explicit (client machines must be explicitly configured to utilize the services of the proxy). Proxies may be implemented for a number of reasons, including logging traffic from end user devices and content filtering websites.

Another common server found in current networks is an **Authentication, Authorization, Accounting / Remote Authentication Dial-In User Service (AAA/RADIUS)** server. AAA or RADIUS servers are used to provide centralized login and accounting services for managing infrastructure devices or for managing access to the internet or internal LANs. Rather than configuring individual user accounts on each device in a network for each user that requires access, administrators can simply configure them to utilize AAA services from the central server, where all user information is stored. This greatly simplifies user account and permissions auditing in enterprise and service provider networks, where hundreds or thousands of user accounts may need to be created and maintained.

Summary

In this chapter, we've explored many of the common cables, connectors, and infrastructure devices that you are likely to come across in a contemporary network. We have discussed different situations where each of them may be used, arming you with some of the knowledge you will need to make decisions about which equipment and cabling is most appropriate for which situations.

Questions

1. A manager has asked their team of network technicians to source a box of twisted-pair cables, which are to be used in an indoor, low-noise environment to provide speeds of 1 Gbps. What type of cable would best fit the manager's requirements?
    1. UTP Cat 3
    2. STP Cat 5e
    3. STP Cat 6a
    4. UTP Cat 5e

2. A network technician has determined that they need to run 80 m of twisted-pair copper cabling near to some high-voltage transmission lines. They require this link to operate at 10 Gbps. Which of the following cable types would most likely fit their needs?

   1. UTP Cat 6
   2. STP Cat 6a
   3. STP Cat 6
   4. STP Cat 5e

3. A manager is planning to connect two remote sites of their business using a WAN connection. The connection needs to span a distance of 8 km. What type of cable would be most suitable for this connection?

   1. STP Cat 6a
   2. SMF
   3. MMF
   4. UTP Cat 5e

4. A network technician is on the phone with a vendor and needs to request transceivers for their router. They require 40 Gbps of capacity on each of the ports of the router. Assuming that the router supports it, which of the following transceivers should be requested?

   1. SFP
   2. SFP+
   3. QSFP
   4. GBIC

5. A network engineer is considering leasing dark fiber from a subsea fiber provider, where they are paying a significant sum of money for each strand of fiber that they lease. Which of the following transceiver types should they consider to keep their costs as low as possible?

   1. Duplex
   2. Bidirectional
   3. Copper
   4. Long distance

6. A network technician has recently taken control of an aging network, and has received several complaints about slow speeds at times when many users are utilizing the network. Upon further inspection, they notice that user devices are connected to the network through hubs. What devices should they invest in first to best alleviate this issue?
    1. Routers
    2. WAPs
    3. Switches
    4. Modems

7. A network administrator is trying to set up a link to a remote office 5 km away. Unfortunately, their switches at both offices only support copper cables. What device will allow them to establish a wired connection to the remote office?
    1. WAP
    2. Media converter
    3. Hub
    4. NGFW

8. A network engineer is planning to better segment their enterprise network, creating several sub-networks for each floor and prioritizing traffic for certain mission-critical functions. Which device would best aid the engineer in this task?
    1. Modem
    2. Router
    3. L2 switch
    4. Proxy server

9. A network technician has gotten tired of continually adding and removing user accounts from every device on his network every time a new staff member joins or leaves the team. What appliance would best solve this issue?
    1. Firewall
    2. Switch
    3. Proxy server
    4. RADIUS server

10. A security administrator has been tasked with purchasing a layer 7 firewall, a VPN concentrator, and an IPS solution. Instead of purchasing individual appliances for each requirement, what should the administrator consider?
    1. A router
    2. A hub
    3. A UTM appliance
    4. A WAP

Further reading

The following sites contain more information on common networking devices and cabling:

- **Basic Home Network And Internet Components, Devices and Services**: `http://www.steves-internet-guide.com/networking-components/`
- **Cabling**: `https://fcit.usf.edu/network/chap4/chap4.htm`

8
Network Virtualization and WAN Technologies

One of the many trends in the field of IT is the topic of virtualization. In `Chapter 6`, *Wireless and Cloud Technologies,* we spoke about cloud computing and provided an overview of the benefits and the various models. The terms *cloud computing* and *virtualization* are quite closely related. Without virtualization, the concept of cloud computing and its delivery would be a huge challenge for cloud engineers.

Another important topic is **Wide Area Network (WAN)**. Have your ever wondered *how a telecommunications provider is able to connect an organization's remote offices, be they located in the same country or on another continent?* In this chapter, we will definitely be focusing on the various types of WAN technologies that **Internet Service Providers (ISPs)** utilize for services for either the home or the business subscriber.

In this chapter, we will dive into virtualization, as well as WAN technologies and services, by taking a look at how it can help improve the posture of an information technology and networking environment. The following topics will be covered during the course of this chapter:

- Virtualization with networking concepts
- Storage technologies
- WAN technologies
- WAN topology
- WAN services

Let's begin!

Virtualization with networking concepts

In today's world, there are many cloud computing solution providers, such as Amazon's **Elastic Compute Cloud (EC2)**, **Amazon Web Services (AWS)**, Microsoft Azure and the **Google Cloud platform (GCP)**. These companies have realized the growing trend over the past years that businesses suffer a huge annual loss when a company's local servers go down. In the IT world, the downtime of a server or network resources means a loss of availability to the services. In some organizations, downtime is equivalent to loss of revenue.

The main question is, *how does cloud computing help improve availability?* Cloud computing solution providers provide a **service level agreement (SLA)** of guaranteed uptime. A simple example is AWS, which has a *service level agreement of providing less than 99.99% but equal to or greater than 99.0%*, as stated in their February 12, 2018, update. More and more solution providers are adding an additional *9* to the end of the percentage of uptime they can provide, thereby increasing their marketability and their service levels as a provider. This means that a solution provider with an SLA of 99% ensures that their services may be down for a maximum of *(60 minutes per hour x 24 hours per day x 365 days per year) = Total uptime annually, using (Total uptime annually x 1%) = annual downtime of cloud solution provider*. This means that there is an approximate or exact value of 5,256 minutes downtime per year, which will result to 87.6 hours of downtime. If a cloud solution provider adds an additional *9* at the end of their SLA, this will decrease the downtime while increasing their availability to 99.9%.

The other question is, *how are cloud service providers able to support so many servers and allow scalability with such simplicity?* This is where the concept of virtualization comes in to support cloud computing technologies. Let's imagine that you work for an organization that has a small data center with 12 physical servers such as the web, email, file server, and so on. Each physical server has the following:

- An operating system
- **Central Processing Unit (CPU)**
- **Random Access Memory (RAM)**
- Storage media
- **Input/output (I/O)** components
- Specific hardware requirements based on the OS platform and other requirements

One of the major challenges for a system/server administrator is when a physical component fails. This results in downtime and therefore affects the availability of the services that are provided from the failed server. There are times where a physical server has all the hardware requirements, such as a bit more RAM and CPU power than what is actually being utilized by the host operating system itself, and at times the server operating system may be idle if it's not being used for a period of time, leaving the remaining resources unused and under-utilized/wasted. This issue is called **server sprawl**:

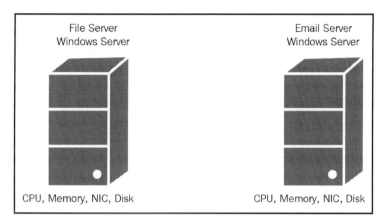

Virtualization takes advantage of these under-utilized and unused resources. One of the main advantages of using virtualization is its ability to support multiple server, desktop, and other operating systems in a single physical hardware platform. It does this by the use of a **hypervisor**.

A hypervisor is considered to be a virtual machine manager, but it's the actual application or program that is added just above the physical hardware layer. The hypervisor is used to create the **virtual machines** (**VMs**) and assigns the appropriate hardware resources to them.

Within a physical hardware platform, there may be multiple CPUs, memory modules, **network interface cards** (**NICs**), and storage/disk controllers; the hypervisor is responsible for the allocation of these resources to each VM:

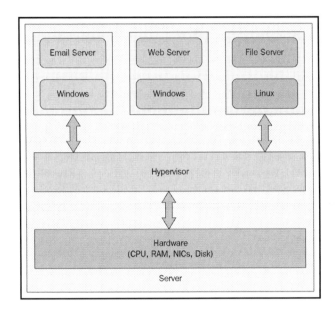

Let's imagine that, as an organization grows, the network infrastructure expands as well, increasing the number of network security appliances and servers. Virtualization can allow a company to virtualize all of their server operating systems and operations into just a few physical servers (hardware platforms), where each would be using a hypervisor. This will not only save on physical space/storage, but will save on cost for maintaining physical servers. Another benefit of using virtualization is if a single VM fails, it does not compromise the availability of the others on the same physical hardware platform.

 The virtual components such as RAM, CPU, storage, NICs, and so on can be dynamically installed, modified, or removed from a virtual machine on a hypervisor.

The following is a list of advantages of using virtualization:

- Reduces the number of physical servers, thereby reducing expenditure for equipment and appliances
- Reduces the space needed to store the physical servers

- Reduces power consumption since fewer physical servers are needed
- Virtualization allows older and legacy operating systems to be run on the hypervisor

Hypervisors

My journey in the field of IT all began when I learned about building, maintaining, and troubleshooting computer systems such as desktops and laptops. At the time, I was enrolled in a CompTIA A+ certification training program. During and after training, I learned and researched a lot of operating systems, such as the old versions of Microsoft Windows, Apple's macOS, and the many flavors of Linux.

I was quite fascinated at this point and wanted to use some flavors of Linux, such as Ubuntu. One main issue I had at the time was having only a single personal computer with Windows installed. I knew that if I needed to install another operating system on my personal computer, I would either need to create another partition on the hard drive or do a clean installation (remove Windows). Since I was a beginner, I was very hesitant about removing my main operating system.

After doing some research on the internet, I came across the concept of virtualization, specifically using a type 2 hypervisor. This allowed me to neither remove my existing operating system nor create another partition on the hard drive. Instead, I needed to install a type 2 hypervisor on top of the Windows OS and later create and manage virtual machines running various OSes. The interesting part about learning about the concepts of virtualization is that we must remember what the main components of a computer system are.

Within a desktop, server, or laptop computer, there are the following layers:

- Operating system
- Services
- Firmware (BIOS/UEFI)
- Hardware (CPU, RAM, HDD, and so on)

The hypervisor appliance/program will be able to provide those four core components virtually to each individual VM. The guest operating systems won't be able to tell the difference in the hardware (for example, AMD versus Intel processor). This is one of the main benefits of the hypervisor. It emulates the hardware and other components, making the guest OS function as though it's currently in its native operating environment.

A VM consists of an OS. The OS within a hypervisor is known as a guest OS, whereas the OS that is installed on the physical computer is known as the host OS:

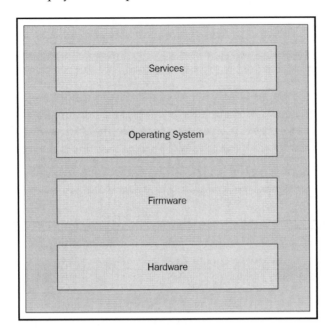

Since we already know that a hypervisor is an application that's used to create VMs, we must not forget about its deployment models. There are two types of hypervisors—**type 1** and **type 2**. Here, we will discuss these types and go over the features of each.

Type 1 hypervisor

The type 1 hypervisor is sometimes called a **bare-metal hypervisor**. This type of deployment is installed directly on the hardware rather than on top of a host OS. The bare-metal or type 1 hypervisor has direct access to all hardware resources. This allows each guest OS, such as the VMs, to interact directly with the hardware, making this type of deployment more efficient than the type 2 model:

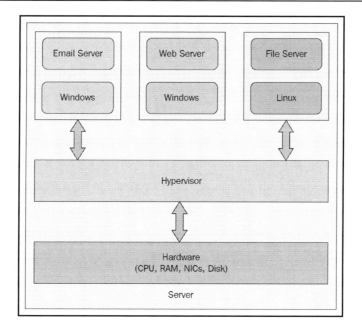

The following is a list of well-known bare-metal hypervisors:

- VMware ESX
- Microsoft Hyper-V server
- Citrix XenServer

Type 2 hypervisor

The type 2 hypervisor is an application that runs on top of an existing host OS such as Microsoft Windows, Apple macOS X, or Linux. This deployment does not allow the hypervisor application to interact directly with the hardware resources such as the processor, RAM, and so on.

However, the host OS still uses hardware resources to function, and any remaining resources are provided to the hypervisor for assignment to any VMs it may contain:

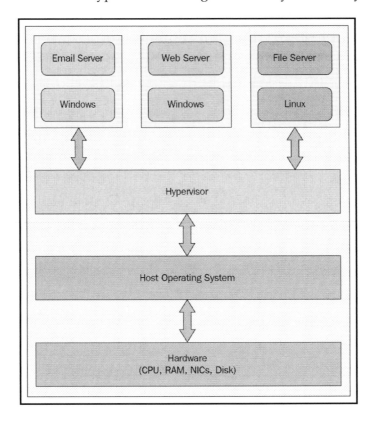

The following is a list of type 2 hypervisors. Note that some are commercial and others are free:

- Microsoft Virtual PC (free)
- VMware Workstation (commercial)
- Oracle VirtualBox (free)
- Mac OS X Parallels (commercial)

Virtual networking components

Creating (spinning up) VMs can be very interesting and a bit exciting, especially, if your duties are similar to those of a virtualization or cloud engineer. However, as aspiring network professionals, we must not forget that our network infrastructure also needs to be able to support a high amount of traffic, scalability, fault-tolerance, and redundancy. We previously mentioned that one of the main benefits of virtualizing servers is being able to reduce the physical storage space for the equipment and save on purchasing dedicated appliances. This concept also applies to networking equipment such as switches, firewalls, routers, and so on.

In this section, we will discuss the concepts of using virtual networking components.

Virtual Switch (vSwitch)

A vSwitch has the same features as a physical switch, but the difference is that the vSwitch exists within a hypervisor. Within many hypervisor applications such as VMware ESX or even Microsoft Hyper-V, they provide a feature so that you can create a vSwitch that can serve many purposes. Let's imagine you want to create a virtualized network where your VMs are a single subnet. Therefore, their NICs would all need to be connected to a single physical switch. However, using the hypervisor, a vSwitch can be created to provide the same effect.

 The switches that are created within a hypervisor have limited capabilities compared to an enterprise-level switch from Cisco or Juniper.

As we can see in the following screenshot, which is of a vSwitch layout on a VMware ESXi hypervisor, there's a vSwitch topology outlining the ports which are both connected to online VMs such as CentOS and pfSense, and the other ports that are connected but the VMs are offline, like the AlienVault SIEM VM:

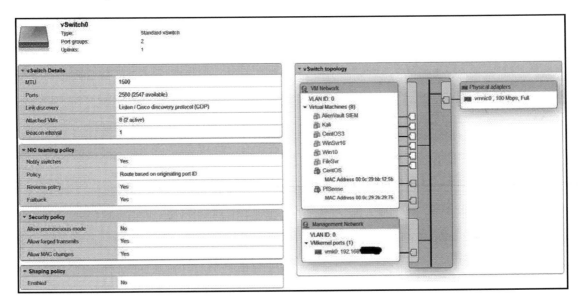

From research, you have probably noticed that Cisco Systems is one of the top vendors and industry leaders—not just in networking appliances but other fields such as security, collaboration, wireless, and even certification. Cisco Systems released their Nexus 1000V vSwitch, which has all the features of a physical Cisco IOS switch, but is able to operate within a hypervisor such as VMware ESXi, vCenter, and so on.

Virtual firewall

Similar to the vSwitch concepts, there is also a virtual firewall model as well. Vendors such as Cisco Systems have been able to provide both physical firewall appliances and virtual appliances, such as their Cisco **Adaptive Security Virtual Appliance (ASAv)** and the Cisco **Next Generation Firewall Virtual (NGFWv)**. Each of these products allows a firewall/security engineer to deploy on a hypervisor, each providing the same features and services as their physical counterparts. Another vendor is pfSense (http://www.pfsense. org), who also provides virtual security appliances that are ready for deployment on virtual and cloud platforms such as Amazon AWS (http://www.aws.amazon.com) and Microsoft Azure (http://www.azure.microsoft.com).

One key point to always remember before setting up a virtual appliance is this: ensure that you have a well-designed network topology diagram; it's simple to take the topology and implement it in a hypervisor application.

The following screenshot is a pfSense firewall deployment on a VMware ESXi hypervisor with four NICs. Each NIC is also a virtual adapter on the firewall. The hypervisor application allows for the creation of multiple network adapters and other components that a system/VM may need. This is a benefit since physical hardware components may be limited to the available ports on a motherboard. The hypervisor removes this limitation and allows the assignment of multiple virtual components to a single VM:

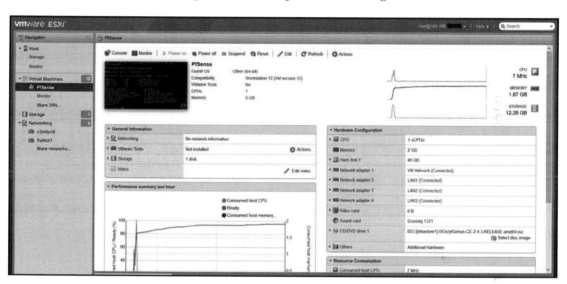

Virtual routers

By now, you may have noticed that almost every operating system, network, and security appliance can be virtualized. Let's not forget about one of the most important devices on a network—the **router**. Most of the routers we have encountered are physical routers, regardless of whether they are from various vendors. However, with the high increase in cloud computing services and virtualization, many vendors have created their own virtual router platforms, which are ready to be deployed on a cloud platform. These include Amazon AWS or even Microsoft Azure platforms.

Two notable vendors are Cisco Systems (http://www.cisco.com) and Juniper Networks (http://www.juniper.net). Cisco has released their Integrated Services Virtual Router and Cloud Services Router 1000V series, while Juniper has also released their vMX Virtual Router, which uses their Junos OS and has the same capabilities as the physical appliances.

These are some major milestones for virtualization in the fields of networking and security. In 2018, Cisco Security Connector Expands EMM/UEM Integrations with VMware Workspace, see the following URL for more information: https://blogs.cisco.com/security/cisco-security-connector-expands-emm-uem-integrations-with-vmware-workspace-one-on-premises.

Storage technologies

The primary purpose of a network is to interconnect various devices or end devices for the purpose of sharing resources. A very important resource to a business or organization is the centralized storage of data for their employees. Whether it's a group project, departmental, or even between various staff members working on the same files or data, collaboration is important. In this section, we will take a look at two particular types of network storage topologies and their characteristics. These are the **Network Attached Storage** (**NAS**) and the **Storage Area Network** (**SAN**) models.

NAS

Unlike traditional file servers, which system administrators seldom deploy using a server operating system such as Windows Server or Linux server, NAS is a single unit that sits on a LAN. The NAS itself does not run traditional operating systems, but rather a firmware that provides management of the unit, allowing an administrator or even a non-technical user to simply configure and add to a LAN. The NAS is comprised of an outer body or shell that's used to house the hard drives. Some NAS units are able to support various number of hard drives, where the minimum is one hard drive.

The higher-priced NAS units are usually a bit larger in size to support multiple hard drives which are interchangeable. Some NAS units provide redundancy of the data store by supporting **Redundant Array of Independent Disks** (**RAID**) to ensure that if there is a failure with a single drive within the hard drive bay, the data is not completely lost but also recoverable. The following is an image of a Netgear NAS unit:

Another benefit of using a NAS unit within a LAN is that the device or the storage folders are accessible through TCP/IP. Once connected to a network, the NAS firmware will seek a DHCP server to obtain an IP address, subnet mask, and default gateway configurations for communication over a TCP/IP network. This means that any TCP/IP-based device will be able to access the resources on the NAS seamlessly without the need for any specialized applications being installed on an end device:

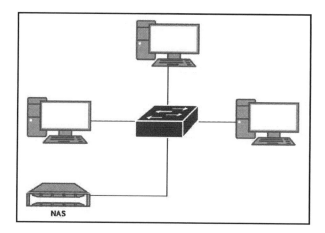

Some NAS vendors are as follows:

- Synology (www.synology.com)
- Western Digital (www.wdc.com)
- Buffalo Americas (www.buffalotech.com)
- NETGEAR (www.netgear.com)

SAN

SAN is a high bandwidth capacity network or an area on the network that contains multiple storage servers for an organization. The SAN can be a subnetwork or an area within a data center that contains not only storage servers but specialized networking appliances and components to ensure that there is very low latency and minimal bottlenecks on the network segment.

Unlike a NAS unit, which is small and compact and is connected directly to a network device such as a switch, a SAN is not just a single unit but rather an entire network from cabling to switches and even high-availability hardware components with redundancy. This is one of the major benefits of a SAN—it's much faster than a NAS, which uses the existing network infrastructure rather than a specialized network that's built with **Fibre Channel** (**FC**) and other recommend components for a SAN. Due to the grade of the components required in a SAN, the overall cost for having such a dedicated high-speed network will be quite costly.

Connection type

Using an unsuitable connector on a fiber or high speed network may result in poor performance. In this sub-section, we will briefly discuss the various connection types in a storage area network.

FC

FC is an area on the network that is able to support very high-speeds for data transmission. The storage servers within the data center are usually connected directly to an FC, which supports transfer rates of approximately 16 to 128 GBps. The FC is primarily used for SCSI commands over a SAN.

The FC is comprised of the following components:

- The storage servers, which are known as the initiators. These will require a fiber channel-compatible network interface card that connects to a specialized fiber channel switch.
- Within the storage servers, there's the actual storage media, which is the target.

Fibre Channel over Ethernet (FCoE)

FCoE integrates into the existing FC infrastructure. The storage server uses an Ethernet adapter rather than using a specialized FC adapter to interface with the network. Since Ethernet is a bit limited regarding communication on a LAN, it is not routable over another subnet. Therefore, using FCoE can only be accessible on a network locally.

Fibre Channel over IP (FCIP)

The difference between FCoE and FCIP is that FCIP allows access through using routing over different subnets. This is unlike FCoE, which provides access only on the same subnet.

Jumbo Frame

The concept of a Jumbo Frame is to allow a large payload of data to be transferred across the network. The typical size of a payload of data is 1,500 bytes; a Jumbo Frame allows up to 9,216 bytes of a payload to be transmitted. This increases the efficiency of the network since fewer packets are being sent on the network.

WAN technologies

When starting a business, you usually start from small, single-office location within a city or a country. As time goes by and you get more customers or clients, the business grows since you need to increase your number of employees so that you can handle more demanding business processes each day. Perhaps your company may start offering new products and services that will require you to expand the physical company in the production, warehousing, and office spaces. This may lead to you creating a branch in another city or country across the world.

In doing so, each branch office may need to access the resources on the corporate network, maybe a centralized storage or perhaps an application server. It would be feasible to run physical cables yourself between your branches, regardless of whether the remote offices are in another city, a different country, or even another region of the world, through the use of WAN technologies. These are used to help an organization expand its physical structure.

What is a WAN? A WAN is created when a LAN is extended over a large geographic network. A WAN allows organizations to share their resources between one branch office and another.

The WAN connection is normally set up and maintained by a local telecommunications provider TELCO. This type of service or connection type is usually owned by the TELCO. An organization can pay for a service so that they can interconnect their remote offices. Whether these remote offices are within a country or across the world, the telecommunication provider has the resources to make it possible.

There are many types of WAN connections, some of which you may have already learned about from discussions with your peers or even from your own research. In this section, we will focus on the following:

- WAN topologies
- WAN service types
- Transmission mediums
- Characteristics of a WAN service
- WAN termination

Let's dive in!

WAN topologies

In a previous chapter, we discussed various network topologies, along with their characteristics and use cases, within the topic of WAN. There are four main topologies that organizations and telecommunication providers deploy. These are as follows:

- **Point-to-Point (P2P)**
- Hub and spoke
- Full mesh
- Dual-homed

P2P

The P2P topology is quite simple. This type of WAN topology is used when there are two remote/branch offices that require interconnectivity between their LAN:

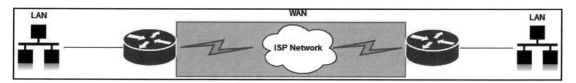

Hub and spoke

In a hub and spoke topology, each remote/branch office has a dedicated WAN connection/link to the corporate headquarters. Each branch office is known as a spoke, while the corporate headquarters is known as the hub. At the hub, the main resources would be located and stored there, which the spokes or branch offices access from the corporate LAN through their dedicated WAN connection. This topology eliminates the need to interconnect the office sites to each other:

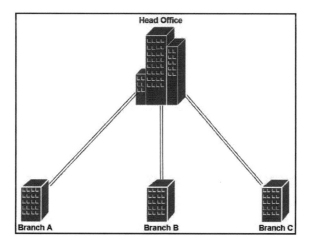

Full mesh

Within the full mesh topology, each office location has a dedicated connection to each other site. This type of topology provides full redundancy in network connectivity between all of its sites. This is a major benefit as opposed to using a hub and spoke topology, where each spoke has a single connection back to the hub. If this single connection goes down, connectivity between the hub and site is lost.

However, having a lot of redundancy in a WAN topology can also have some disadvantages, such as the following:

- Each WAN link/connection from the telecommunication provider is a cost. More connections equals more expenditure for an organization.
- Since each site has a dedicated connection/link to every other site, as more sites are created as the organization grows, the more links are needed from each site to interconnect the new sites. When there's an issue with a link, the troubleshooting process can be challenging as the full mesh topology can eventually become complex and difficult:

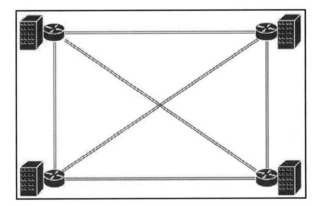

Dual-homed

In a dual-homed topology, the hub has two routers and each spoke site has dual connections going to each of the two routers at the hub. This design provides redundancy using the hub and spoke topology. The disadvantage of using this design is the addition of each redundant link per site (spoke):

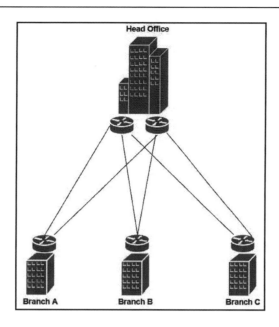

WAN service types

In this section, we will discuss the various types of WAN services that are provided by most telecommunication providers.

Integrated Services Digital Network (ISDN)

ISDN is a communication standard that is used for transmitting both voice and data over a **Public Switched Telephone Network (PSTN)** using digital signals rather than an analog signal. The PSTN is a collection of both voice and public telephone networks which are interconnected for commercial use by a telecommunication provider. This is sometimes known as the **Plain Old Telephone Service (POTS)**.

There are two types of interfaces that are used in ISDN:

- **Basic Rate Interface (BRI)**: This type of interface is used for small businesses and home subscribers. BRI provides *2 x 64* KBps channels for transporting both voice and data traffic. These are known as the **Bearer Channels** or the **B Channels**, while a single 16 KBps channel is used for signaling. This is known as the **Delta Channel** or the **D Channel**.

- **Primary Rate Interface (PRI)**: The PRI is quite similar to the BRI. However, PRI provides *23 B* channels each, which are 64 KBps, and a single D channel of 64 KBps in North America. Combining the 23 B channels and the single D channel, an ISDN PRI can support up to 1.544 MBps of bandwidth. In European countries and various parts of the world, PRI also supports 30 B channels and a single D channel, providing up to 2.048 MBps.

The local loop is the actual cable that is either copper or fiber optic, which is connected from the subscriber's modem or router back to the local service provider exchange.

Leased lines

A leased line is a dedicated connection that uses a P2P type of topology for interconnecting two sites. The name refers to the fact that an organization (subscriber) pays a monthly fee to a service provider to ensure that the link is always available for the duration of the service agreement. Regardless of whether the subscriber uses the connection or not, it's always available.

T1/T3

The T-carrier lines are usually used in North America. These are as follows:

- T1—supports 1.544 MBps
- T3—supports 43.7 MBps

E1/E3

The E-carrier links are mainly used in European countries:

- E1—supports 2.048 MBps
- E3—supports 34.368 MBps

Digital Subscriber Line (DSL)

DSL is a type of broadband service that allows an ISP to offer high-speed internet access to their subscribers. DSL uses the existing copper telephone lines, but uses a much higher frequency to provide faster transmission speeds between the ISP and the subscriber. With a DSL service, a consumer can use their telephone (landline) while browsing the internet. Unlike dial-up, DSL is an always-on internet service.

DSL allows multiple subscriber lines to be multiplexed into a single high-capacity connection at a **DSL access multiplexer** (**DSLAM**), which is on the telecommunication provider's network.

There are two types of DSL:

- Symmetrical DSL
- Asymmetrical DSL

Symmetrical DSL: This is where both the upload and download speeds are equal in value. For example, the upload speed is 512 KBps while the download speed is 512 KBps.

Asymmetrical DSL: This is more popular among residential subscribers. In asymmetrical DSL, the upload speed is lower than the download speed. For example, the upload speed is 256 KBps while the download speed is 512 KBps.

Metropolitan Ethernet

The Ethernet was originally developed to operate on a LAN. Over the past years, the standard for Ethernet has been updated and telecommunication providers are able to provide Ethernet connectivity over their WAN technologies. One of the famous variations is known as the Metropolitan Ethernet, or Metro Ethernet. An ISP or TELCO is able to provide a WAN connection for their customers within the ISP/TELCO network at a reduced cost.

The Metro Ethernet WAN connectivity has been replacing most of the other WAN technologies as it's simpler to integrate into existing networks, provides higher data rates, and is cheaper.

 A Metro Ethernet WAN is limited to only be within a service provider network. If a WAN is needed beyond a service provider's network, a **Multiprotocol Label Switching** (**MPLS**) circuit is needed.

Cable broadband

A cable broadband service uses the existing coaxial cable that is used by the cable company to distribute their television service to subscribers. Similar to DSL, cable broadband is an always-on service that does not require the subscriber to initiate the connection; the cable modem handles the auto connection of the service. The cable modem is able to translate a digital signal into a broadband frequency, which is then sent over the cable television network. This signal is then terminated at the telecommunication provider's head office which is known as the headend using a **Cable Modem Termination System** (**CMTS**).

Dial-up

In the early days of the internet, most ISPs offered their internet connection across existing telephone lines. The subscriber (yourself) would pay a fee to the ISP. This fee was either based on your usage, such as number of hours you used per month, or a monthly rate. The subscriber would require a modem (modulator/demodulator) to covert the analog signal from the telephone line to a digital signal and vice versa. The modem would literally dial-in to the ISP network to create the connection between your computer to the ISP network and the internet. However, the average dial-up modem operated at 56 KBps, and the connections speeds were lower. While connected to the internet, the telephone wouldn't be operational, unless you had a specialized splutter device, which was used to separate the signals.

MPLS

MPLS is another type of WAN technology that is used in a lot of modern international WAN circuits. Within an MPLS network, all traffic is tagged/labeled similarly to using VLANs on a switch network. MPLS uses labels, which allows multiple types of network protocols to use the infrastructure, thereby removing any limitations. This is opposed to other WAN technologies, which may be able to transport certain traffic types or network protocols. Once traffic enters an MPLS network, whether it's IP, **Asynchronous Transfer Mode** (**ATM**), Frame Relay, or Metro Ethernet, all traffic is labelled.

MPLS allows ISPs to create a WAN connection beyond borders, spanning over regions, and passing through multiple ISPs. This is an international circuit.

ATM

ATM is an older WAN protocol that has the capability of transferring voice, video, and data across both public and private networks. It handles the transportation of payloads by using a cell-based structure, where each cell is of a fixed length, that is, 53 bytes.

Frame Relay

Frame Relay is another older WAN technology that is used to interconnect each branch office/site of an organization. It utilizes a single interface on a router by creating multiple sub-interfaces, which are then used to connect each branch/site using **Permanent Virtual Circuit** (**PVC**). These virtual circuits allowed for the transmission of both voice and data traffic, while providing up to 4 MBps for most telecommunication providers.

In a Frame Relay network topology, whenever a virtual circuit is created, it uses a **data-link connection identifier** (**DLCI**), which is unique on the network and is used to identify a peer router.

Point-to-Point Protocol (PPP)

PPP uses a standard method for transporting multiple protocols over P2P WAN links. A major benefit of PPP is the fact that it is open source, which means that it is operable among many vendors. PPP uses two sub protocols, one of which is the **Link Control Protocol** (**LCP**), which is responsible for establishing, maintaining, and terminating the logical connection over the P2P connection. Once LCP establishes the link, control is then passed on to the **Network Control Protocol** (**NCP**), which are responsible for configuring and establishing various network protocols, such as IPv4 and IPv6.

Point-to-Point Protocol over Ethernet (PPPoE)

The PPP is mainly used on serial links and ISDN networks. One benefit of using PPP is its ability to assign IP addresses to the remote peer at the end of the PPP link. Another benefit is being able to use PPP for link authentication, such as using the **Challenge-Handshake Authentication Protocol** (**CHAP**). This would ensure that a PPP peer needs to provide a valid username and password combination before establishing a logical link.

Telecommunication providers utilize PPP due to its benefits such as link authentication, since it provides accountability for network usage and its link management features in the protocol itself. Since Ethernet links are not supported over PPP, the PPPoE protocol provides a solution where ISPs are able to provide their service to subscribers. This is done by encapsulating PPP frames inside an Ethernet frame for communication between the subscriber and the ISP network.

Most home users have a DSL connection in their home. This is usually a DSL modem that connects to the ISP network using PPP. However, on the LAN side or the subscriber network, there is Ethernet. The DSL will encapsulate the Ethernet frames into PPP frames for transportation to the ISP.

Dynamic Multipoint VPN (DMVPN)

Cisco Systems has created a VPN solution for interconnecting multiple sites/remote offices in a much easier and scalable manner. A typical VPN allows one site to connect to another, creating a hub and spoke topology where all traffic from one spoke must pass through the hub, and then to the destination. With a DMVPN, each spoke is able to communicate directly with another spoke/remote office. Whenever traffic is destined from one spoke to another, a DMVPN is established between the peers.

Transmission mediums

Many types of mediums are used in WAN connections. In this section, we will take a look at each of the various types.

Satellite

Sometimes, an ISP is unable to provide their physical infrastructure, such as the local loop, to a potential subscriber of their service. At times, a remote office may be a bit out-of-the-way, since there aren't any service providers. This will definitely be an issue for an organization that requires that all of their remote offices are connected to the headquarters.

One solution is to use a **Very Small Aperture Terminal** (**VSAT**). VSAT is able to provide a private WAN connection via satellite communication. VSAT technology has a few limitations, some of which are as follows:

- The signal from the dish on your company's or house's roof must travel an approximate distance of 35,786 kilometers to the orbiting satellite in space and back. This will create higher latency.
- A line of sight is needed for better signal strength.

Wireless

There are many types of wireless internet and WAN connectivity methods. The following are typically used:

- **Satellite internet**: This type of internet/WAN connection utilizes VSAT technologies. Rather than a subscriber's satellite dish pointing to an orbiting satellite in space, ISPs are putting up exchange points at strategic locations that will be able to relay a signal locally across a country or city. However, using this type of setup also inherits the higher latency and line-of-sight limitations.
- **WiMAX**: Some ISPs provide WiMAX for customers who are on the go. WiMAX is defined by IEEE 802.16, which is used to provide high-speed internet (broadband) access using wireless technologies. The ISP would provide a pocket-size hotspot to the subscriber, which would connect to a nearby cellular tower. This is used to relay the internet service through the ISP network.
- **3G and 4G**: Telecommunication providers are utilizing their existing cellular network infrastructure to not only provide voice communication but also high-speed internet access on their customers mobile devices such as smartphones, tablet computers, laptops, and any other wireless compatible device. The subscriber device connects to the TELCO's cellular antennas, which then connects to the TELCO and the internet. However, the signal between the mobile device and the cellular tower is important to monitor, since if the signal gets weaker, the speed of the internet connection will also lower.

 The terms 3G and 4G mean third and fourth generation of cellular network access. LTE is a newer version of cellular network access, but is a later version of 4G.

Copper cable

Most networks use copper cabling due its very low cost and easy installation. However, using copper cables has a few limitations, such as their maximum distances and signal interfaces. Since this media operates at the Physical Layer of the OSI model, data is sent across using an electrical signal along the wire. The receiving device is able to decode and reassemble the signals back into data.

The main types of copper cables are as follows:

- **Unshielded Twisted Pair (UTP)**
- **Shielded Twisted Pair (STP)**
- Coaxial

Fiber optic

Most high-capacity networks, whether they are private or public networks, use optical fiber for transmitting data over very long distances. Unlike copper cables, which are susceptible to interference and cross-talk, fiber optic cables are immune to any sort of interference. Within a fiber optic cable, at the center, is a core which is either plastic or glass. Light is sent into a single strand of fiber, which is used for encoding bits of data through the core itself. The receiving device at the other end of the cable will terminate and decode the message back into data.

The following are some use cases for fiber optics:

- Enterprise networks
- **Fiber to the Home (FTTH)**
- Submarine cable networks

WAN termination

The following are the components which are usually found at the termination points of a WAN connection:

- **Demarcation point**: This is the point at which the support from the service provider ends. This point can be identified at the point where the service provider interconnects their network with the subscriber. If the ISP supplied a modem to access their services, it is at the modem where the demarcation point is.

- **Data Communications Equipment (DCE)**: The DCE is a device that resides on the ISP network which provides an interface to connect to their subscribers.
- **Data Terminal Equipment (DTE)**: On the subscriber end of the local loop, a DTE is used to terminate the connection or signal from the DCE on the ISP end.
- **Customer Premises Equipment (CPE)**: This is the equipment owned by the customer, such as a router.
- **Channel Service Unit/Data Service Unit (CSU/DSU)**: This is used when a telecommunication provider supplies a digital leased line to a subscriber. The CSU is used to terminate the signals that are received on the leased lines, whereas the DSU is used to convert the signal to be usable on a LAN and vice versa.

Summary

In this chapter, we took a look at various types of virtualization technologies, from different types of hypervisors to deployment models, and the important benefits of using virtualization within an IT infrastructure. Be it a small or large organization, virtualization can improve IT efficiency and save on expenditures.

Furthermore, we saw how telecommunication providers are able to interconnect not just organizations and businesses but people too using various services and technologies together, either through physical cables or wireless technologies. By now, you should have a clear understanding of what takes place within a telecommunication provider's network and the various WAN services that exist and their characteristics.

In the next chapter, we will look at the aspects of business continuity and disaster recovery concepts, which will focus on ensuring the high availability of network resources.

Questions

1. In virtualization, a _____ is installed directly on the hardware of a server appliance.
    1. Type 1 hypervisor
    2. Type 2 hypervisor
    3. Guest operating system
    4. Service

2. What are two benefits of using virtualization within an organization?
    1. Improves network performance
    2. Saves cost on additional hardware
    3. Improves end user productivity
    4. Reduces the storage spaces needed for additional servers

3. Which type of storage device can be connected directly to a TCP/IP network?
    1. HDD
    2. SSD
    3. Flash drive
    4. NAS

4. Which type of technology is used to extend a LAN over a large geographic distance?
    1. Switch
    2. Router
    3. WAN
    4. WLAN

5. Which WAN topology provides the highest redundancy?
    1. Hub and spoke
    2. Mesh
    3. Point-to-point
    4. Star

6. Which type of WAN technology is used where an ISP is unable to implement either copper or fiber optic cables in a remote location?
    1. DSL
    2. ISDN
    3. VSAT
    4. T1

7. Which WAN technology uses a cell structure for communication?
    1. DSL
    2. Cable
    3. Frame Relay
    4. ATM

Further reading

Read the following articles for more information:

- For more knowledge on virtualization, VMware offers free self-paced training at the following URL: `https://mylearn.vmware.com/mgrReg/plan.cfm?plan=33611 ui=www_edu`

- Check out **Introduction to Virtualization** course at Packt Publishing at the following URL: `https://www.packtpub.com/application-development/introduction-virtualization-one-hour-crash-course-video`

9

Business Continuity and Disaster Recovery Concepts

Contemporary networks require engineers and technicians to not only perform the initial configuration and maintenance of physical networking infrastructure, but also to develop appropriate documentation and diagrams; to create proper operating, recovery, and change management procedures; and to implement robust scanning, monitoring, and logging systems for their networks. In this chapter, we will first discuss the importance of creating network documentation and diagrams, after which we will introduce the concept of business continuity and disaster planning. Lastly, we will examine some common scanning, monitoring, and patching processes to be followed in the proper management of a network.

We will cover the following topics in the chapter:

- Role of documentation and diagrams
- Business continuity and disaster recovery
- Common operational processes

The role of documentation and diagrams

Although it may seem a trivial concept, proper documentation and diagrams serve to differentiate properly managed and structured networks from *thrown-together* networks. Documentation allows new staff to be brought up to speed quickly, allows non-technical staff to understand the design of the network, and helps potential customers and clients of the business to build confidence in the network.

In this section, we will first discuss some general documentation and diagramming concepts, after which we will dive into the documentation required for physical infrastructure on the network. We will lastly explore some of the common operational procedures that you are likely to come across while administering a network.

General documentation and diagramming concepts

A network diagram is a visual depiction of the infrastructure that constitutes a network. Network diagrams can range from being concise, focusing on only the most essential components of a particular function, to being incredibly large and complex, covering the entire end-to-end network. Regardless of the size of the diagram, it is important to use standard symbols for devices. This allows readers to easily understand the devices within the network and the general function that each one provides. For example, the following diagram illustrates (using some common symbols) a simple network showing several components connected to a switch:

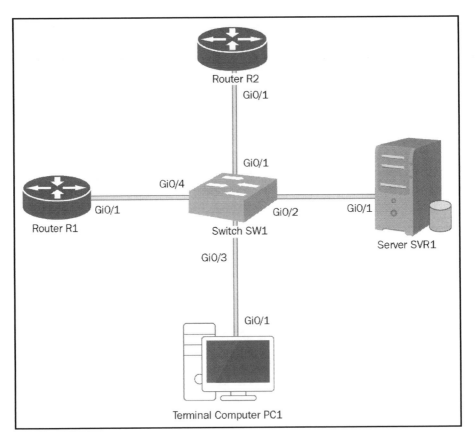

Another important concept in the realm of diagramming is the difference between logical and physical diagrams. Physical diagrams illustrate all of the physical components involved in a particular network or section of a network, whereas logical diagrams focus on the functionality of different devices on the network, including only the components and configurations that are relevant to that functionality. For example, the preceding diagram may be classified as a physical diagram, as it includes the cables and ports used to connect the equipment involved in this network. Physical diagrams usually include wiring and port locations on the network, illustrating exactly which cables are used to connect equipment and which ports the cables connect to on equipment.

On the other hand, the following diagram shows one possible logical diagram of this network, illustrating the layer 3 connectivity between **Router R1** and **Router R2**:

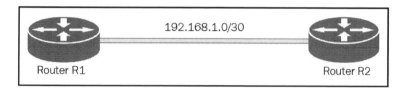

Note that the ports and cabling are not included in this diagram, and that the switch has been removed entirely since it does not perform functions at layer 3 in this particular configuration.

In the following subsection, we will examine some more of the documentation commonly required for physical network infrastructure.

Physical infrastructure documentation

In addition to the physical network diagrams discussed in the previous section, network administrators are often required to document and diagram several other physical components that constitute their network.

One such diagram is a rack diagram. These diagrams are used to document the placement of equipment in data center racks, helping administrators to keep track of their equipment and helping them plan for future expansion in their data centers. Each rack constitutes a particular number of spaces for mounting equipment called **Rack Units (RUs)**. Equipment may require a single unit or several units in a rack. Rack diagrams allow administrators to keep track of free us in racks and to locate equipment in a rack. The following diagram shows an example of a rack diagram:

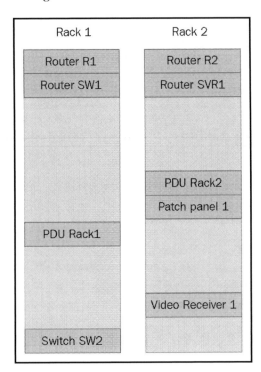

Another bit of documentation commonly required is the **Intermediate Distribution Frame (IDF)/Main Distribution Frame (MDF)** diagram. The MDF is a frame or rack that serves as the termination point for lines from telephone companies, managing connections between the central office and one or several IDFs. IDFs then connect to user equipment within the enterprise. IDF/MDF diagrams illustrate the connections from the telephone exchange to the MDF, from the MDF to the IDF(s), and from the IDFs to the user equipment within the enterprise.

Additionally, network administrators are usually required to add labeling to all of their infrastructure. This labeling helps administrators to differentiate between similar pieces of equipment and to understand the function that each of their devices performs on their network. For example, an administrator may install several routers in a network that are exactly the same make and model, requiring the placement of labels such as **R1**, **R2**, and so on to differentiate between them. Labeling conventions can be as simple or as complex as they need to be, including, for instance, designations for physical locations or owners of the equipment. Labeling is not limited to devices alone, but may also be placed on racks, cables, patch panels, and cabinets, helping administrators to document and identify anything in their network that they need to keep track of.

Lastly, it is important for administrators to implement an inventory management system. This system helps administrators keep track of all of their important physical assets such as their devices, cables, connectors, transceivers, and labels, allowing them to place orders for additional assets before they run out and preventing overstocking of any assets.

In addition to keeping track of physical assets, it is also important to develop documentation for all of the common processes that staff follow when working on the network. We will examine some of these processes in the next subsection.

Operational documentation

The most common processes that network staff follow in their day-to-day operations are commonly documented as **Standard Operating Procedures** (**SOPs**). SOPs are simply a set of step-by-step instructions to be followed by staff in order to accomplish a particular task. SOPs aid organizations in improving efficiency, in reducing the probability for human error, and in training new employees. In the context of network management, SOPs may reduce network outages and downtime by ensuring that all employees follow the same list of predefined steps when managing infrastructure.

In addition to SOPs, administrators should also implement clear procedures governing change management. Change-management procedures stipulate processes to be followed in implementing any change on a production (in-use) network. Many technicians are accustomed to making changes to equipment and cabling *on the fly*, changing configuration with minimal prior planning or consultation. However, these changes often carry serious inherent risks, making change management an essential part of minimizing downtime in a network. It is therefore imperative that administrators develop a proper change management process that incorporates aspects such as peer review (getting other members of staff to verify the intended changes), change-management advisory boards (which assess the impact and risk of any proposed change to the network), and proper planning (implementing the change during off hours and having a clearly defined rollback procedure). Another important part of change management is the documentation of baselines in the network. A baseline is simply a fixed point of reference for a particular system or function in a network. By creating baselines in the network, administrators are able to test functionality or measure performance after a change is implemented and ensure that the network was not adversely affected by the change. Baselines may be created in a number of areas including security systems, network configuration, and network performance.

Although documentation and diagrams are an important part of maintaining highly available networks, there are many other aspects to be considered in the quest for high availability in networks and business continuity as a whole. In the next section, we will discuss some of these aspects as they relate to networking systems.

Business continuity and disaster recovery

Business continuity refers to the capability of an enterprise to keep its core business functions and processes running during times of outages and disasters. Disaster recovery, on the other hand, refers to the upkeep of **Information and Communications Technology (ICT)** infrastructure of the enterprise, focusing on restoring this infrastructure as quickly as possible following any type of disastrous event. In this section, we will examine notions related to both these concepts. We will first discuss several terms related to the design of high-availability networks, after which we will examine reliability in power delivery and various recovery processes. Lastly, we will define a few common metrics related to these concepts.

Designing high-availability networks

Any network designed around the concepts of stability and reliability must incorporate a large amount of fault tolerance. **Fault tolerance** refers to the ability of a system to continue to operate normally, in spite of the failure of one of more of its constituent parts. Fault tolerance is closely related to both the concept of high availability, which is the ability of a system to operate properly and continuously for an extended period of time, and the concept of a single point of failure, which refers to any one component or entity in a system whose failure can affect the operation of the entire system.

Network administrators often purchase particular components and implement several types of configurations in order to design highly available, fault-tolerant systems. One commonly implemented configuration is load balancing. **Load balancing** is a configuration technique that aims to disseminate workloads among all of the available resources. This technique is commonly implemented in servers. Incoming traffic from clients is initially directed at the load balancer, which then utilizes its preconfigured balancing algorithm to determine which of its backend servers will receive the traffic. The following diagram illustrates this concept:

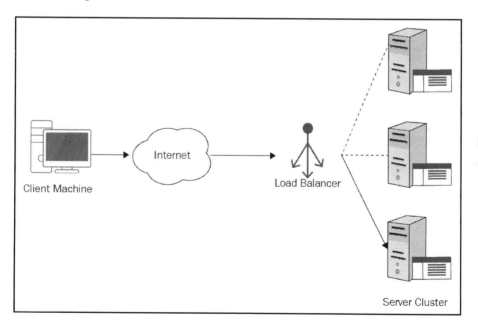

Common load balancing/scheduling algorithms include **round-robin** (a simple algorithm where requests are distributed to servers in a sequential manner as they arrive), weighted round-robin (as with round-robin, but servers are assigned different weightings and the ones with higher weightings receive larger shares of incoming requests), and least-connection (servers with smaller numbers of client connections are preferred over saturated servers).

This diagram also introduces the concept of clustering, which is another technique commonly used to provide high availability. **Clustering** refers to the aggregation of several nodes into a group, such that the group of nodes behaves as though it were a single node. For example, the preceding diagram illustrated a server cluster, where each server delivered content to clients in the same manner as a single server would. Clustering adds a degree of fault tolerance to a system as long as the cluster is configured correctly. For example, a cluster can be configured such that, even if a single node in the cluster fails, the other nodes continue to provide the overall function of the cluster, with the other nodes simply absorbing the increased workload.

Another technique commonly used to provide fault tolerance is **Network Interface Card (NIC)** teaming. NIC teaming refers to a technique in which several NICs on a server are combined into a group, with the aim of providing higher capacity or improved fault tolerance to the server. When configured to provide increased fault tolerance, NIC teaming balances traffic across all of the NICs and links in the group, allowing for traffic to continue flowing if any of the individual NICs in the group fails. This concept of combining several links into one highly available link can also be implemented on network equipment (such as switches) through the concept of port aggregation.

Port aggregation allows for the combination of several physical ports on devices into one logical port on the device. This process can be performed through particular protocols on devices such as the **Link Aggregation Control Protocol (LACP)**. The following diagram illustrates a simple combination of both of these concepts, showing how three NICs in a server may teamed and combined with a port channel on a switch consisting of three physical ports:

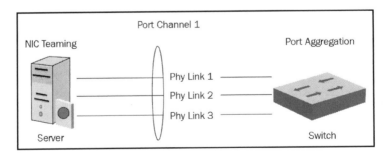

Redundancy in power delivery

A highly reliable network cannot function if none of the networking components are energized. For this reason, network administrators often build redundancy into their power delivery system as well, from the distribution grid all the way up to the **Power Supply Unit** (**PSU**) in their devices. In this subsection, we will examine some of the ways in which administrators ensure that their equipment is fed power continually.

Starting from the outermost part of the power distribution grid, networks in data centers are usually designed to be fed power from multiple electrical distribution circuits. Depending on the proximity of the data center to the nearest power generation stations and substations, utility providers may be able to provide completely separate grids, utilizing different power generation stations, substations, transmission lines, and transformers for each feed. In this manner, any of the components along that chain could fail, and the center will continue to receive power from the alternate circuit(s). However, in many situations, this complete redundancy may be too costly, requiring the utility provider to combine some aspects of the grid for each circuit.

Regardless of how many electrical circuits are brought in from the distribution grid, the majority of data centers also include at least one generator, to provide power to equipment in times when the feed from the utility fails. These generators may be fueled by a number of sources (such as diesel or natural gas) and are typically connected to the electrical network of the data center through an **Automatic Transfer Switch** (**ATS**). This ATS automatically detects when the utility power has failed and switches the power source to the backup generator, often starting the generator in the process.

Uninterruptible Power Supplies (**UPSes**) are usually placed after the ATS. UPSes consist of energy storage components such as batteries, charging these components when they are fed with electrical power, and providing output power from these components when the input power fails. Depending on the construction of the UPS, connected devices may be connected directly to the input power source and only switch to battery backup when the input power source fails, or they may be consistently connected to the batteries, with the UPS continually recharging the batteries as they deplete. In addition to providing a backup power supply, many UPSes also provide additional functionality to connected components such as over-voltage protection.

Power Distribution Units (PDUs) usually connect to UPSes, providing several outlets through which devices can connect. PDUs may also provide additional functionality, such as monitoring and load balancing. Rather than connecting a single PSU to a single PDU, many network administrators opt to install multiple PDUs in their rack, ensuring that each piece of equipment is also fitted with multiple PSUs and then connecting each PSU to a different PDU. The following diagram illustrates a simple electrical system that combines all of these concepts:

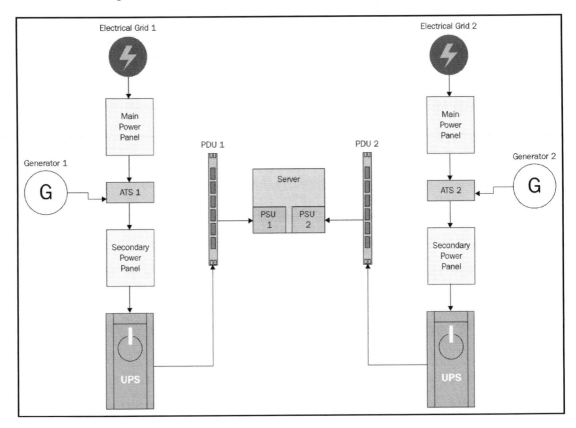

Recovery processes

In the event of a critical disaster at an enterprise's primary business location, it may be necessary for the enterprise to move all of its staff to a backup location to ensure business continuity. These backup locations can be categorized into one of three groups, depending on how they are equipped and run:

- A hot site is a complete mirror image of an enterprise's primary location, containing all of the equipment and data required for the staff to begin working again with little to no downtime. Hot sites contain the latest backups of data and configurations of equipment.
- A warm site contains all of the physical infrastructure of the primary location, but requires staff to restore backups and configurations manually, meaning that recovery times are longer than with a hot site.
- A cold site is a backup site that simply reserves space for the enterprise. Infrastructure must be transferred to the site and backups must then be restored.

Although cold sites require the longest times to restore business functions, they also have the lowest costs associated with them. Enterprises must therefore balance cost with redundancy, choosing the most appropriate solution for themselves according to how quickly they wish to be back up and running.

In addition to making a choice for backup sites, network administrators must also make a choice of which method of data backup they wish to employ. Three of the main methods are as follows:

- **Full backups**: All data in every file selected for backup is preserved every time a backup cycle is performed. This method allows data to be restored quickly, since every backup contains all of the data required for restoration (requiring only one restoration to be performed); however, this method also requires the most time to perform and requires the most space on backup media.
- **Incremental backups**: A backup that records only the files that have been added or changed since the last backup. A full backup is performed first, and incremental backups then record the changes that occur after that initial full backup. Incremental backups therefore require much less space and time to restore, as they record only the changes that have occurred since the last backup (either incremental or full). However, they also require much more time to restore, requiring first the restoration of the last full backup, then the restoration of all subsequent incremental backups.

- **Differential backups**: This backup method provides a compromise between full and incremental backups. With this method, a full backup is performed initially. Then, on each subsequent backup cycle, a differential backup is run, recording the changes made since the last full backup. In this way, restoration is quicker than with an incremental backup, requiring only the full backup and the last differential backup. This method also requires less space and time than continuous full backups.

It is also important to be familiar with snapshots. Snapshots record the state of a system at a particular instance in time. They do not actually back up (copy) the data within the system, but merely records how the data is organized within the system at the instant it is taken. Since they do not replicate data, snapshots are commonly used for recording different versions of a system. However, this lack of replication also means that they are not full backup solutions by themselves. It is therefore important to utilize other backup solutions in tandem with snapshots.

Availability metrics

Network administrators must be aware of several important metrics that relate to availability in their systems:

- **Mean Time To Repair (MTTR)**: MTTR can be defined as the average time that it takes to diagnose and fix a repairable piece of equipment, in an effort to restore regular operation of that equipment. Equipment with lower MTTRs therefore contribute to higher availability, as they can be brought back to operation in a smaller space of time.
- **Mean Time Between Failures (MTBF)**: This is an estimate of the time between two subsequent failures of equipment. It is also a term applicable to equipment that can be repaired, whereas **Mean Time To Failure (MTTF)** is used to refer to non-repairable equipment. Systems with higher MTBFs contribute to higher availability, as these systems can operate for longer periods before failing.
- **Recovery Time Objective (RTO)** and **Recovery Point Objective (RPO)**: These are two other important metrics in the realm of availability. RTO refers to the maximum allowable time that a system may be down, before impact on business operations becomes too severe, while RPO refers to the maximum amount of data that is allowed to be lost before serious impact on business operations manifests.

Lastly, several organizations explicitly state their availability requirements and objectives in formal documentation called **Service Level Agreements (SLAs)**. These SLAs commonly dictate availability in terms of a percentage or in terms of nines. For example, a company may claim to have three nines of availability, meaning that their systems are operational for 99.9% of the year, which means that the systems are only allowed to be down for 8.77 hours in a year.

As part of achieving such high availability metrics, enterprises must continually monitor and analyze output from devices on their network, ensuring that problems on devices are solved and alarms cleared, vulnerabilities are patched, and performance SLAs are being met. In the next section, we will examine some of these important operational processes.

Common operational processes

In this section, we will examine some of the most common processes that network administrators must continually undertake to ensure that their networks are performing optimally.

Scanning and patching processes

As part of proper preventative maintenance on a network, it is important that security and network administrators set up a regular scanning schedule, or implement an automated scanning tool for devices on their network, in order to quickly identify vulnerabilities and unnecessary services on devices within their network.

Vulnerability scanners search for known security weaknesses on the network, giving the administrator an opportunity to patch the system before malicious personnel exploit these vulnerabilities. Port scanning attempts to identify unnecessary services running on a system by searching for open ports on the system, allowing the administrator to disable the unnecessary services and therefore reduce the attack surface (the sum of all possible points of attack) of the identified device.

Patch management forms an integral part of this preventative maintenance. **Patch management** refers to the complete process of obtaining, testing, and rolling out patches to a particular system or group of systems. This process aims to ensure that functionality on production systems is not adversely affected by the installation of patches, and is achieved through proper testing on non-critical test systems. Proper patch management also aims to ensure that functionality can be restored quickly by rolling back a patch, in the event that the patch causes unwanted effects on the system.

In addition to these scanning and patching processes, network administrators must also implement continuous monitoring in their network, so that they are quickly notified of significant events that occur on devices. In the following subsection, we will examine some of the processes that are implemented for continuous monitoring.

Continuous monitoring

Log files are messages from a device that contain information about significant events concerning the device. They are the device's way of communicating its problems. Network administrators must thus ensure that they regularly check the log files from their devices. These log files can be checked locally (on the machine), or through a remote log management system such as a Syslog Server or a **Security Information and Event Management (SIEM)** tool. These log management systems usually provide more functionality than simply listing logs from devices, often allowing administrators to set up notifications and alerts when devices send logs about critical events on the network. The following screenshot illustrates some entries in a log management system:

```
2018-11-23 21:37:33.000       172.16.31.1
%SEC_LOGIN-4-LOGIN_FAILED: Login failed [user: http] [Source: 54.38.241.164] [localport: 22] [Reason: Login Authentication Failed] at 01:
37:33 TRI Sat Nov 24 2018

2018-11-23 21:37:33.000       172.16.31.1
%SEC_LOGIN-4-LOGIN_FAILED: Login failed [user: http] [Source: 54.38.241.164] [localport: 22] [Reason: Login Authentication Failed] at 01:
37:33 TRI Sat Nov 24 2018

2018-11-23 21:37:32.000       172.16.31.1
%SEC_LOGIN-4-LOGIN_FAILED: Login failed [user: http] [Source: 54.38.241.164] [localport: 22] [Reason: Login Authentication Failed] at 01:
37:32 TRI Sat Nov 24 2018

2018-11-23 21:37:32.000       172.16.31.1
%SEC_LOGIN-4-LOGIN_FAILED: Login failed [user: http] [Source: 54.38.241.164] [localport: 22] [Reason: Login Authentication Failed] at 01:
37:32 TRI Sat Nov 24 2018

2018-11-23 21:37:32.000       172.16.31.1
%SEC_LOGIN-4-LOGIN_FAILED: Login failed [user: http] [Source: 54.38.241.164] [localport: 22] [Reason: Login Authentication Failed] at 01:
37:32 TRI Sat Nov 24 2018
```

Another common method of monitoring devices is through the **Simple Network Management Protocol (SNMP)**. Three versions of SNMP currently exist (four if you include both SNMPv2 and SNMPv2c):

- SNMPv1
- SNMPv2/SNMPv2c
- SNMPv3

Different devices support different versions of this protocol, with SNMPv3 being the most up to date and the most secure. An SNMP system consists of an agent (installed on the managed device) and a manager, which is typically included as part of a **Network Management System** (**NMS**). The SNMP manager can issue both GET requests (to poll the agent and retrieve data) and SET requests (to change variables on the agent), with the agent issuing RESPONSE messages for both these requests. The agent is also able to proactively send data to the manager using **TRAPS**. Through this SNMP system, administrators are able to monitor important **Key Performance Indicators** (**KPIs**)/metrics on devices such as CPU usage, interface error rates (number of frames received with errors), bandwidth or throughput through a link (the traffic through a link, commonly expressed as a multiple of bits per second), utilization (traffic through a link in relation to the total capacity of that link), and packet drops (packets that have failed to reach their destination). Each variable on a device that can be polled or changed is known as an **Object Identifier** (**OID**). A **Management Information Base** (**MIB**) is a collection of these OIDs arranged hierarchically. The following screenshot shows some output from an NMS, illustrating traffic on an interface:

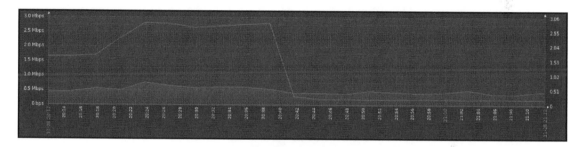

Through a combination of all of these methods of continuous monitoring, administrators can establish baselines for their devices and their network as a whole, using the gathered data to record the norms and trends in the metrics that they are interested in. This baselining process allows the administrator to easily notice when significant deviations from the norm occur. The administrator may then investigate the root cause of the deviation by checking SIEM or other log-management software, or by capturing live data on the network and performing more in-depth traffic analysis using a protocol analyzer.

Summary

In this chapter, we have highlighted the importance of proper documentation and diagramming, discussing how documentation helps serve as a guide to new staff or as a reference to the network administrator himself at a later date. We also illustrated some common examples of diagrams that administrators require (such as rack diagrams), and discussed the importance of these diagrams in maintaining and understanding a network. We also discussed critical concepts related to business continuity and disaster management, showing how redundancy forms the cornerstone of modern, highly available networks, allowing core functions to continue in spite of the failure of a single component. We also discussed several recovery processes that may be performed in the event of a disaster. Lastly, we examined some of the most common processes that personnel perform while maintaining their networks.

Questions

1. A technician is looking at a network diagram and comes across the following symbol:

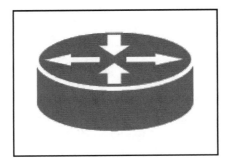

What type of device does this most likely represent?

   1. Switch
   2. Router
   3. Server
   4. UPS

2. A network administrator has realized that his network has grown too large and he is losing track of all of the connections and interfaces that he has connected. What type of diagram would most help him with this situation?

   1. Logical
   2. Physical
   3. Security
   4. Geographical

3. A manager has realized that he is losing track of which devices are arriving at and leaving his warehouse. He wants to implement an improved system that will help him know what items are present in the warehouse. Which of the following would be of help in this situation?

   1. Network diagram
   2. SIEM
   3. Inventory management system
   4. Router

4. A manager is planning to hire two new technicians into his team, but is worried that he does not have enough time to show them the common procedures that his team performs. Which of the following types of documentation would help him?

   1. SOP
   2. MOU
   3. BIA
   4. Contract

5. A CEO is worried that his business processes may be brought down by the failure of a particular piece of equipment during a disaster. What concept is he trying to address to ensure higher availability?

   1. Power outage
   2. SFP
   3. SPoF
   4. SLA

6. A CTO wants to ensure that his staff always have access to a second facility, fully stocked with all their required equipment and up-to-date copies of their data repositories. What type of backup site does he require?
   1. Warm site
   2. Hot site
   3. Cold site
   4. Full backup

7. A database manager performs full backups on his data every Friday night, and incremental backups on every other night. A disaster causes him to lose his database during the day on Wednesday. How many restorations must be performed to recover the data?
   1. 1
   2. 3
   3. 5
   4. 6

8. Why would an IT administrator test patches in a non-critical system before rolling it out to his production environment?
   1. To check system temperatures
   2. To check security baselines
   3. To ensure that business continuity is not affected
   4. To ensure that his antivirus does not reject the patch

9. A technician wants to monitor the traffic through a specific interface on a router. What protocol is most likely to provide this data?
   1. LDAP
   2. IPv6
   3. SNMP
   4. ICMP

10. A network administrator notices that a device is continually rebooting every few hours. What should be his next course of action?
    1. Replace the device
    2. Check the power connectors to the device
    3. Check the network connectors to the device
    4. Check the logs on the device

Further reading

The following link shows some additional information regarding diagram types on networks: `https://www.auvik.com/media/blog/network-documentation-best-practices/`.

10
Network Identity Management and Policies

In previous chapters, we took a look at various technologies and protocols that are used in a network; some are to help us extend the reach of network infrastructure such as a **Wide Area Network (WAN)**. However, not all organizations are able to afford the cost of maintaining/outsourcing this type of infrastructure. As an upcoming networking professional or enthusiast, it's important to learn and understand other types of network technologies that can be used to aid us in a similar situation.

A topic that is commonly overlooked in the technical field of **Information Technology (IT)** is policies in an organization, more specifically, the IT policies that govern how IT operations are executed in the organization and how they are used to preserve the integrity and security of the environment.

In this chapter, we will take a look at the following topics:

- **Virtual Private Network (VPN)**, both IPsec and SSL
- Various VPN topologies
- Various remote access methodologies
- Identity polices and best practices

Let's begin!

Remote access methodologies

At times, in the field of networking or systems administration, there is a need for remote access between devices. As a simple example, imagine you are a systems/network administrator at a local company and one of your main responsibilities in the organization it to configure, deploy, and maintain the company's servers. Usually, the servers would be physically stored either in a private/public data center or on the company's premises. At times, you may not be close to the server to make adjustments to the configuration, such as if you're at another branch office of the company working on an on-site project, but require access to the servers. This situation would be challenging if you always require physical access to systems whether they are servers, network appliances, or virtual machines.

This is where remote access management comes to save the day. There are various methods and protocols that allow you or an administrator of an appliance to remotely manage a device across a network. This improves efficiency in the management of appliances on the network, and employee productivity.

Another responsibility of a network administrator is to ensure each branch (site) of the organization is interconnected in some way or an other, to ensure all the remote offices are able to access the resources of the head office/headquarters location, as the most critical server may be housed on-premises.

At times, WAN may be not be suitable for connecting the branches together for many reasons; one factor may be cost as the charges by a telecommunication provider may be out the of the scope for the planned budget or the organization would like to have a backup/redundant connection in the event the primary link may fail at any point in time. VPN is one of the top recommended solutions for an organization with multiple branches.

Further into this section, we will be covering various remote access methodologies and VPN frameworks, protocols, topologies, and use cases.

Let's dive in!

VPN

Let's imagine that you recently got a new job as a network/system administrator for a local start up company, which has one location at the moment. Since it's a single location, all their various servers reside locally on-site and two of your responsibilities are to manage the servers and network infrastructure.

Being a start up company, a single location is sufficient but in due time the business will grow as it may offer new products and services, and hire more employees to assist in the management of daily business. As time passes, the company does expand to another location (site B) in another city. Since the first location (site A) already has all the mission critical applications, resources, and servers, the Managing Director made it the Head Office or Headquarters for the company. You are assigned a new task: interconnect the two sites to allow the resources from site A be shared to site B in a secure manner.

In `Chapter 8`, *Network Virtualization and WAN Technologies*, we discussed various WAN technologies and services. One quick solution you're possibly thinking about is to use a WAN connection from an **Internet Service Provider** (**ISP**). There are a few things to consider when determining a suitable solution for the business needs; these are cost, reliability, support, and configuration complexity. The benefits of using a solution from a service provider such as WAN connection is the backend support, since it's a managed service from an ISP and their team of engineers are proactively monitoring the quality and reliability of the link. However, the downside is that the cost for a managed service may be a bit steep for some businesses. The cost can vary based on the bandwidth capacity of the link, the **service level agreement** (**SLA**), features, and even the number of sites.

An alternative to using a WAN solution from a service provider is using a VPN. A VPN creates a secure connection or tunnel through an untrusted network; all traffic that passes through the tunnel is encrypted by default until it is decrypted at the other end of the tunnel. A VPN focuses on the following:

- Confidentiality
- Integrity
- Authentication
- Anti-replay attacks

Most **small and medium-sized** (**SMB**) and enterprise vendor routers and firewall appliances support VPN capabilities. Using a VPN will allow the company or organization to save money, providing there are already supported devices at each internet edge location. An **internet edge** is where an organization's private network connects with the internet or service provider's network.

VPN simply requires each location that is to use the VPN service to have a static public IP address, which does not change. If it does, the VPN tunnel will be broken between the participating peer routers/firewalls. The downside of using a VPN is that the support and management is usually done by the members of the local IT department. Therefore, in most cases, in-house VPN is needed.

VPN's can be established with dynamic IP's. This is dependent on using a service like dynamic DNS.

In this section, we will discuss various VPN technologies, frameworks, topologies, and use cases in a production environment.

There are two types of VPN: **Internet Protocol Security (IPsec)** and **Secure Sockets Layer (SSL)** VPNs.

IPsec

During your journey in networking, you will eventually come across the term IPsec, and if you are going into the field of network security in the future, you will definitely be applying IPsec as part of your job role. The main question is *what exactly is IPsec and what does it do?*

IPsec is a framework, better known as a suite of protocols, which are used together to ensure confidentiality (data encryption), integrity (hashing), and authenticity (PSK and RSA digital certificates) of the data flowing through a VPN tunnel.

Confidentiality

Confidentiality in real life is keeping a secret from others that are not intended to hear or know. In the networking field, it is known as data encryption. By using special encryption algorithms and an encryption key, only the person with the correct decryption key is able to read the contents.

Encryption

Encryption is the process of encoding a plain-text message in an encrypted format known as cipher text. Whether data is stored on a computer or network in the plain-text format, it is readable by anyone who has access to it. If all data is always in a plain-text format, whether it is stored on a system or moving across a network, there won't be any privacy (confidentiality). Let's imagine you want to check your bank account information using your bank's online banking facilities. When you visit the bank's website, you are required to enter your username for identity and the password to complete the authentication phase.

If there is no mechanism between your device, such as a computer, and the bank's website to provide data encryption for users who are supplying their usernames and passwords, a malicious user or hacker who may be sitting in the middle observing your traffic as it passes across the network, without privacy/encryption, will be able to obtain it and use the information for malicious purposes.

There are two types of encryption algorithms that are used for data encryption: **symmetric** and **asymmetric** algorithms.

Symmetric algorithm

When using a symmetric algorithm for data encryption, the algorithm uses a unique secret key to encrypt the data, converting it into cipher text. However, the same key is used to decrypt the cipher text. The issue with using symmetric encryption is that if the key is lost or stolen, the cipher text is compromised:

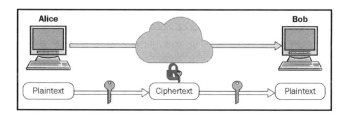

A simple example of using a symmetric algorithm is using a padlock to secure a room. A unique (secret) key is used per lock, but if this key is lost or stolen, the contents of the room may be comprised by an unauthorized person.

Asymmetric algorithm

Unlike symmetric encryption, which uses the same secret key to both encrypt and decrypt a message (data), asymmetric encryption uses two different keys, one for encryption and another for decryption. The benefit of using asymmetric encryption is that if one key is lost or stolen, the message (data or cipher text) is not compromised:

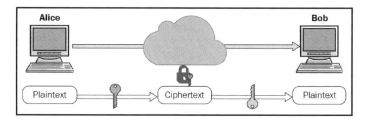

Integrity

In the real world, integrity is to ensure that the state of something does not change. Within a network, messages are constantly passing across a network, either a local area network or the internet; communication is always taking place. However, an important factor is to ensure that the content of each message is not altered or modified in any way during its transmission. In the computing world, hashing algorithms are used to ensure the integrity of data on a system or across a network.

There are currently two notable hashing algorithms—**Message Digest 5 (MD5)** and the **Secure Hashing Algorithm (SHA)**:

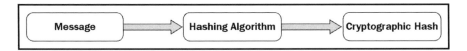

Authentication

A critical part of the computing and networking world is proving our identity to a system. One fundamental method of securing a system is enabling authentication, which involves providing user credentials, which the system can use to identify us. Let's imagine you want to check your email accounts or banking details, or log in to a computer. These systems contain your details and other sensitive information, which should be kept private from others. A system may not be able to identify you on the same basis as human-to-human interaction; however, using a user account and password combination, a system can validate the identity of a person.

An analogy might be that a person who is not authorized to log in to a corporate computer may enter an incorrect username and password combination, which does not exist, therefore the system will not grant them access to any resources. When a valid user account is provided, the system will be unlocked and make the necessary resources available to the valid user.

In an IPsec VPN configuration, there are two methods that are used to provide authentication:

- **Pre-Shared Key (PSK)**: The PSK is a shared secret between peers, such as a password
- **Digital certificate**: The digital certificate is comparable to an identification card on a network, which is exchanged between peers before a VPN tunnel can be established

Anti-replay

Each packet that is sent across an IPsec VPN link is tagged with a unique sequence number to assist the receiving device in the reassembly process. Sometimes, not all packets are received in the same order in which they were originally sent by the sender.

A hacker or malicious user can either predict or obtain the sequence number of the packet and craft his/her packet, insert the valid sequence number, and send it. The anti-replay feature detects a packet with the same sequence number as one that has already entered the tunnel, so the packet will not be allowed to enter.

Diffie-Hellman

Before VPN can be established, each peer must provide their identity by authenticating to each other. Since VPNs are used to establish a secure tunnel over an unsecure/untrusted network, VPN peers must exchange their secret keys in a secure manner. Diffie-Hellman is an algorithm that is designed to exchange cryptographic keys over an unsecure/untrusted network.

IPsec protocols

IPsec uses two protocols, which encapsulate the IP packet for its journey through the IPsec VPN tunnel.

Authentication Header (AH)

The AH protocol has the ability to provide both data integrity and authentication for all traffic traversing the IPsec tunnel. Each bit of a message that enters the tunnel at either end is hashed and the IPsec AH is added to the original IP header of the packet. However, the AH protocol does not provide confidentiality (encryption) for messages that are transmitted over the VPN tunnel.

Encapsulation Security Payload (ESP)

Unlike AH, which only provides authentication and integrity, ESP provides confidentiality, authentication, and integrity for all datagrams that enter the IPsec tunnel.

Further information on IPsec can be found in the **CCNA Security 210-260 Certification Guide** by *Packt Publishing* (`https://www.packtpub.com/ networking-and-servers/ccna-security-210-260-certification- guide`).

SSL

To have a clear understanding of an SSL VPN, we will use the following scenario. You work at a local company as the network administrator. Part of your role is to manage all the network appliances and some of the internal servers, which are on-premises in the private data center. However, the senior management team of the company requires access to a few applications running on some servers locally (in the private cloud). Whether the members of the senior management team are currently in the office or traveling, or at home, they always want access to these applications.

The benefit of using an SSL VPN is the ability create a remote access VPN through a web interface portal using SSL; this will give VPN users access to internal or predefined resources. The login portal can be accessed using any modern web browser; users can simply access it by specifying either an IP address or a domain name.

The following screenshot displays an SSL VPN login portal from a Cisco **Adaptive Security Appliance (ASA)**:

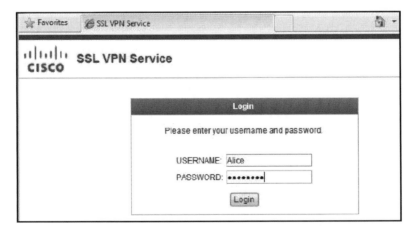

Once a user is logged in with a valid user account, privileges are assigned and resources are presented. This type of VPN is suitable for users such as the senior management team, since it's very simple to use and requires almost zero user training. All a user would need is a modern web browser and an internet connection.

The following screenshot displays the resources available to the user, `Alice`, after she has logged in through the SSL VPN web portal:

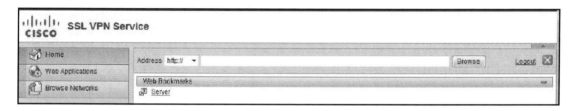

This type of VPN eliminates the need for any specialized software to be installed on a VPN user's system. However, this type of VPN only secures the traffic between the web browser and the VPN concentrator (router or firewall). It does not provide optimal protection for any other traffic between the user's system and the internet. The user's system is vulnerable to various types of malware and could be infected with spyware, which secretly monitors the user's activity.

Let's discuss another deployment/use case for the SSL VPN. Let's imagine you're the network security engineer for a local organization and one of your executive staff had to leave on a sudden business trip to another country. During this trip, he realized there are some files that are important and he needs access to them before the scheduled meeting; furthermore, he would also like access to a few other resources on the corporate network. Unfortunately, you didn't have the time to install a VPN client on his laptop before he left.

An SSL VPN can be used to deliver not only applications but also deploy VPN clients securely to clients over an unsecure network. Upon logging in on the SSL VPN web portal, the firewall has the ability to check whether the client device has a VPN client installed or not; if one isn't detected, the firewall will attempt to deploy the VPN client to the client device.

The following screenshot displays after a user has logged in to a SSL VPN portal. The Cisco ASA is checking whether the client system has all the necessary applications, and is attempting to deploy the items that are not present on the local system:

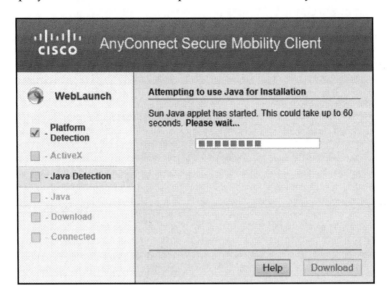

Transport Layer Security (TLS)

Over time, there have been many versions of the SSL protocol, each of which has its known set of vulnerabilities; this includes the latest, SSL version 3. As newer cyber threats emerge, there was a need to create a superior replacement protocol for SSL; this is known as **Transport Layer Security (TLS)**.

Most secure web protocols such as **Hyper Text Transfer Protocol Secure (HTTPS)** have adapted and in most cases use TLS as their preferred encryption protocol. The current version of TLS is TLS 1.3.

VPN topologies

There are two main types of virtual private network deployments, the site-to-site and the remote access models.

Site-to-site VPN

At the start of this chapter, we looked at a scenario where a system/network administrator needed to find a cost-efficient service for connecting an organization's remote offices. The solution was a VPN. This type of VPN is known as a site-to-site VPN. All traffic destined for the remote LAN (remote office) is sent through the VPN tunnel, so users are able to access resources seamlessly as though available locally on their own network in the office; however, the site-to-site VPN tunnel is transparent to all users.

The requirements for a site-to-site VPN are as follows:

- An internet connection at each remote office that needs to be configured to use a VPN.
- At each location, either a firewall or a router with IPsec capabilities to create the VPN.
- Most importantly, a static IP address to ensure the peers' IP addresses are fixed. If one peer IP address changes without notification, the entire VPN link is broken:

You can enable **site-to-site (S2S)** VPN using dynamic IP's with a service such as dynamic DNS.

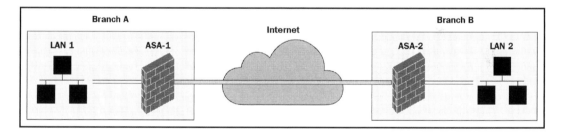

Remote access VPN

Another type of VPN is the remote access VPN. This deployment model allows employees who are not physically on the company's premises to remotely access corporate resources and network securely over an untrusted network such as the internet.

Let's take a look at a few scenarios for using a remote access VPN in an organization. Let's imagine you are a network engineer for a service provider and part of your job requires you to travel a lot to various enterprise clients to deploy various IT solutions on behalf of your company/employer. At times, you may require access to the corporate LAN for certain resources when you're away on a business trip or at a customer site. One of the major concerns about accessing the corporate LAN is security. You, as the off-site engineer, would require a secure connection to the corporate network, but all you have is an internet connection, which is untrusted.

The remote access VPN is usually configured on an **Integrated Services Router** (**ISR**) with security features such as VPN capabilities or a firewall at the internet edge of the organization. This appliance would allow remote users to establish a secure tunnel through the internet to the security gateway, that is, the router or firewall. However, for the user's device, whether it's a laptop or another mobile device, a VPN client is required to be installed and configured:

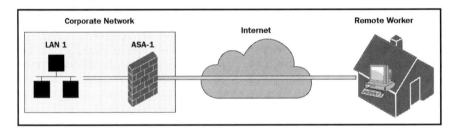

A remote access VPN allows a user with an internet connection, whether the user is in a coffee shop working on a document, a teleworker at home who requires access to the resources on the corporate servers on a daily basis, or an executive member of staff who is on a business trip using a hotel's Wi-Fi network, to ensure that all traffic destined for the corporate network will be sent across VPN. This mitigates any eavesdropping attacks that may attempt to breach confidentiality (privacy). All other traffic destined for the internet does not use the VPN tunnel.

The following is an screenshot of the **Cisco AnyConnect Secure Mobility Client**:

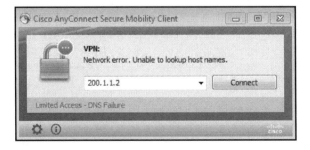

Once the VPN user enters either the domain name or the public IP address of the VPN concentrator (router or firewall), the user will be prompted to enter valid credentials:

Once established, the remote user has access to the corporate network as if the user is currently on the premises of the company and is connected to the corporate local area network.

If you're interested in setting up your own remote access VPN, take a look at OpenVPN at `www.openvpn.net`. On their community page, you'll find the Community Edition of their VPN Server applications for various operating system types with accompanying documentation.

Remote Desktop Protocol (RDP)

RDP was developed by Microsoft and remains a propriety protocol for their systems. Unlike VPN, which creates an encrypted tunnel for all traffic to be securely exchanged between devices, RDP is a bit different. RDP allows a user to securely access a Microsoft system remotely over a network, using the Remote Desktop Connection Manager, which provides a **graphical user interface (GUI)**.

This is convenient for system administrators to remotely control a system such as Microsoft Windows Server. Rather than the user having to be present at the physical server appliance, the user can simply open the Remote Desktop Connection Manager from any Microsoft Windows system.

To open the Remote Desktop Connection Manager on Windows, follow these steps:

1. Hit the Windows key + *R*, which will open the **Run** window

2. Secondly, type `mstsc` in the **Run** window and click on **OK**:

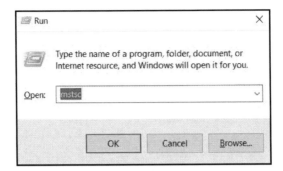

Once the manager window opens, simply enter either the IP address or the host name of the system you would like to establish an RDP connection to:

In the previous screenshot, the server I was attempting to establish is
KEVTA4.SERVERPLUS.LOCAL, which was on serverplus.local, and the user account is
test. Once connected, the GUI window loads up the server's interface as if you were
physically connected.

Secure Shell (SSH)

SSH is a secure remote terminal access protocol that uses port 22 by default on a device that
runs the SSH daemon/service. By default, SSH encrypts all its traffic, which prevents any
eavesdropping attacks such as a **man-in-the-middle** (**MITM**) attack or the sniffing of
network packets, which focuses on obtaining sensitive information such as user accounts,
passwords, and so on.

There are many devices that support the SSH protocol, such as servers, switches, routers,
firewalls, and so on. SSH allows an administrator to remotely configure and manage an
appliance; unlike the **Remote Desktop Protocol** (**RDP**), which is a propriety protocol, SSH
is freely available for general use. Furthermore, SSH provides Terminal access, or in other
words, a **command-line interface** (**CLI**).

Using a CLI has its benefits, such as improved security and efficiency. Script kiddie hackers
are not too versed in system administration or advanced hacking techniques and rely
heavily on hacking tools that provide a GUI. If a device is accessible via a command-line
interface, this will be a challenge for the script kiddie hacker. Another benefit is that a GUI
on a system uses more system resources, such as CPU and RAM, to present information in
a very friendly user interface.

SSH is the preferred network protocol for remotely managing network appliances, for its
security and simplicity benefits. All a user would need is an SSH client such as **PuTTY**
(www.putty.org) or **SecureCRT** (www.vandyke.com), but there are many other SSH clients
widely available, both freeware and commercial. Most Linux operating systems have a
built-in SSH client in their architecture that is accessible through the Terminal window.

The following screenshot shows the PuTTY interface; here, we are attempting to connect to a remote server on the internet; however, the server is using port 2220 for the SSH protocol:

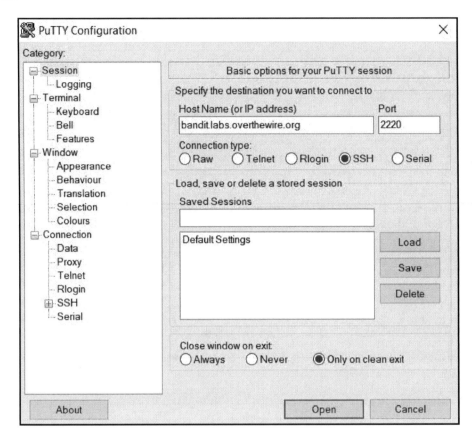

Once the SSH client (PuTTY) attempts to establish an SSH session, the public keys are exchanged to prove the authenticity of the remote host:

Once the public key is accepted, the Terminal interface is presented as seen here in the following screenshot:

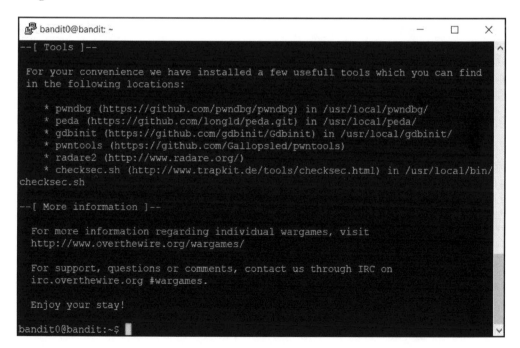

At this point, the user can manage the server remotely and securely.

Telnet

Telnet is another terminal access network protocol, which operates on port 23 by default. Unlike SSH, which provides encryption, Telnet traffic is unencrypted and is highly not recommended to be used when connecting to another device for remote administration. This is a major security issue, as a malicious user or hacker can see all the traffic passing across the network by simply using a sniffer such as Wireshark:

The following screenshot shows the PuTTY interface; here, we are attempting to connect to a remote server on the internet:

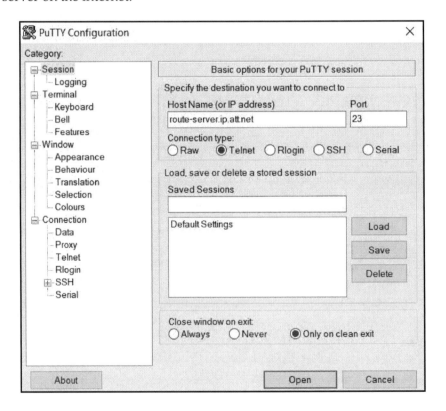

The router interface shown was used from the results of the BGP **Looking Glass (LG)** project made available by various ISPs globally to help others have a better understanding of the **Border Gateway Protocol (BGP)**.

The following screenshot displays the Terminal interface for the remote device:

```
route-server.cbbtier3.att.net - PuTTY                          —    □    ×
12.122.120.7    2001:1890:ff:ffff:12:122:120:7    Fort Lauderdale, FL
12.122.125.6    2001:1890:ff:ffff:12:122:125:6    Los Angeles, CA
12.122.125.44   2001:1890:ff:ffff:12:122:125:44   New York, NY
12.122.125.106  2001:1890:ff:ffff:12:122:125:106  Philadelphia, PA
12.122.125.132  2001:1890:ff:ffff:12:122:125:132  Phoenix, AZ
12.122.125.165  2001:1890:ff:ffff:12:122:125:165  San Diego, CA
12.122.126.232  2001:1890:ff:ffff:12:122:126:232  San Francisco, CA
12.122.125.224  2001:1890:ff:ffff:12:122:125:224  Seattle, WA
12.122.126.9    2001:1890:ff:ffff:12:122:126:9    St. Louis, MO
12.122.126.64   2001:1890:ff:ffff:12:122:126:64   Washington, DC


*** Please Note:
Ping and traceroute delay figures measured here are unreliable, due to the
high CPU load experienced when complicated show commands are running.

For questions about this route-server, send email to: jayb@att.com

*** Log in with username 'rviews', password 'rviews' ***

login: rviews
Password:

--- JUNOS 17.1R1-S1 built 2017-04-07 08:21:13 UTC
rviews@route-server.ip.att.net>
```

However, if an attacker is intercepting or monitoring network traffic, the attacker can reassemble the packets to see the session and transaction data in plain text. The following is a capture of another Telnet session; using Wireshark, we can see the following screenshot:

```
Wireshark · Follow TCP Stream (tcp.stream eq 0) · telnet-cooked.pcap

.......... ..!..".."....#..%..%......... ..!.."..".......P. ...."....b........b....        B.
................."......'.....#..&..&..$..&..&..$.. .....#.....'.......... .9600,9600....#.bam.zing.org:
0.0....'..DISPLAY.bam.zing.org:0.0......xterm-color...........!.............."............
OpenBSD/i386 (oof) (ttyp2)

login: fake
......Password:user

......Last login: Sat Nov 27 20:11:43 on ttyp2 from bam.zing.org
Warning: no Kerberos tickets issued.
OpenBSD 2.6-beta (OOF) #4: Tue Oct 12 20:42:32 CDT 1999

Welcome to OpenBSD: The proactively secure Unix-like operating system.

Please use the sendbug(1) utility to report bugs in the system.
Before reporting a bug, please try to reproduce it with the latest
version of the code.  With bug reports, please try to ensure that
enough information to reproduce the problem is enclosed, and if a
known fix for it exists, include that as well.

$ /sbin/ping www.yahoo.com
PING www.yahoo.com (204.71.200.67): 56 data bytes
64 bytes from 204.71.200.67: icmp_seq=0 ttl=241 time=69.885 ms
64 bytes from 204.71.200.67: icmp_seq=1 ttl=241 time=73.591 ms
64 bytes from 204.71.200.67: icmp_seq=2 ttl=241 time=72.302 ms
64 bytes from 204.71.200.67: icmp_seq=3 ttl=241 time=73.493 ms
64 bytes from 204.71.200.67: icmp_seq=4 ttl=241 time=75.068 ms
64 bytes from 204.71.200.67: icmp_seq=5 ttl=241 time=70.239 ms
..........
.--- www.yahoo.com ping statistics ---
6 packets transmitted, 6 packets received, 0% packet loss
round-trip min/avg/max = 69.885/72.429/75.068 ms
$ ls
$ ls -a
.             ..          .cshrc    .login    .mailrc   .profile  .rhosts
$ exit
```

The red text is sent from the client side and the blue text is sent from the Telnet server. We can see that the user entered the username `fake` and password `user` on the Telnet-enabled device. Furthermore, we are able to see all the activities that have taken place during this session.

 Wireshark has a repository of freely available sample captures to assist network professionals and enthusiasts in learning about network protocol analysis. These captures are at the following URL through the Wireshark website at `https://wiki.wireshark.org/SampleCaptures`.

HTTPS

As mentioned previously in this book, HTTPS allows secure communication of web-based content between a client's web browser and a web server. HTTPS has also been implemented in a lot of network and security appliances for easier configuration and management of the device:

Many small business appliances provide an HTTPS management interface; this eliminates the need for the administrator to know any particular commands for setting up the appliance. Instead, it allows for simplicity; the administrator can simply connect to the device directly, or access it over the network by simply entering the IP address of the appliance on any modern web browser.

The following is a screenshot of a wireless router, which is managed primarily through its web interface:

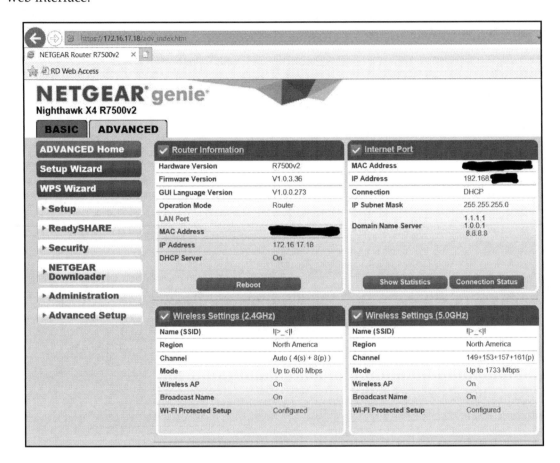

Furthermore, each setting can be adjusted by simply clicking on the desired category and feature:

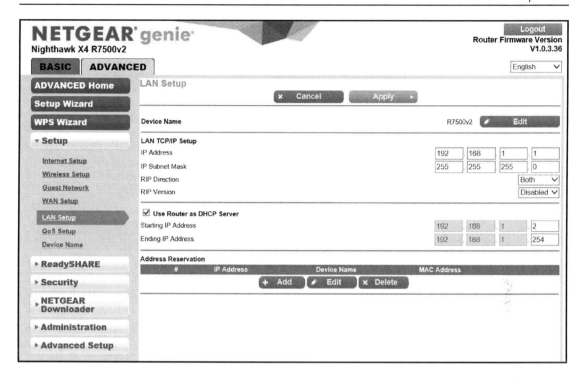

Once again, without learning any complex commands for a specific vendor's appliance, the web interface is always a simpler method to administer a device.

The following is the management plane of VMware ESXi:

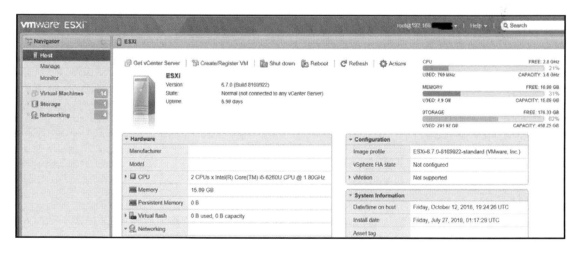

We can see once more that an administrator is able to see statistics of the appliance and apply further configurations.

 HTTPS operates on port 443 by default.

Identity policies and best practices

As an upcoming networking enthusiast or professional, it is important to understand the corporate side of an organization as it plays a vital role in information technology. During the course of your reading on the *Network+* certification, you'll notice security and availability are quite important to protect the organization's assets and ensure resources are available to members of staff.

Whenever an organization hires a new person to join their corporate team, the human resources department ensures the new employee understands the corporate policies, guidelines, procedures, and any repercussions if there are any breaches in the policy by an employee.

The purpose of a policy is to ensure a person, department, or organization adopts principles of actions. Guidelines are a general method for doing something and are not mandatory for executing a task. A procedure is an official method for executing a task. In each organization, there are various departments, each of which has its own set of guidelines and procedures for doing certain tasks.

In a corporation, the human resources department must ensure each employee understands and executes their duties efficiently on a daily basis. These policies, guidelines, and procedures are documented in the organization's human resources manual, which is usually given to new employees on their first day of employment. Some organizations ensure new employees read and understand it thoroughly and sign an official receipt to this effect.

Many organizations also have a full-fledged IT department to manage their entire IT infrastructure from desktops to servers and network appliances, and most IT managers create an IT security policy manual, which usually accompanies the human resources manual for all employees. The objective of this security policy manual is to ensure the company's assets are protected and to assist in minimizing risks and threats while having the minimum impact on the company's business operations.

Some of the policies that are commonly found in the IT security policy handbook are as follows:

- **Acceptable Use Policy (AUP)**
- **Bring Your Own Device (BYOD)** policy
- Internet access policy
- Password policy
- Remote access policy
- User account policy
- Wireless network policy

AUP

AUP is designed to protect an organization's assets such as the employees, IT systems and infrastructure, intellectual property, and their customers. The AUP outlines the uses of IT resources and systems by employees, data security and management, unacceptable use, and enforcement. In general, AUP is created by the owner of a system to restrict the methods in which the system can be accessed and used, while providing some guidelines and procedures. This policy is usually presented to new employees.

BYOD policy

BYOD policy is a set of rules, guidelines, and policies designed to govern how employee-owned devices such as tablets, smartphones, laptops, and so on can be used on the corporate IT network. The BYOD policy outlines the eligibility of who can use their personal device on the corporate network, which devices are allowed, what services are made available, the security for data protection, and acceptable use.

Internet access policy

Internet access policy outlines the rules and guidelines on appropriate use of the organization's network for internet access. The policy outlines unacceptable use, which may be inappropriate or illegal.

Password policy

Password policies are used to outline the standard for creating very strong passwords, protecting a user's passwords, and ensuring they are frequently changed to ensure a high degree of confidentiality. Some policies force a user to set a password that is a minimum length of 12 characters, and contains at least one capital letter, number, and special symbols. This would ensure the complexity of any user password is difficult for a hacker to guess or break.

Remote access policy

Remote access policy is used to set the standard with which an employee is able to connect to the organization's corporate network. It is to ensure the potential exposure of any sensitive information is reduced as it may cause damage to the organization's corporate portfolio and reputation.

User account policy

User account policy is used to outline how employees user accounts are managed in the organization's IT systems. These include email systems and administrative accounts. The policy outlines how a user account should be created and activated, and what privileges are to be assigned based on management authorization, user account expiry, and deletion procedures.

Wireless network policy

Wireless network policy outlines the policies for using wireless technologies, services, and administration of devices in the organization. It is to ensure security, optimal performance, and reduced interference.

If you're interested in further understanding and developing IT security policies for an organization, the SANS Institute has a rich repository of templates available at `https://www.sans.org/security-resources/policies`.

Summary

To recap, we opened the chapter by discussing the purpose of a VPN and how it can assist an organization, whether large or small, to connect their branch offices securely over the internet. Furthermore, we took a look at various deployment models for real-world use cases of each type of deployment. We then dove a bit into other methods of remotely administering and managing a system over a network in a secure fashion. We saw the importance of having policies implemented in an organization to assist in the preservation and security of the network infrastructure, assets, and data.

In the next chapter, we will discuss various network security concepts.

Questions

1. Which type of policy should an organization implement to govern the use of smart devices?
   1. Remote access policy
   2. Acceptable use policy
   3. Bring your own device policy
   4. User account policy

2. Which type of policy should an organization present to a new employee who is joining the workplace?
   1. Remote access policy
   2. Acceptable use policy
   3. Bring your own device policy
   4. User account policy

3. Which type of policy should an IT department follow when managing employees' user accounts?
   1. Remote access policy
   2. Acceptable use policy
   3. Bring your own device policy
   4. User account policy

4. Which type of VPN can be used to interconnect two remote offices?
   1. Site-to-site
   2. Remote access
   3. SSL
   4. TLS

5. Which is the most secure protocol, used for remotely accessing a device over a Terminal interface?
   1. SSH
   2. TLS
   3. Telnet
   4. SSL

6. Which of the following is a sub-protocol of the IPsec framework?
   1. TLS
   2. SSL
   3. ESP
   4. Diffie-Hellman

7. Which of the following provides privacy?
   1. Confidentiality
   2. Integrity
   3. Availability
   4. Anti-replay

11
Network Security Concepts

Around the world, each day, we are constantly hearing about cyber attacks occurring, some of which are announced through many local international news bodies, cyber security news websites, and cyber security threat websites, while others are kept hidden for various reasons. The need for cyber security professionals and training is critical now more than ever, and will continue to increase as technologies become increasingly advanced.

Whether you're a seasoned network engineer, an IT technician, an enthusiast, or simply starting your studies in networking, security threats and attacks exist everywhere. No network infrastructure exists that's fully secure because each minute, hour, or day, a new cyber threat emerges. If your network isn't protected or you don't have any countermeasures implemented to mitigate new and existing threats, your network is a gold mine for hackers. Nowadays, a company's data is very valuable, and hackers are interested in compromising this invaluable asset. In this chapter, we are going to focus on both wireless and network security concepts.

In this chapter, we will be covering the following topics:

- Wireless encryption standards
- Authentication and security on a wireless network
- Network attacks and threats
- Securing networking devices
- Mitigation techniques

Let's dive in!

Wireless security

In this section, we will focus our attention on the importance of wireless security, and then we'll dive in to learning and understanding various wireless encryption standards and technologies that are used to help secure the transmission of traffic on a wireless network. We will also look at different wireless authentication and authorization methods that will aid you in designing and implementing a safer wireless network for your home or office.

Wireless encryption standards

In this section, we are going to dive in to various encryption standards that are used on wireless networks.

Wired Equivalent Privacy (WEP)

WEP is an encryption standard that was used in early generations of wireless networks. WEP uses the RC4 Cipher, which provided a 40-bit key for data encryption. In 2002, various security flaws were discovered, which allowed an attacker to compromise the encryption key. Due to the weak encryption key, WEP can be compromised within a few hours. It's not recommended to use a WEP encryption standard on wireless networks anymore.

Wi-Fi Protected Access (WPA)

WPA was created in 2002 to fix the security flaws of **Wired Equivalent Privacy** (**WEP**). WPA uses **Temporal Key Integrity Protocol** (**TKIP**), which applies the RC4 encryption cipher for data privacy. Furthermore, the **initialization vector** (**IV**) is larger on each packet and uses a hash value to produce an encryption key of 128-bits. TKIP uses the secret key combined with the IV; this produces the TKIP value, which changes frequently between the client and the wireless router/access point.

Additionally, a sequence counter is used as a countermeasure for any replay attacks that are attempted by a hacker or a malicious user. Each packet sent between the wireless router/access point and the client device contains integrity checking, which is done through a 64-bit key to prevent and detect any modifications of packets between the sender and receiver. However, as with a lot of technologies, TKIP has its vulnerabilities and was later disapproved during wireless security implementations in 2012.

Wi-Fi Protected Access 2 (WPA2)

The WPA2 wireless security encryption standard uses the **Advanced Encryption Standard** (**AES**) for data encryption rather than the RC4. This is an upgrade for data security. Furthermore, WPA2 applied the **Counter Mode with Cipher Block Chaining Message Authentication Code Protocol** (**CCMP**), which replaced the need for TKIP. The CCMP uses a 128-bit key for its data encryption by using the AES, which creates data blocks of 128-bit in size. Due to larger data blocks and stronger encryption algorithms being used in WPA2, more computing resources are required.

CCMP provides the following during wireless transmissions:

- Confidentiality
- Authentication
- Access control

Authentication and security on a wireless network

In this section, we will cover various wireless authentication and security methods on a wireless network.

Extensible Authentication Protocol (EAP)

EAP is a framework that allows a client to authenticate to a wireless network. The **Internet Engineering Task Force** (**IETF**) has many **Request for Comments** (**RFC**) standards for the EAP framework.

EAP Flexible Authentication via Secure Tunneling (EAP-FAST)

One version of EAP Cisco that was proposed was the **Lightweight EAP** (**LEAP**), which was considered to be lightweight and secure. However, Cisco has since updated their framework to the EAP-FAST, which improved security on the wireless network.

EAP Transport Layer Security (EAP-TLS)

The EAP-TLS provides strong security. TLS has since gained popularity as the successor of the **Secure Sockets Layer** (**SSL**). With improved security features, EAP-TLS was widely implemented in wireless devices.

EAP Tunneled Transport Layer Security (EAP-TTLS)

This version of the TLS tunnel allowed organizations to tunnel other authentication methods and protocols through the EAP tunnel.

Protected Extensible Authentication Protocol (PEAP)

PEAP was developed by various technology vendors such as Cisco, RSA security, and Microsoft. PEAP allows EAP within a TLS tunnel, however it was most commonly implemented in EAP-MSCHAPv2 on Microsoft systems, which allows for authentication to Microsoft's MS-CHAPv2 databases.

On your wireless router or access point, under the Wireless security settings, you will have various security modes to choose from, such as **None**, **WEP**, **WPA**, **WPA2**, and so on. After choosing a security mode, the device will allow you to choose an encryption standard, such as **TKIP**, **AES**, or both:

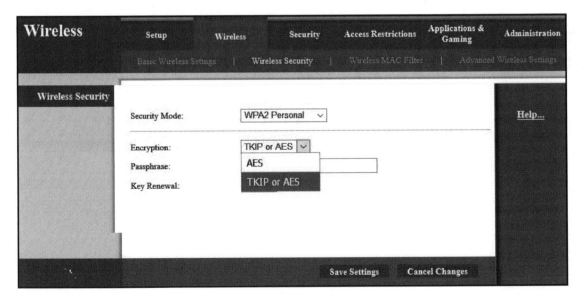

If you choose the security mode as **None**, then this would be classed as an open network, allowing anyone to connect to your network without supplying any password or user credentials.

After choosing the encryption mode, the device will allow you to set a **Pre-Shared Key** (**PSK**) (better known as a WPA2-PSK), which is used during the authentication phase between the wireless router/access and the client. The WPA2 security mode uses a 256-bit key for data encryption of all traffic to and from the client.

In WPA2-Enterprise, the wireless router/access functions as an **authenticator**. The client that provides the user credentials to access the wireless network is known as the supplicant. The client would send their username and password combination to the wireless router; the wireless router/access point would then query an **Authentication, Authorization, and Accounting** (**AAA**) server for a valid user account. If the user credentials were accepted/found, the AAA server would notify the authenticator, which would allow the client to authenticate. Policies/privileges are also applied to the user during this phase. Each action taken by the user is logged for accountability.

 AAA is a framework that can be delivered using either a **Remote Authentication Dial-In User Service** (**RADIUS**) or a **Terminal Access Controller Access Control System** (**TACACS**) server.

MAC filtering

A wireless router can filter a **Media Access Control** (**MAC**) address, which is either allowed or denied access to the wireless network. However, attackers have found a way to spoof an authenticated client's MAC address. This allows an attacker to bypass the filtering access control list feature on the wireless router/access point.

The following screenshot shows client devices (stations) that are currently authenticated to a wireless router (**Basic Service Set Identifier** (**BSSID**) is the MAC address and the **Extended Service Set Identifier** (**ESSID**) is the name of the network).

Please note that parts of the MAC addresses and the ESSID have been blocked out for privacy concerns:

```
CH  2 || Elapsed: 2 mins || 2018-10-28 18:58

BSSID             PWR RXQ  Beacons    #Data, #/s  CH  MB   ENC  CIPHER AUTH ESSID

38:4C:4F:           0   0      565       103    0   2  195  WPA2 CCMP   PSK          WiFi T28R

BSSID             STATION          PWR    Rate    Lost    Frames  Probe

38:4C:4F:         B0:C0:90:         -1    1e- 0      0       43
38:4C:4F:         5C:C3:07:        -82    1e- 1e     0       35
38:4C:4F:         DA:A1:19:        -92    0 - 1      0       17            WiFi T28R
```

Geofencing

Geofencing is where you restrict or allow features when the device is in a particular area using a client's **Global Positioning System** (**GPS**) location service. For example, if a wireless client is outside a geographic area, some features may not work. Therefore, geofencing ensures that users are in a particular area so that they can use a device or feature.

Network attacks and threats

In this section, we will dive in to understanding various network security attacks and threats that attackers use in an attempt to diminish a service or compromise an organization's assets for various reasons.

Denial-of-Service (DoS)

In a lot of places around of the world, whenever a government or an organization does something of which citizens or employees are not generally accepting, they usually have a protest or a corporate strike. At times, these protests lead to planning an organized strike where the citizens or employees of an organization plan to not show up at their relevant workplace. The strike itself is to deny customers from accessing the services provided by a company or organization.

In the digital world, a DoS attack is also applicable. Let's take a look at a simple case study of the famous hacktivist group Anonymous. Just to clarify, **hacktivism** is the use of computers to promote some sort of political agenda or a social change either locally or internationally. Back in 2003, Anonymous was formed through the famous image board website (http://www.4chan.org). During this time, 4chan allowed members to create threads and post without using a particular username. This allowed everyone to post as Anonymous, and therefore a person's identity could be concealed for privacy and anonymity. Some of their attacks involved a network stress test tool named the **Low Orbit Ion Cannon** (**LOIC**). This was used to make a political stand against various US politicians some years ago. A group organized their campaign on the 4chan website, where everyone posted anonymously, and provided instructions and procedures for taking down various websites:

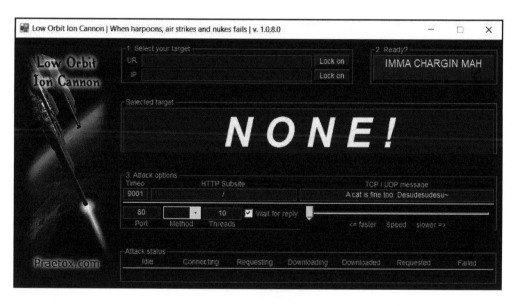

The tool was used to send a continuous stream of TCP or UDP packets to a single server or website. The recipient, upon having received each packet, will need to process and respond accordingly and eventually stop responding to legitimate requests.

Let's imagine you are a public speaker and that all of the people who are part of your audience start to ask you questions continuously without stopping. You would have to process each question one at a time, and then respond. Eventually, the amount of incoming traffic (questions) will be overwhelming and you, the recipient (server), will not be able to respond and eventually become bombarded.

There are three main types of DoS attacks:

- Reflective
- Amplified
- Distributed

Reflective

In a reflective attack, the attacker sends unsolicited requests to a server by using the victim's IP address as the attacker's source IP address. This impersonation process is known as **spoofing**. When the server receives the request from the attacker, it sends its replies to the source IP address within the IP packets it has received. Therefore, all of the responses will go to the victim's machine rather than the attacker's:

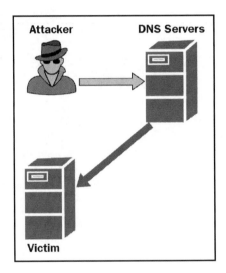

Amplified

The amplified attack is similar to the reflective attack. In an amplified attack, the attacker spoofs the IP address of the victim and sends a continuous stream of unsolicited messages (requests) to multiple servers, such as DNS servers. When each server processes each packet, they all respond to the victim's machine. The victim's machine will constantly be flooded with messages from various online servers:

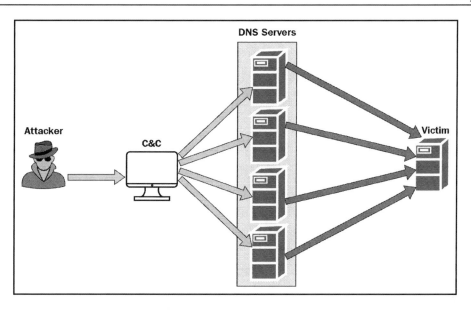

Distributed

In a **Distributed Denial-of-Service (DDoS)** attack, the victim receives a continuous stream of unsolicited messages from multiple sources. This type of attack is similar to the amplified attack. On March 1, 2018, **The Hacker News** (www.thehackernews.com) reported one of the biggest DDoS attacks to ever take place. This was a 1.35 TBs which hit the famous GitHub website (www.github.com):

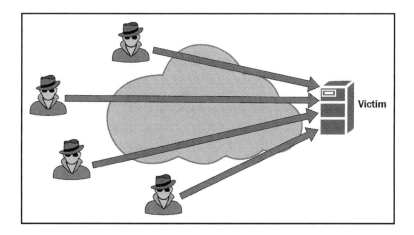

Social engineering

Social engineering is the art of manipulating or convincing a person to reveal private or confidential information about someone or something. Most of the time, the victim is unable to tell whether they are providing sensitive information to the attacker.

The following are the phases in which an attacker executes a social engineering attack:

1. The attacker performs reconnaissance on the target/potential victim.
2. The attacker develops a relationship with the victim (employees). This is used to build trust.
3. Finally, the attacker exploits their relationship with the victim.

Social engineering does not only occur in people as a human-based attack, but also digitally through computers, which are used to assist in manipulating or tricking a potential victim. A simple example of a human-based social engineering attack would be an attacker calling into an IT help desk within an organization and pretending to be a senior executive staff member (impersonation) and asking the IT help desk agent to reset the victim's user account to a specific password. Due to the trust the agent has for the executive staff, he/she won't be too concerned about questioning the person who is making the request.

To prevent a social engineering attack, an organization must ensure the following:

- That sufficient training is provided to each employee
- That there are appropriate security policies, procedures, and controls in place
- That there is regulated access and monitoring of information

Other forms of human-based social engineering attacks are as follows:

- **Dumpster diving**: The attacker searches through someone's or an organization's trash for sensitive information, which can then be used for impersonation.
- **Tailgating/piggybacking**: The attacker follows an authorized person through a door to a secure area. When walking through a doorway, a lot of people usually hold the door open for the person behind them as a form of politeness. However, this type of attack takes advantage of a person's good nature. In tailgating, the attacker usually has a fake ID during the process. During piggybacking, the attacker usually pretends he/she has forgotten their ID badge and hopes that the potential victim allows the attacker access to the secure area.

A popular TV show that aired during 2007–2013, **Burn Notice**, often displayed a lot of human-based social engineering engagements.

Computer-based social engineering is where an attacker uses a computer or mobile system to manipulate a potential victim.

Some examples of computer-based social engineering attacks are as follows:

- **Phishing**: Someone sends a fake email pretending to be an authorized entity, such as a bank requesting to change your account details.
- **Spear phishing**: Similar to phishing, spear phishing focuses on specific individuals within an organization.
- **Whaling**: This is another form of phishing. However, this attack is focused on high profile employees such as stakeholders, directors, executive members, and so on.
- **Smishing**: This form of social engineering is a mobile-based attack that uses **short message service** (**SMS**) as its delivery platform.

One of the many tools used in a computer-based social engineering attack is known as the **Social-Engineer Toolkit** (**SET**), which was developed by TrustedSec (`www.trustedsec.com`). The SET has been included in many cyber security conferences, such as for DEFCON and Black Hat. The following is a screenshot of the welcome window of the SET:

As you can see in the following screenshot, a malicious user, or a penetration tester, has several options for crafting a simple yet sophisticated attack for a potential victim:

```
Select from the menu:

 1) Spear-Phishing Attack Vectors
 2) Website Attack Vectors
 3) Infectious Media Generator
 4) Create a Payload and Listener
 5) Mass Mailer Attack
 6) Arduino-Based Attack Vector
 7) Wireless Access Point Attack Vector
 8) QRCode Generator Attack Vector
 9) Powershell Attack Vectors
10) SMS Spoofing Attack Vector
11) Third Party Modules
```

Insider threat

In each organization, whether large or small, there is at least one employee who is disgruntled about their current position within the organization. A disgruntled employee is one of the biggest threats to any company, as this person already knows the organization's procedures, systems, and has access to the company's assets such as financial and customer records, confidential information, and so on. A lot of the time, whenever an employee leaves a company on bad terms, they usually have the idea of causing the organization some sort of harm upon their resignation or termination.

An employee with bad intentions can potentially research hacking techniques and attempt to take down or destroy the company's data or reputation. However, there are times where a hacker may pretend to be a regular candidate at a job interview in the hopes of getting a job within an organization. Once the hacker obtains employment within the company, he/she can install their backdoor within the organization's network. The backdoor would both exfiltrate data and allow the hacker to access the company's network remotely.

Whenever an organization's network and systems are compromised, over 90% of the attacks originate from within the company. It is easier for a hacker to compromise a network or system from inside rather than outside. If the attacker has to send malicious traffic to an organization's network over the internet, there's a very high possibility that the firewall at the perimeter of the company will detect and block the malicious traffic. If the traffic is missed by the firewall, the **Intrusion Prevent System** (**IPS**) appliance will be able to catch and block it as well. If the attack originates from within, both the firewall and IPS appliances won't see the traffic as it won't be passing through either device.

At times, the insider threat can be a person, a malicious software, and/or a device that looks like a regular network device or component that's part of the network but in reality is not.

Let's go over some of the devices that hackers implant on a network.

The following looks like a network adapter bridging two cables together. However, it is actually a tiny box that has the area of a box of matches. One of its features is that it can capture network traffic that can later be analyzed using a tool called Wireshark. It literally functions as an inline sniffer, and is known as a **Packet Squirrel**:

The following device looks like a USB Ethernet adapter, which tricks a regular person into not tampering with it as they believe that the IT department has placed it on the computer system. One of the functions of this device is to remotely access the company's network from the internet while pivoting an attacker, capturing network traffic, and so on. This is known as a LAN Turtle, and can be used by a malicious user or attacker as a network implant so that they can gain backdoor access into the physical network:

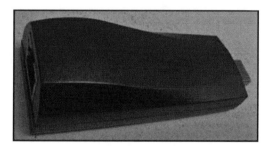

Logic bomb

A logic bomb is a type of virus that remains in a dormant state until a particular action is executed on the system it has infected. *How can a logic bomb be used in a real-world situation?* Let's imagine a hacker has compromised a server that has very important and confidential data on the local drives. The hacker installs a backdoor and a logic bomb. As I previously mentioned, a *backdoor* is a doorway in the operating system that is used to allow a hacker entry into the system. When the hacker has completed his/her objectives on the compromised system, the last step is to cover their tracks, removing any logs, files, and traces that show that the intruder was in the system and what he/she was doing.

At times, an organization may have an internal incident response team or hire an external team to perform digital forensics on the compromised system to determine what happened and who did the crime. This is where the logic bomb plays its role. During the acquisition phase (obtaining evidence) which is performed by the forensics experts on the live system, the logic bomb may be triggered to unleash its payload, which may wipe the entire hard drive of the organization and remove any further evidence.

Rogue Access Point (AP)

One of the many popular methods of wireless hacking is setting up a rogue AP. A rogue AP is used by a hacker who uses a wireless router of his/her own, and creates a **Service Set Identifier (SSID)** or a network name in the hopes of attracting people to connect to it. The name of the SSID would be something that would definitely attract users, such as VIP Access, Free Wi-Fi, or even the name of a popular coffee house. The goal is to get people to connect and, while they are browsing the internet, the hacker intercepts all their network traffic, looking for any sensitive or confidential information.

A simple mitigation technique is to not connect to any wireless networks that have a suspicious name or you do not trust. Sometimes, upon seeing an open wireless network, somebody might think it's a gold mine that has free internet access. However, to a hacker, it's bait, and their gold mine would be the victim's traffic and data, which is intercepted.

Evil twin

An evil twin is similar to the rogue access point model, but the evil twin is either a wireless router or an access point that's deployed on a company's network by a hacker or a malicious user. This method allows the hacker to capture sensitive data while mobile users access the company's network.

On a lot of **local area networks** (**LANs**), the network/system administrator usually sets up a **Dynamic Host Configuration Protocol** (**DHCP**) server to automatically distribute IP configurations to clients who are physically connected to the network. If the network/system administrator does not have any sort of **Network Access Control** (**NAC**) systems in place, as defined by IEEE 802.1X, or even monitoring the DHCP/ARP pools on the network, a disgruntled employee can connect his/her access point to the network, set it up to advertise the company's SSID network name, and capture other workers' traffic without anyone realizing an inside threat exists.

This little, pocket size device is used by both hackers and penetration testers for auditing wireless networks. The following device is known as the Wi-Fi Pineapple:

Countermeasures for both rogue APs and evin twin deployments are as follows:

- Conduct regular wireless audits using a Wi-Fi spectrum analyzer such as insider (www.metageek.com) to scan for any suspicious wireless routers in range
- Train staff in wireless security awareness

War-driving

Some of us, upon getting our first Wi-Fi enabled device such as a laptop, would probably have the thought of driving around the neighborhood looking for anyone with an open wireless network for *free internet access*. A hacker would probably attempt to do the same, driving around a community or neighborhood looking for any open wireless networks, connecting to it, and intercepting the traffic or compromising the network devices with malicious intentions.

Usually, the devices used in a war-driving scenario would be a laptop either preloaded with a penetration testing Linux distribution such as Kali Linux (www.kali.org) and a high-gain wireless antenna, which supports wireless packet injection and monitoring.

The following are some countermeasures for war-driving:

- Ensure that your wireless network is secured by using strong encryption standards
- Ensure that your password for the wireless network is very strong
- Do not leave your wireless network open
- Do not place wireless routers or access points close to the outer perimeter of a compound or a building

Ransomware

At the time of writing this book (2018), we are currently in the age of ransomware attacks. Over the past few years, a new generation of malware has surfaced in the wild (internet). Once a system has been infected with this malware, it's quite difficult to restore the compromised data.

So, *how exactly does ransomware work?* Hackers usually compromise an online server and inject their malicious code into the server or files on the server. Then, a regular user (potential victim) accesses the resources on the server or simply visits the website, and either the user downloads a malicious file without knowing it is harmful on his/her system, or the malicious code on the web server attempts to push itself on the potential victim's systems. Regardless of which method is used, once the malicious file executes on the victim's system, it immediately begins to encrypt the entire local drives using a secret key (passphrase or a digital certificate). While this is being done, it attempts to spread across the network. When the system is encrypted with ransomware, it become unusable, with a single screen presented to the victim, informing them to pay a ransom. The ransom would be something of monetary value, either asking the victim to provide their credit card details or to pay in some sort of crypto-currency such as Bitcoin.

During the compromised phase, the ransomware agent on the infected system usually attempts to communicate with a **Command and Control** (**C&C**) server for updates. These updates include newer versions of the malware itself to ensure that cyber security professionals do not easily decrypt the files, disinfect the system, and update the encryption key. This is a smart method that hackers are using to make money since companies value their data a lot. Imagine that a server that has all of the financial records of an organization on it got hit by a ransomware; the impact would be critical. Attempts can be made to remove and disinfect the system, but if the ransomware agent is receiving updates from the C&C server, it make the removal process very difficult. Some organizations take the easy way out, that is, paying the ransom. However, there is no guarantee that the hackers will supply the decryption key.

In 2017, the WannaCry ransomware rocked the world very hard. It demanded a ransom that was only payable in the form of $300-$500 worth of Bitcoins by the victims. This particular ransomware took advantage of a Windows SMB exploit, which allowed the ransomware to spread rapidly across the internet. However, the author of the WannaCry ransomware published an updated version known as WannaCry 2.0, which reduced the chances of preventing it.

 Further information on the WannaCry ransomware can be found at The Hacker News (`https://thehackernews.com/2017/05/how-to-wannacry-ransomware.html`).

Some countermeasures for ransomware are as follows:

- Implement a next generation firewall.
- Implement endpoint security and ensure that virus definitions are up-to-date.
- Implement anti-ransomware protection on end devices.
- Ensure that your systems have the latest patches and updates installed.
- Implement data backup and retention policies. If a victim does not pay the ransom, he/she can still restore data from a last *known* good backup.

DNS poisoning

As we have already discussed, DNS is used to resolve hostnames to IP addresses. Imagine that you have to remember the IP address of every server on the internet that is hosting your favorite website. It would be a challenge for anyone to remember so many IP addresses. Within an organization, system administrators use DNS internally on their corporate network by providing each device with a unique name, and the DNS Servers records are created to point a host name to an IP address. DNS can be used to assist in many situations, such as remote desktops. Imagine that you're a system administrator at a local company, and a user has logged a ticket stating that there is an issue with an application on their system. Instead of physically going to the location of the user, the system admin can simply ask the user for the host name of the system rather than the IP address. The DNS server would resolve the host name to the current IP address and allow the system administrator to connect remotely.

However, if a hacker is able to comprise a DNS server and modify the DNS records, an unsuspecting user may visit an incorrect website, even though the host name is accurate. At this point, you may be wondering what the impact and effects of an attacker performing DNS poisoning on an organization or an individual are. To explain this further, I'll briefly tell you about a security incident I personally encountered a few years ago at a local organization.

At the time, I was simply a Network Specialist, who had received a complaint from an employee of the finance department stating that they were unable to access the internet. Upon checking their network connection, the internet was working fine. However, the real issue was that the user was unable to access the company's online banking account. I'd asked the user to show me the website they were trying to access. The shocking thing was that the website access was accurate, but the pages that were presented were not of the bank's. This was a clear indication that the host name was being resolved to another public IP address where an attacker was attempting to catch user account details.

For a security incident of this nature to occur, the DNS records of the DNS Server used by the victim were either compromised and modified or the DNS Server IP configurations were modified on the victim's computer and were resolving entries on the attacker's DNS Server.

There are many records in a DNS Server. The following are the most commonly used entries:

Record Type	Description
A	The Address Mapper or the "A" record is used to map a hostname to an IPv4 address
AAAA	The quad A records maps a hostname to an IPv6 address
CNAME	The CNAME is used to create alias for the domain name
MX	The MX records is used to specify the mail exhange servers
NS	The Name Server (NS) records is used to specify the authoritative name server
PTR	The Pointer (PTR) record is used to resolve an IP to a hostname
SOA	The Start of Authority (SOA) record has information stored in the DNS zone and its recorrds
TXT	The Text (TXT) record contains text string which my used to proof identity on a domain

Using the `nslookup` command on Windows, you can troubleshoot DNS issues. By simply executing the `nslookup` command, you current DNS Server settings will be presented:

```
C:\>nslookup
Default Server: one.one.one.one
Address: 2606:4700:4700::1111
```

Furthermore, the `ipconfig /all` command on Windows provides your DNS Server IP configurations:

```
DNS Servers . . . . . . . . . . . : 2606:4700:4700::1111
                                    2606:4700:4700::1001
                                    1.1.1.1
                                    1.0.0.1
```

The following are some public DNS servers that you can use:

- **Cisco OpenDNS** (`www.opendns.com`)
- **Google Public DNS** (`https://developers.google.com/speed/public-dns`)
- **Cloudflare DNS** (`https://1.1.1.1`)

ARP poisoning

One of the most popular protocols that exists between the Data Link and the Network Layers of the OSI reference model is the **Address Resolution Protocol** (**ARP**). ARP mostly operates at the Data Link layer, with its purpose being to resolve IP address to **Media Access Control** (**MAC**) addresses. You may be wondering, *why do devices on a network need to resolve IP addresses to MAC addresses?* A switch is a layer 2 device, and is only able to read the layer 2 header of the frame. This part of the frame contains only MAC addresses, and so if devices are using the **Internet Protocol** (**IP**) to communicate on a local network, the switches will not be able to read the Network Layer header which contains the IP addresses. Therefore, all communication that occurs on a local network uses layer 2 addressing uses MAC addresses instead.

Let's imagine that your laptop or desktop computer wants to communicate to a website such as `www.google.com`. Your computer would send its traffic to its default gateway, which is a router. However, your end device inserts the MAC address of the default gateway as the destination MAC address on the Frame. When the default gateway receives the bits, it will see the destination MAC address is its own and will further process the datagram up to the Network Layer (layer 3 of the OSI reference model) to take a look at the destination IP address within the packet header. Upon sending the datagram to its destination, the router will now remove the existing layer 2 header information and replace the source MAC address with its own, and give the destination as the next-hop or the next device to receive it. This process continues until the datagram is delivered to its final destination.

Using the `arp -a` command on Windows, we can see the current ARP entries of the local device:

```
C:\>arp -a

Interface: 172.16.17.8 --- 0x17
  Internet Address      Physical Address      Type
  172.16.17.6           f0-27-2d-             dynamic
  172.16.17.18          9c-3d-cf-             dynamic
  172.16.17.255         ff-ff-ff-ff-ff-ff     static
  224.0.0.22            01-00-5e-00-00-16     static
  224.0.0.251           01-00-5e-00-00-fb     static
  224.0.0.252           01-00-5e-00-00-fc     static
  239.255.255.250       01-00-5e-7f-ff-fa     static
  255.255.255.255       ff-ff-ff-ff-ff-ff     static
```

Using the `show ip arp` command on a Cisco IOS device, we can once again see the current ARP entries:

```
R1.TT#show ip arp
Protocol  Address         Age (min)  Hardware Addr   Type   Interface
Internet  192.168.1.1        -       00E0.F9A0.CE01  ARPA   GigabitEthernet0/0
Internet  192.168.1.2        0       00D0.585E.8753  ARPA   GigabitEthernet0/0
Internet  192.168.1.10       0       00E0.F79B.DE34  ARPA   GigabitEthernet0/0
Internet  192.168.2.1        -       00E0.F9A0.CE02  ARPA   GigabitEthernet0/1
Internet  192.168.2.2        0       00D0.58BB.AC01  ARPA   GigabitEthernet0/1
Internet  192.168.2.10       0       0002.1686.D920  ARPA   GigabitEthernet0/1
```

To view the ARP cache on Linux devices, use the `arp -a` command.

ARP poisoning is where an attacker sends intentional **Gratuitous ARP** messages to a potential victim's machine, in effect, causing the victim's machine to update the ARP cache. As we saw previously, the ARP cache has an IP-to-MAC mapping, where the ARP poisoning attack forces a victim's machine to change the MAC addresses for specific IP addresses in the cache. Therefore, the victim's traffic will be sent to another device rather than the actual device on the network.

The Gratuitous ARP is sent as an advanced notification of an update for an IP-to-MAC resolution. This would cause the receiving device to update its ARP cache.

Let's take a look at the following diagram to get a better understanding of an ARP poisoning attack. Whenever **PC1** wants to send traffic out to the internet, its sends BB:BB:BB:BB:BB:BB to its default gateway by using the router's MAC address. The router, in return, will record the **PC1** MAC address, AA:AA:AA:AA:AA:AA. Let's imagine that an attacker has joined the network, as shown in the following diagram. The attacker is attempting an ARP cache poisoning attack. The attacker's machine will send a Gratuitous ARP message to PC1, telling it that the default gateway's IP-to-MAC mapping has been updated to 192.168.1.1–CC:CC:CC:CC:CC:CC:

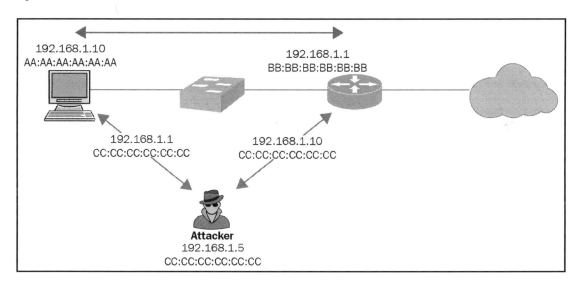

The effect of this change on **PC1** will be that all of the traffic destined outside of the local network and the default gateway will now be sent to the attacker's machine. Furthermore, the attacker will send a Gratuitous ARP message to the router, informing the MAC that the address of 192.168.1.10 has been updated to CC:CC:CC:CC:CC:CC. Therefore, returning traffic for 192.168.1.10 will now be sent to the attacker machine. This is both an ARP cache poisoning and a **man-in-the-middle (MITM)** attack as all traffic between **PC1** and the router will be passing through the attacker.

Deauthentication

Whenever we connect to a wireless network using a mobile device such as smartphone, laptop, and so on, this connection is known as an association between the client and the wireless router/access point. A deauthentication attack focuses on bumping out all of the wireless devices that are connected to a wireless router/access point. From an attacker's point of view, the attacker machine does not need to be connected/associated to the target wireless network, instead being within range of the wireless signal. The effect of this type of attack is to create a **Denial-of-Service (DoS)** attack for the clients who are connected to the wireless network.

Brute force

Let's imagine you're a construction worker that's been hired to break down a wall. Unfortunately, you don't have any heavy machinery equipment to aid in the process, but you have a sledge hammer. You know this won't be enough, because after the first strike at the wall, you haven't done any damage. If you continue striking the wall with the same sledge hammer, you'll eventually notice that the wall begins to crack and shatter. This is the effect of brute force.

So, *how does a brute force attack work in the digital world*? Let's imagine that an attacker is trying to crack a password for a login portal for a victim's web server. Let's take a look at the following login page for the Joomla web framework:

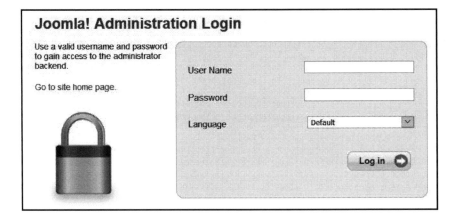

If an attacker has figured out the username of a user, he/she can try all of the possible passwords in the **Password** field on the portal. This is provided that the website administrator has not modified the administrator in any way. This would mean that the attacker machine will slam in all password possibilities until the correct password is found.

A brute force attack is always or mostly successful. However, the downside is that the time it takes to crack the system is very long.

Virtual Local Area Network (VLAN) hopping

VLAN means that devices that are physically connected to a network can be logically segmented into virtual networks. Let's think of this as follows—all of the devices within a building are connected to the same physical network but logically, within the switches, each department is on their own IP networks and VLANs. Imagine that a device within the Sales department sends a broadcast message—only the devices within the Sales department will receive it since all of the other departments are on logically separated networks (VLANs).

VLAN hopping allows an attacker to access network resources and traffic of other VLANs, which would normally be inaccessible. VLAN hopping attacks occur on switches that have their physical ports configured to be converted into a trunk port automatically. A trunk allows multiple VLAN traffic to simultaneously pass across the network.

The Cisco **Dynamic Trunking Protocol** (**DTP**) is susceptible to VLAN hopping attacks. The attacker can establish a physical connection to a switch and inject specially crafted IEEE 802.1Q frames into the switch port. If auto-trunking is enabled, the port will be converted into a trunk. This would then allow the attacker to access all VLANs on the network.

Exploits versus vulnerabilities

It's quite important to understand the difference between a vulnerability and an exploit. A vulnerability is a weakness or flaw in a system, while an exploit is a piece of software or code that is used to take advantage of a vulnerability on a target system.

Let's take a look at a vulnerability on a system. The following is partial Nmap scan results for a vulnerable system:

```
Starting Nmap 7.70 ( https://nmap.org ) at 2018-06-19 11:17 EDT
Nmap scan report for 192.168.0.222
Host is up (0.078s latency).
Not shown: 969 closed ports
PORT     STATE SERVICE        VERSION
21/tcp   open  ftp            vsftpd 2.3.4
| ftp-anon: Anonymous FTP login allowed (FTP code 230)
|_ftp-bounce: bounce working!
| ftp-syst:
|   STAT:
| FTP server status:
|       Connected to 192.168.0.55
|       Logged in as ftp
|       TYPE: ASCII
|       No session bandwidth limit
|       Session timeout in seconds is 300
|       Control connection is plain text
|       Data connections will be plain text
|       vsFTPd 2.3.4 - secure, fast, stable
|_End of status
22/tcp   open  ssh            OpenSSH 4.7p1 Debian 8ubuntu1 (protocol 2.0)
```

We can see that TCP port 21 is open, which is providing FTP services by using the vsftpd 2.3.4 daemon on the target host. After performing some research online, we found that there is a known vulnerability for the vsftpd 2.3.4 daemon, which will allow for Backdoor Command Execution.

Securing networking devices

Earlier in this chapter, we discussed a number of security threats that can occurs on a network. As an upcoming network professional, it is very important to understand how to secure and mitigate these threats and vulnerabilities on a network infrastructure. In this section, we are going to take a look at applying some simple and effective controls on a system and network to assist in preventing and mitigating these security threats.

Changing default credentials

Whether you have purchased a computer or a network appliance, these devices have default accounts that allow the owner to log in to the administrator or root account. In some cases, users do not change or disable the default accounts or passwords that have been implemented, which is usually classed as a security vulnerability on a network.

Not changing the default configurations on a device could lead to a security breach on the network, and the complexity of the attack would be simple for either guessing the password or checking the manufacturer's website for default account and password information.

Microsoft Windows

After a clean installation of the Windows operating system, there's the primary account, which is the administrator. During the installation, it's not mandatory to assign a password to this account. Without a password assigned, anyone with either physical or remote access to the device would be able to login successfully without providing any user credentials. To check for any hidden accounts on Windows, use the `net user` command in Command Prompt:

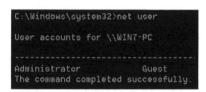

To get further information on a particular user account, use the `net user` command, followed by the account name:

```
C:\Windows\system32>net user Guest
User name                    Guest
Full Name
Comment                      Built-in account for guest access to the computer/d
omain
User's comment
Country code                 000 (System Default)
Account active               No
Account expires              Never

Password last set            10/25/2018 11:44:37 AM
Password expires             Never
Password changeable          10/25/2018 11:44:37 AM
Password required            No
User may change password     No

Workstations allowed         All
Logon script
User profile
Home directory
Last logon                   Never

Logon hours allowed          All

Local Group Memberships      *Guests
Global Group memberships     *None
The command completed successfully.
```

Furthermore, to manage local user accounts, simply navigate to **Control Panel** | **User Accounts**.

Linux

On the Linux operating system, the administrator account is known as the root. Similar to the administrator user account on Windows, the root user account has the highest privileges in Linux. During the Linux process of most Linux-based operating systems, the installation wizard prompts you to set a unique password for the root account and allows the creation of a standard user account. This ensures that the user logs in to the operating system using the standard user account for general usage. However, if further privileges are required to perform an action, the root account has be involved temporarily.

To quickly change the login password for an account in Linux, open Terminal and run the `passwd` command.

Other devices

Whether you're administering a server, network devices, or even security appliances, all of these devices usually come with a factory set default account. Without changing the default passwords on these devices, a malicious user or hacker can compromise the devices easily. Imagine that a system/network administrator has deployed various devices within the network to improve the IT infrastructure. All of the devices are configured and providing optimum performance, but the IT personnel didn't bother to change the default user account information on any of the network appliances on the network. One day, a disgruntled employee emerges and is about to submit his/her resignation, but before doing so, the person did some research online to learn how to hack into various network devices and servers. Having the default user credentials enabled on each system made the attack very easy for the non-technical employee to access and take down various segments of the network.

Avoiding common passwords

In 2014, I had the privilege of looking at a router's configuration files after a cyber attack had occurred at a reputable organization in the region. The attack is known as **toll-fraud**, which results in a company's telephone bill being extremely high due to unaccountable international calls. After reviewing the configurations of the compromised router, it seemed that the person who had made the configurations or set the device password actually used a very common, guessable password.

This was a clear indication that the attacker didn't need to perform any sort of complex attack or password cracking techniques, but simply guess the password based on the manufacturer of the device. As a result of not having a proper password policy and applying basic security practices, the organization had to spend thousands of dollars remediating any damage that was done within their network and the high cost of the telephone bill. This is the result of setting common passwords on devices.

Device hardening

Firmware is a piece of software that is permanently programmed into the read-only memory of an electronic component. It's quite important to update/upgrade the firmware on a system since an updated version will contain fixes for any bugs within the program and security issues, and will implement newer features from the vendor. Firmware updates can be found on the device manufacturer's website.

Installing device updates, patches, hotfix, and service packs on an operating system will assist in minimizing the attack surface and reduce the threat landscape within an organization. These updates are frequently released by software companies as a continuous service to ensure that any bugs and security issues are resolved as quickly as possible.

Device hardening is not only focused on installing updates but also on applying baseline policies across all systems and devices within the organization. This ensures that the minimum security standards are applied to everyone and each device as it will aid in minimizing security threats and risk.

Disabling unnecessary services

As you have learned in the previous chapters, whenever there are services running on an operating system, there are logical network ports assigned to each unique service. Having unnecessary services active on a system poses a security vulnerability on the device. From an attacker's point of view, each open port on a system is a doorway into the operating system. Leaving a doorway open in reality can be an invitation for an intruder.

Disabling services in Windows

To determine what services are currently running on Windows, open the **Run** prompt, type `services.msc`, and click on **OK**:

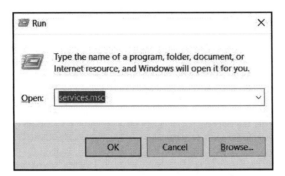

Next, you'll see the **Services** window (snap-in), displaying all of the services that are available, both enabled and disabled, on the local system:

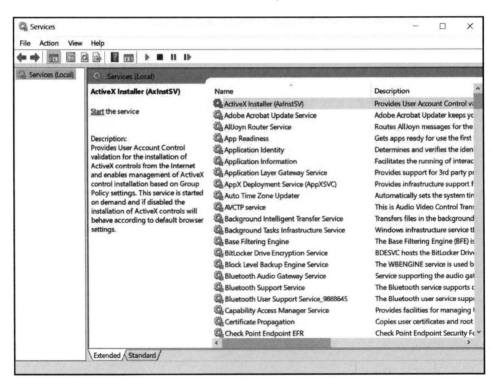

By double clicking on a service, another window will open, providing further details about the particular service, including the **Startup type** and **Service status** options that allow you start, stop, pause, resume a service, and manage whether its starts on boot or is simply disabled:

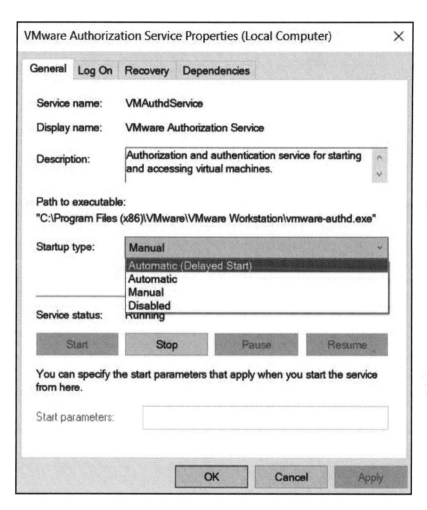

Using the `netstat` command in Command Prompt, you'll be able to view various network statistics on the local machine. Let's use `netstat -n` to view all remote connections, including their state, source, and destination port number, and the protocol type:

```
TCP    172.16.17.8:49699      52.165.170.112:443    ESTABLISHED
TCP    172.16.17.8:58129      162.125.18.133:443    ESTABLISHED
TCP    172.16.17.8:59183      13.107.6.254:443      ESTABLISHED
TCP    172.16.17.8:59265      23.195.64.119:443     ESTABLISHED
TCP    172.16.17.8:59291      143.204.31.156:443    FIN_WAIT_1
TCP    172.16.17.8:59450      131.253.33.254:443    ESTABLISHED
TCP    172.16.17.8:60012      13.107.49.254:443     FIN_WAIT_1
TCP    172.16.17.8:60014      13.107.3.254:443      ESTABLISHED
TCP    172.16.17.8:60024      34.248.150.116:443    ESTABLISHED
```

Let's take this a step further. This time, we're going to use the process ID and match it with the services found in Task Manager. First, use the `netstat -ano` command:

```
TCP    172.16.17.8:49699      52.165.170.112:443    ESTABLISHED    6356
TCP    172.16.17.8:58129      162.125.18.133:443    ESTABLISHED    7672
TCP    172.16.17.8:59183      13.107.6.254:443      ESTABLISHED    4860
TCP    172.16.17.8:59265      23.195.64.119:443     ESTABLISHED    4860
TCP    172.16.17.8:59450      131.253.33.254:443    ESTABLISHED    4860
TCP    172.16.17.8:60014      13.107.3.254:443      FIN_WAIT_1     4860
TCP    172.16.17.8:60024      34.248.150.116:443    ESTABLISHED    3152
TCP    172.16.17.8:60711      204.79.197.254:443    FIN_WAIT_1     4860
TCP    172.16.17.8:60714      13.33.69.164:443      ESTABLISHED    4860
TCP    172.16.17.8:60788      52.1.221.21:443       ESTABLISHED    7672
TCP    172.16.17.8:60918      162.125.18.133:443    ESTABLISHED    7672
TCP    172.16.17.8:61418      162.125.34.137:443    ESTABLISHED    7672
```

Now, open Windows **Task Manager** and go to the **Services** tab. There, you'll see that each of the services has a **Process ID (PID)** value, which can be cross-referenced to the `netstat –ano` results:

Name	PID	Description	Status	Group
RpcSs	1044	Remote Procedure Call (RPC)	Running	rpcss
RpcEptMapper	1044	RPC Endpoint Mapper	Running	RPCSS
EventSystem	1076	COM+ Event System	Running	LocalService
LSM	1092	Local Session Manager	Running	DcomLaunch
WinDefend	1100	Windows Defender Antivirus Service	Running	
jhi_service	1200	Intel(R) Dynamic Application Loader Ho...	Running	
wlidsvc	1292	Microsoft Account Sign-in Assistant	Running	netsvcs
NcbService	1412	Network Connection Broker	Running	LocalSystemNe...
TimeBrokerSvc	1420	Time Broker	Running	LocalServiceNe...
Schedule	1472	Task Scheduler	Running	netsvcs
ProfSvc	1508	User Profile Service	Running	netsvcs
UserManager	1640	User Manager	Running	netsvcs
LMS	1700	Intel(R) Management and Security Appli...	Running	
mpssvc	1712	Windows Defender Firewall	Running	LocalServiceNo...
CoreMessagingRegistrar	1712	CoreMessaging	Running	LocalServiceNo...
BFE	1712	Base Filtering Engine	Running	LocalServiceNo...
NVDisplay.ContainerLocalSy...	1888	NVIDIA Display Container LS	Running	
EventLog	1972	Windows Event Log	Running	LocalServiceNe...
SysMain	2044	Superfetch	Running	LocalSystemNe...
SENS	2096	System Event Notification Service	Running	netsvcs
igfxCUIService2.0.0.0	2120	Intel(R) HD Graphics Control Panel Servi	Running	
AudioEndpointBuilder	2156	Windows Audio Endpoint Builder	Running	LocalSystemNe...
FontCache	2164	Windows Font Cache Service	Running	LocalService

Task Manager — File Options View

Processes | Performance | App history | Startup | Users | Details | Services

Fewer details | Open Services

Linux

On Linux-based systems, the `netstat` utility is also available, and will assist in discovering running services and open ports:

```
root@printer:~# netstat -a
Active Internet connections (servers and established)
Proto Recv-Q Send-Q Local Address           Foreign Address         State
tcp        0      0 0.0.0.0:ssh             0.0.0.0:*               LISTEN
tcp        0      0 localhost:postgresql    0.0.0.0:*               LISTEN
tcp6       0      0 [::]:http               [::]:*                  LISTEN
tcp6       0      0 [::]:9876               [::]:*                  LISTEN
tcp6       0      0 [::]:ssh                [::]:*                  LISTEN
tcp6       0      0 localhost:postgresql    [::]:*                  LISTEN
udp6       0      0 localhost:44187         localhost:44187         ESTABLISHED
```

Furthermore, you can use the `service service-name start` command to enable a service and the `service service-name stop` command to stop a running service, like so:

```
root@printer:~# service postgresql start
```

Cisco

A Cisco IOS switch or router is capable of providing services such as SSH, DHCP, and so on. As we mentioned previously, application layer protocols communicate with the Transport Security Layer to open TCP and UDP ports. The `show control-plane host open-ports` command provides network statistics, similar to the `netstat` command on Windows:

```
R2#show control-plane host open-ports
Active internet connections (servers and established)
Prot        Local Address      Foreign Address                    Service    State
 tcp              *:23                  *:0                         Telnet    LISTEN
 udp              *:67                  *:0                  DHCPD Receive    LISTEN
```

Network scanning

Another method of determining running services and open ports on a system is to use a network scanner. **Network Mapper**, better known as **Nmap**, is renowned for its advanced capabilities in determining not only open ports, but being able to identify vulnerabilities, the operating system being used, services versions, and so on, on a target system.

The following is an output from an Nmap scan against a system. Here, we can see the various ports and their corresponding services:

```
Starting Nmap 7.70 ( https://nmap.org ) at 2018-06-19 11:35 EDT
Nmap scan report for 192.168.0.219
Host is up (1.6s latency).
Not shown: 969 closed ports
PORT      STATE SERVICE
21/tcp    open  ftp
22/tcp    open  ssh
23/tcp    open  telnet
25/tcp    open  smtp
53/tcp    open  domain
80/tcp    open  http
110/tcp   open  pop3
111/tcp   open  rpcbind
119/tcp   open  nntp
139/tcp   open  netbios-ssn
143/tcp   open  imap
445/tcp   open  microsoft-ds
465/tcp   open  smtps
512/tcp   open  exec
513/tcp   open  login
514/tcp   open  shell
563/tcp   open  snews
587/tcp   open  submission
993/tcp   open  imaps
995/tcp   open  pop3s
1099/tcp  open  rmiregistry
1524/tcp  open  ingreslock
2049/tcp  open  nfs
2121/tcp  open  ccproxy-ftp
3306/tcp  open  mysql
5432/tcp  open  postgresql
5900/tcp  open  vnc
6000/tcp  open  X11
6667/tcp  open  irc
8009/tcp  open  ajp13
8180/tcp  open  unknown

Nmap done: 1 IP address (1 host up) scanned in 109.28 seconds
```

 Network scanning is considered to be intrusive and an invasion of privacy. Please do not scan a system without legal permission.

Disabling physical ports

We've been talking about logical ports a lot thus far, but we must not forget about disabling any unused physical ports on a device either. Leaving physical ports active can allow a malicious user or hacker to physically connect specialized devices to a network to create physical backdoor access.

The following device, as mentioned in the *Insider threat* section of this chapter, is known as a **LAN Turtle**, and is a device that can be used as a network implant within an organization's network:

On networking appliances, once it has a managed switch, router, firewall or another device, the management interface allows the administrator to enable and disable ports accordingly. It is a good network security practice to disable any unused ports on a system or device.

On a Cisco switch or router, the `show ip interface brief` command displays all of the ports on the device, along with their status. The `Status` column shows the layer 1 (Physical) status of each interface. There are three possible statuses:

- `up`: The port is active and is receiving an electrical signal from another connected device.
- `down`: The port is active, but is not receiving an electrical signal. This occurs when there is no device connected to the port or there is no cable connected to the interface.
- `administratively down`: This means that the device's administrator has manually shut down this interface from the operating system:

```
R1.TT#show ip interface brief
Interface            IP-Address       OK? Method Status                 Protocol
GigabitEthernet0/0   192.168.1.1      YES manual up                     up
GigabitEthernet0/1   192.168.2.1      YES manual up                     up
GigabitEthernet0/2   unassigned       YES unset  administratively down  down
Vlan1                unassigned       YES unset  administratively down  down
```

The following screenshot shows how you can access an interface and manually shut down the port:

```
R1.TT(config)#interface gigabitEthernet 0/1
R1.TT(config-if)#shutdown
```

After the port has been disabled, using the `show ip interface brief` command once more, we can see that the status has now changed to `administratively down`, as expected:

```
R1.TT#show ip interface brief
Interface            IP-Address      OK? Method Status                Protocol
GigabitEthernet0/0   192.168.1.1     YES manual up                    up
GigabitEthernet0/1   192.168.2.1     YES manual administratively down down
```

 To enable an interface on a Cisco IOS device, use the `no shutdown` command on the interface.

Mitigation techniques

Let's talk about the various mitigation techniques that are used for security threats on a network infrastructure a little bit more.

Network segmentation – Demilitarized Zone (DMZ)

Most organizations have servers that are accessible by users of the public internet. Some of these servers are web servers and email servers. It's definitely not recommended to allow any traffic originating from the internet to access your internal, private network. Creating a DMZ to place these publicly accessible servers is highly recommended.

The DMZ is a semi-trusted segment of the company's network that allows users from the internet limited access to devices in this area, which is why it's the best possible location to place the publicly accessible servers on the organization's network:

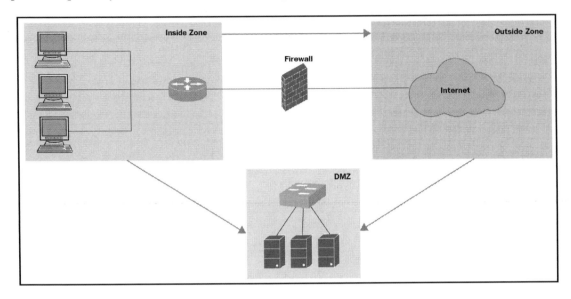

Traffic originating from the **Inside Zone** is allowed in both the DMZ and the **Outside Zone**. Traffic originating from the internet is not allowed to the **Inside Zone**, while specific traffic is allowed to only the DMZ. Traffic originating from the DMZ is not allowed in the **Inside Zone**.

Network segmentation – VLANs

As mentioned in `Chapter 5`, *Routing and Switching Concepts*, we spoke about VLAN. By default, all ports are assigned to VLAN 1 on a managed switch. As an upcoming networking professional, leaving all ports on the same VLAN will result in a logical flat network without any segmentation. This would lead to unnecessary broadcast messages, which will reduce the network's performance and increase the risk of a network security incident.

Furthermore, using VLANs on a physical network will assist in improving the security posture of the network. Let's imagine that each department within an organization is on a unique VLAN. If an intruder plugs his/her attacker machine into a switch port, only that logical segment may be compromised until the attacker finds a way to perform VLAN Hopping. Having multiple VLANs also allows **Access Control Lists (ACLs)** to be implemented on the routers that handle the inter-VLAN routing of traffic. The ACLs can be used to either permit or deny traffic originating from one VLAN to another.

On a Cisco IOS switch, to view the current VLAN, use the `show vlan brief` command:

```
SW1#show vlan brief

VLAN Name                             Status    Ports
---- -------------------------------- --------- -------------------------------
1    default                          active    Fa0/1, Fa0/2, Fa0/3, Fa0/4
                                                Fa0/5, Fa0/6, Fa0/7, Fa0/8
                                                Fa0/9, Fa0/10, Fa0/11, Fa0/12
                                                Fa0/13, Fa0/14, Fa0/15, Fa0/16
                                                Fa0/17, Fa0/18, Fa0/19, Fa0/20
                                                Fa0/21, Fa0/22, Fa0/23, Fa0/24
                                                Gig0/1, Gig0/2
1002 fddi-default                     active
1003 token-ring-default               active
1004 fddinet-default                  active
1005 trnet-default                    active
```

There is always a minimum of five VLANs. VLAN 1 has all of its ports assigned to VLAN 1 by default, while VLANs 1002, 1003, 1004, and 1005 are reserved for Token Ring and **Fiber Distributed Data Interface** (**FDDI**) VLANs. These VLANs cannot be deleted or removed from the switch.

Creating a VLAN on a switch is quite simple. Just use the `vlan vlan-ID` command, as shown in the following screenshot:

```
SW1(config)#vlan 10
SW1(config-vlan)#name Sales
SW1(config-vlan)#exit
SW1(config)#vlan 20
SW1(config-vlan)#name IT
SW1(config-vlan)#exit
```

VLANs are represented by a number on the switch. Giving it a name helps us understand the purpose of the VLAN:

```
SW1#show vlan brief

VLAN Name                             Status    Ports
---- -------------------------------- --------- -------------------------------
1    default                          active    Fa0/1, Fa0/2, Fa0/3, Fa0/4
                                                Fa0/5, Fa0/6, Fa0/7, Fa0/8
                                                Fa0/9, Fa0/10, Fa0/11, Fa0/12
                                                Fa0/13, Fa0/14, Fa0/15, Fa0/16
                                                Fa0/17, Fa0/18, Fa0/19, Fa0/20
                                                Fa0/21, Fa0/22, Fa0/23, Fa0/24
                                                Gig0/1, Gig0/2
10   Sales                            active
20   IT                               active
1002 fddi-default                     active
1003 token-ring-default               active
1004 fddinet-default                  active
1005 trnet-default                    active
```

To assign an interface to a VLAN, we can use the following sequence of commands:

```
SW1(config)#interface fastethernet 0/1
SW1(config)#interface fastethernet 0/1
SW1(config-if)#switchport mode access
SW1(config-if)#switchport access vlan 10
SW1(config-if)#switchport nonegotiate
SW1(config-if)#no shutdown
SW1(config-if)#exit
```

`interface fastethernet 0/1` has now been assigned to VLAN 10, as shown in the following screenshot:

```
SW1#show vlan brief

VLAN Name                             Status    Ports
---- -------------------------------- --------- -------------------------------
1    default                          active    Fa0/2, Fa0/3, Fa0/4, Fa0/5
                                                Fa0/6, Fa0/7, Fa0/8, Fa0/9
                                                Fa0/10, Fa0/11, Fa0/12, Fa0/13
                                                Fa0/14, Fa0/15, Fa0/16, Fa0/17
                                                Fa0/18, Fa0/19, Fa0/20, Fa0/21
                                                Fa0/22, Fa0/23, Fa0/24, Gig0/1
                                                Gig0/2
10   Sales                            active    Fa0/1
20   IT                               active
1002 fddi-default                     active
1003 token-ring-default               active
1004 fddinet-default                  active
1005 trnet-default                    active
```

Changing the native VLAN

The native VLAN in a switch network has a particular purpose, as opposed to the data VLANs. The native VLAN is responsible for transporting all untagged traffic. *What is untagged traffic on a network?* Whenever traffic enters a switch port, the datagram is tagged with the VLAN-ID that's been assigned to the interface. All of the traffic in a managed switch remains tagged until it exits an interface that is directly connected to its intended recipient. Then, the VLAN tag is broken off by the switch. Self-generated traffic or traffic generated by a switch (untagged traffic) is placed on an unused VLAN on the trunk. This unused VLAN is known as the **native VLAN**.

By default, the native VLAN is VLAN 1. As a security practice, it is not recommended to use VLAN 1 for anything on your network. If all of the devices within your organization are on VLAN 1, and if a hacker gains access to your network, whether physically or remotely, he/she can access all of your devices with ease. Having your network segmented via the use of VLANs improves efficiency and security on the network.

The following screenshot shows you how to create a native VLAN on a Cisco IOS switch:

```
SW1(config)#vlan 99
SW1(config-vlan)#name Native
SW1(config-vlan)#exit
```

The following screenshot shows you how to assign the native VLAN and set specific VLANs to use the trunk port on a Cisco IOS switch:

```
SW1(config)#interface gigabitEthernet 0/1
SW1(config-if)#switchport mode trunk
SW1(config-if)#switchport trunk native vlan 99
SW1(config-if)#switchport trunk allowed vlan 10,20
SW1(config-if)#switchport nonegotiate
SW1(config-if)#no shutdown
SW1(config-if)#exit
```

The following screenshot shows you the verification of VLAN information on a `trunk` interface:

```
SW1(config)#interface gigabitEthernet 0/1
SW1(config-if)#switchport mode trunk
SW1(config-if)#switchport trunk native vlan 99
SW1(config-if)#switchport trunk allowed vlan 10,20
SW1(config-if)#switchport nonegotiate
SW1(config-if)#no shutdown
SW1(config-if)#exit
```

Spanning Tree Protocol (STP) threat mitigation techniques

STP threat mitigation techniques are as follows:

Bridge Protocol Data Unit (BPDU) guard

BPDU guard is used to prevent BPDUs from entering a switch port. This features is recommended if the switch is using `portfast` on a particular interface. It assists in preventing a hacker from injecting malicious BPDU messages into the switch in the hopes of adjusting the root bridge to the attacker's machines and manipulating layer 2 traffic.

The following screenshot shows you how to assign the `portfast` and BPDU guard features under an access port on a Cisco IOS switch:

```
SW1(config)#interface fastEthernet 0/4
SW1(config-if)#switchport mode access
SW1(config-if)#switchport access vlan 10
% Access VLAN does not exist. Creating vlan 10
SW1(config-if)#spanning-tree portfast
%Warning: portfast should only be enabled on ports connected to a single
host. Connecting hubs, concentrators, switches, bridges, etc... to this
interface  when portfast is enabled, can cause temporary bridging loops.
Use with CAUTION

%Portfast has been configured on FastEthernet0/4 but will only
have effect when the interface is in a non-trunking mode.
SW1(config-if)#spanning-tree bpduguard enable
SW1(config-if)#no shutdown
SW1(config-if)#exit
SW1(config)#
```

Root guard

The root guard is placed at the local interfaces of both the root bridge and the secondary root bridge that connects to other switches except themselves. The root guard's features is used to enforce the placement of root bridges on a network.

The following screenshot shows you how to apply the root guard feature under an interface in a Cisco IOS switch:

```
SW1(config)#interface fastEthernet 0/24
SW1(config-if)#spanning-tree guard root
SW1(config-if)#no shutdown
SW1(config-if)#exit
```

DHCP snooping

DHCP snooping is applied on switches to prevent a hacker from installing a rogue DHCP server on the network. If an attacker has successfully installed a rogue DHCP server on the network, he/she would be able to inject unsolicited DHCP messages to all connected client devices. As you learned in Chapter 2, *Network Ports, Protocols, and Topologies* a DHCP server provides IP configurations to clients on the network, and are as follows:

- Host IP address
- Subnet mask
- Default gateway
- DNS servers

Imagine that a hacker has installed his/her rogue DHCP server on the network, which sends clients a different default gateway that the hacker is able to intercept and re-route or even exhaust the DHCP Pool of IP addresses.

Tools such as **Yersinia** have the capability of performing a stress test on a DHCP server:

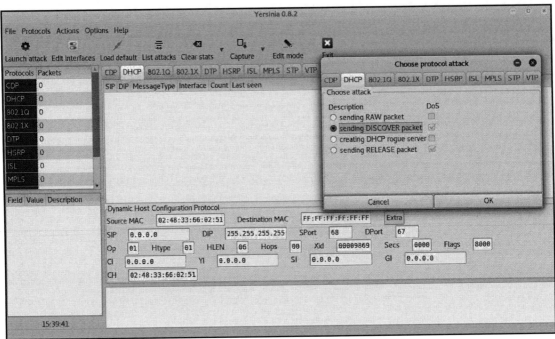

DHCP Snooping prevents DHCP Offer and DHCP Acknowledgment messages from entering the switch network. When DHCP snooping is enabled on a switch network, all ports are immediately converted into untrusted ports that are used to block all DHCP Offer and DHCP Acknowledgment messages. Trusted ports are assigned to the DHCP server and trunk ports only.

To configure DHCP snooping on a Cisco switch, use the following commands:

```
SW1(config)#ip dhcp snooping
SW1(config)#interface fastEthernet 0/1
SW1(config-if)#ip dhcp snooping trust
SW1(config-if)#exit
SW1(config)#interface range fastEthernet 0/2 - fastEthernet 0/24
SW1(config-if-range)#ip dhcp snooping limit rate 6
SW1(config-if-range)#exit
SW1(config)#ip dhcp snooping vlan 10,20,30
```

The `show ip dhcp snooping` command is used to verify trusted and untrusted ports assignment, while the `show ip dhcp snooping binding` command disables the IP-MAC address binding, interface, and VLAN membership.

Honeypot and honeynet

A **honeypot** is an autonomous system/device on a network that assists IT security professionals in identifying who is trying to probe or attack the company's systems. A honeypot behaves like a real computer/server on the network in the hopes of misleading an intruder.

A **honeynet** is a segment on the network that is made up of multiple honeypot devices, thereby emulating a vulnerable network.

These devices generate logs and monitor the activities of the intruder. A network security professional can use this information to better protect and implemented security controls and countermeasures within the organization.

Penetration testing

Each day, new and more sophisticated threats are emerging, and organizations are considering the fact that they could be breached. Penetration testing involves an organization hiring a penetration tester to actually hack their network legally. The purpose is to discover any hidden vulnerabilities within the organization, how an actually attacker would break in, and what assets could be compromised. This concept helps the organization better secure their network infrastructure and improve their security posture by implementing various security policies and countermeasures on the network.

Some of the most well-known penetration testing certification bodies are as follows:

- **EC-Council**: **Certified Ethical Hacker (CEH)**
- **SANS GIAC**: Network Penetration Testing and Ethical Hacking
- **Offensive Security**: **Offensive Security Certified Professional (OSCP)**

Summary

We opened this chapter by discussing what happens when a client device makes an association with a wireless router/access and the various wireless security standards that are currently being used in organizations globally. Later in this chapter, we took a look at identifying common network attacks and threats and understanding the benefits of applying recommended practices to help mitigate various threats on a network infrastructure.

In the next chapter, we will be covering security in the TCP/IP stack, and explain the vulnerabilities that exist in each layer of TCP/IP.

Questions

1. In wireless security, which encryption standard uses TKIP?
    1. WEP
    2. WPA
    3. WPA2
    4. CCMP

2. Cisco developed which of the following protocols for wireless authentication?
    1. EAP-FAST
    2. EAP-TLS
    3. PEAP
    4. EAP

3. An attacker is trying to exhaust a web server by sending a continuous stream of fake requests. What is the attacker trying to do?
    1. Network scanning
    2. Install a virus
    3. DoS
    4. Create a backdoor

4. An attacker has called an organization's help desk, pretending to be someone else to gather confidential information. What is the attacker attempting to do?
    1. Tailgating
    2. Piggybacking
    3. Social engineering
    4. Insider threat

5. A type of virus that is triggered after a predefined set of actions has occurred is known as what?
    1. Ransomware
    2. Logic bomb
    3. Spyware
    4. Insider threat

6. A malware that encrypts and holds a victim's data as hostage is known as what?
    1. Ransomware
    2. Logic bomb
    3. Spyware
    4. Insider threat

7. Which DNS record is responsible for specifying an email server?
    1. SOA
    2. NS
    3. CNAME
    4. MX

8. Which command is used to view the ARP cache on a Windows system?
    1. `arp -n`
    2. `arp -a`
    3. `netstat -a`
    4. `netstat -n`

Further reading

Further information on understanding network security concepts and implementation of security appliances, check out the *CCNA Security 210-260 Certification Guide* by Packt at `https://india.packtpub.com/in/networking-and-servers/ccna-security-210-260-certification-guide`.

12
TCP/IP Security

In the past few chapters, we have discussed a lot of topics related to network security from network identity management to attacks and threats. In this chapter, we are going to cover further vulnerabilities within the **Transmission Control Protocol/Internet Protocol (TCP/IP)** stack. In the early days, during the creation of protocols and TCP/IP, security was not a concern. Cyber criminals and cyber terrorists wasn't even a thing, and the term *hacker* referred to a person who was a computer wizard and not what is known today, as a person with malicious intentions who uses a computer system to execute harmful tasks. As time passes and the technology evolves, there are more cyber threats each day.

The former CEO of Cisco Systems once said the following:

> *"There are two types of companies: those that have been hacked, and those who don't know they have been hacked."*

Each day, a new vulnerability is discovered in many systems around the world by many persons, whether they are a software developer, cyber security professional, threat hunter, malicious user, or hacker. We will start by exploring the various flaws a hacker can exploit at each layer of the TCP/IP stack to compromise a system or network, then we'll look at methods for securing the network infrastructure using a step-by-step approach.

In this chapter, we will be covering the following topics:

- Vulnerabilities on each layer of the TCP/IP stack
- Securing the TCP/IP stack using a **Defense in Depth (DiD)** approach

Let's begin!

Vulnerabilities at the Application Layer

The Application Layer of the TCP/IP stack consists of the **Application, Presentation,** and **Session** Layers of the OSI reference model. As we learned before, whenever a computer wants to send traffic (datagrams) to the network, the creation of the **Protocol Data Units (PDUs)** begins at the top of the TCP/IP stack, the Application Layer:

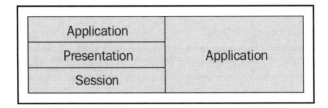

The following are some of the application layer protocols which we should pay close attention to on our network:

- **File Transfer Protocol (FTP)**
- Telnet
- **Secure Shell (SSH)**
- **Simple Mail Transfer Protocol (SMTP)**
- **Domain Name System (DNS)**
- **Dynamic Host Configuration Protocol (DHCP)**
- **Hypertext Transfer Protocol (HTTP)**

Each of these protocols was designed to provide the function it was built to do, and with a lesser focus on security. Malicious users and hackers are able to compromise both the application that utilizes these protocols and the network protocols themselves.

An example of an application is the **Seattle Lab Mail (SLMail)** 5.5 mail server, which has a known recorded vulnerability, *CVE-2003-0264*. According to the **Common Vulnerabilities and Exposure (CVE)** database (https://cve.mitre.org), CVE-2003-0264 is described as follows:

> *"Multiple buffer overflows in SLMail 5.1.0.4420 allow remote attackers to execute arbitrary code via (1) a long EHLO argument to slmail.exe, (2) a long XTRN argument to slmail.exe, (3) a long string to POPPASSWD, or (4) a long password to the POP3 server."*

This exploit takes advantage of the **Post Office Protocol (POP)** in the SLMail application.

Cross Site Scripting (XSS)

XSS focuses on exploiting a weakness in websites. In an XSS attack, the malicious user or hacker injects client-side scripts into a web page/site that a potential victim would trust. The scripts can be **JavaScript**, **VBScript**, **ActiveX**, and **HTML**, or even Flash (ActiveX), which will be executed on the victim's system. These scripts will be masked as legitimate requests between the web server and the client's browser.

XSS focuses on the following:

- Redirecting a victim to a malicious website/server
- Using hidden Iframes and pop-up messages on the victim's browser
- Data manipulation
- Data theft
- Session hijacking

Let's take a deeper look at what happens in an XSS attack:

1. An attacker injects malicious code into a web page/site that a potential victim trusts. A trusted site can be a favorite shopping website, social media platform, or school or university web portal.
2. A potential victim visits the trusted site. The malicious code interacts with the victim's web browser and executes. The web browser is usually unable to determine whether the scripts are malicious or not and therefore still executes the commands.
3. The malicious scripts can be used obtain cookie information, tokens, session information, and so on about other websites that the browser has stored information about.

4. The acquired details (cookies, tokens, sessions ID, and so on) are sent back to the hacker, who in turn uses them to log in to the sites that the victim's browser has visited:

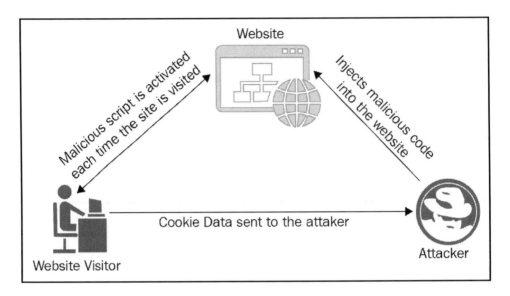

There are two types of XSS attacks:

- Stored XSS (persistent)
- Reflected (non-persistent)

Stored XSS (persistent): In this attack, the attacker injects a malicious script directly into the web application or a website. The script is stored permanently on the page, so when a potential victim visits the compromised page, the victim's web browser will parse all the code of the web page/application fine. Afterwards, the script is executed in the background without the victim's knowledge. At this point, the script is able to retrieve session cookies, passwords, and any other sensitive information stored in the user's web browser, and sends the loot back to the attacker in the background.

Reflective XSS (non-persistent): In this attack, the attacker usually sends an email with the malicious link to the victim. When the victim clicks the link, it is opened in the victim's web browser (reflected), and at this point the malicious script is invoked and begins to retrieve the loot (passwords, credit card numbers, and so on) stored in the victim's web browser.

SQL injection (SQLi)

SQLi attacks focus on parsing SQL commands into an SQL database that does not validate the user input. The attacker attempts to gain unauthorized access to a database either by creating or retrieving information stored in the database application. Nowadays, attackers are not only interested in gaining access, but also in retrieving (stealing) information and selling it to others for financial gain.

SQLi can be used to implement the following:

- **Authentication bypass**: Allows the attacker to log in to a system without a valid user credential
- **Information disclosure**: Retrieves confidential information from the database
- **Compromise data integrity**: The attacker is able to manipulate information stored in the database

Lightweight Directory Access Protocol (LDAP) injection

In `Chapter 2`, *Network Ports, Protocols, and Topologies,* we mentioned the purpose of LDAP. Just to recap briefly, LDAP is designed to query and update directory services, such as a database like Microsoft Active Directory. LDAP uses both TCP and UDP port `389` and LDAP uses port `636`. In an LDAP injection attack, the attacker exploits the vulnerabilities within a web application that constructs LDAP messages or statements, which are based on the user input. If the receiving application does not validate or sanitize the user input, this increases the possibility of manipulating LDAP messages.

Cross-Site Request Forgery (CSRF)

This attack is a bit similar to the previously mentioned XSS attack. In a CSRF attack, the victim machine/browser is forced to execute malicious actions against a website with which the victim has been authenticated (a website that trusts the actions of the user).

To have a better understanding of how this attack works, let's visualize a potential victim, **Bob**. On a regular day, Bob visits some of his favorite websites, such as various blogs, social media platforms, and so on, where he usually logs in automatically to view the content. Once Bob logs in to a particular website, the website would automatically trust the transactions between itself and the authenticated user, Bob. One day, he receives an email from the attacker but unfortunately Bob does not realize the email is a phishing/spam message and clicks on the link within the body of the message. His web browser opens the malicious URL in a new tab:

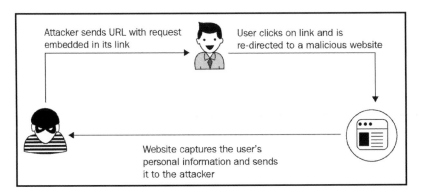

The attack would cause Bob's machine/web browser to invoke malicious actions on the trusted website; the website would see all the requests are originating from Bob. The return traffic such as the loot (passwords, credit card details, user account, and so on) would be returned to the attacker.

Session hijacking

When a user visits a website, a cookie is stored in the user's web browser. Cookies are used to track the user's preferences and manage the session while the user is on the site. While the user is on the website, a session ID is also set within the cookie, and this information may be persistent, which allows a user to close the web browser and then later revisit the same website and automatically log in.

However, the web developer can set how long the information is persistent for, whether it expires after an hour or a week, depending on the developer's preference. In a session hijacking attack, the attacker can attempt to obtain the session ID while it is being exchanged between the potential victim and the website. The attacker can then use this session ID of the victim on the website, and this would allow the attacker to gain access to the victim's session, further allowing access to the victim's user account and so on.

Cookie poisoning

As mentioned previously, a cookie stores information about a user's preferences while he/she is visiting a website. **Cookie poisoning** is when an attacker has modified a victim's cookie, which will then be used to gain confidential information about the victim such as his/her identity.

DNS

During the course of this book, we've mentioned DNS a couple of times and we saw how DNS can be used to help us reach various devices and websites more easily, by simply specifying the host name. Just as technologies and protocols advance, hackers always seem to find a way to use these good technologies for bad purposes and cyber-crimes.

Distributed Denial-of-Service (DDoS)

A DDoS attack can occur against a DNS server. Attacker sometimes target **Internet Service Providers (ISPs)** networks, public and private **Domain Name System (DNS)** servers, and so on to prevent other legitimate users from accessing the service. If a DNS server is unable to handle the amount of requests coming into the server, its performance will eventually begin to degrade gradually, until it either stops responding or crashes. This would result in a **Denial-of-Service (DoS)** attack.

Registrar hijacking

Whenever a person wants to purchase a domain, the person has to complete the registration process at a domain registrar. Attackers do try to compromise users accounts on various domain registrar websites in the hope of taking control of the victim's domain names. With a domain name, multiple DNS records can be created or modified to direct incoming requests to a specific device. If a hacker modifies the **A** record on a domain to redirect all traffic to a compromised or malicious server, anyone who visits the compromised domain will be redirected to the malicious website.

Cache poisoning

Whenever a user visits a website, there's the process of resolving a host name to an IP address which occurs in the background. The resolved data is stored within the local system in a cache area. The attacker can compromise this temporary storage area and manipulate any further resolution done by the local system.

Typosquatting

McAfee (`https://securingtomorrow.mcafee.com`) outlined typosquatting, also known as **URL hijacking**, as a type of cyber-attack that allows an attacker to create a domain name very close to a company's legitimate domain name in the hope of tricking victims into visiting the fake website to either steal their personal information or distribute a malicious payload to the victim's system.

Let's take a look at a simple example of this type of attack. In this scenario, we have a user, Bob, who frequently uses the Google search engine to find his way around the internet. Since Bob uses the `www.google.com` website often, he sets it as his homepage on the web browser so each time he opens the application or clicks the Home icon, `www.google.com` is loaded onto the screen. One day Bob decides to use another computer, and the first thing he does is set his favorite search engine URL as his home page. However, he typed `www.gooogle.com` and didn't realized it. Whenever Bob visits this website, it looks like the real website. Since the domain was able to be resolved to a website, this is an example of how *typosquatting* works.

It's always recommended to use a trusted search engine to find a URL for the website you want to visit. Trusted internet search engine companies focus on blacklisting malicious and fake URLs in their search results to help protect internet users such as yourself.

Vulnerabilities at the Transport Layer

In this section, we are going to discuss various weaknesses that exist within the underlying protocols of the Transport Layer.

Fingerprinting

Whenever a crime occurs, local authorities such as the police would conduct fingerprint analysis to determine, or narrow the scope of identifying, the perpetrator. In the cyber security world, fingerprinting is a bit similar on a computer platform. Fingerprinting is used to discover open ports and services that are running open on the target system. From a hacker's point of view, fingerprinting is done before the exploitation phase, as the more information a hacker can obtain about a target, the hacker can then narrow its attack scope and use specific tools to increase the chances of successfully compromising the target machine.

However, fingerprinting isn't always used by hackers or those with malicious intent. This technique is also used by system/network administrators, network security engineers, and cyber security professionals alike. Imagine you're a network administrator assigned to secure a server; apart from applying system hardening techniques such as patching and configuring access controls, you would also need to check for any open ports that are not being used. As mentioned in `Chapter 2`, *Network Ports, Protocols, and Topologies*, each network protocol running at the Application Layer of the TCP/IP stack binds itself with a logical port within the operating system to accept incoming traffic.

Let's take a look at a more practical approach to fingerprinting in the computing world. We have a target machine, `10.10.10.100`, on our network. As a hacker or a network security professional, we would like to know which TCP and UDP ports are open, the services that use the open ports, and the service daemon running on the target system. In the following screenshot, we've used `nmap` to help us discover the information we are seeking. The NMap tools delivers specially crafted probes to a target machine:

```
root@kali:~# nmap -sV 10.10.10.100
Starting Nmap 7.70 ( https://nmap.org ) at 2018-11-09 15:33 EST
Nmap scan report for 10.10.10.100
Host is up (0.00026s latency).
Not shown: 977 closed ports
PORT      STATE  SERVICE    VERSION
21/tcp    open   ftp        vsftpd 2.3.4
22/tcp    open   ssh        OpenSSH 4.7p1 Debian 8ubuntu1 (protocol 2.0)
23/tcp    open   telnet     Linux telnetd
25/tcp    open   smtp       Postfix smtpd
53/tcp    open   domain     ISC BIND 9.4.2
80/tcp    open   http       Apache httpd 2.2.8 ((Ubuntu) DAV/2)
```

Enumeration

In a cyber attack, the hacker uses enumeration techniques to extract information about the target system or network. This information will aid the attacker in identifying system attack points. The following are the various network services and ports that stand out for a hacker:

- Port `53`: DNS zone transfer and DNS enumeration
- Port `135`: Microsoft RPC Endpoint Mapper
- Port `25`: **Simple Mail Transfer Protocol (SMTP)**

DNS enumeration

DNS enumeration is where an attacker is attempting to determine whether there are other servers or devices that carry the domain name of an organization. Let's take a look at how DNS enumeration works. Imagine we are trying to find out all the publicly available servers Google has on the internet. Using the `host` utility in Linux and specifying a host name, `host www.google.com`, we can see the IP address `172.217.6.196` has been resolved successfully. This means there's a device with a host name of `www.google.com` active. Furthermore, if we attempt to resolve the host name, `gmail.google.com`, another IP address is presented but when we attempt to resolve `mx.google.com`, no IP address is given. This is an indication that there isn't an active device with the `mx.google.com` host name:

```
root@kali:~# host www.google.com
www.google.com has address 172.217.6.196
www.google.com has IPv6 address 2607:f8b0:4006:800::2004
root@kali:~# host gmail.google.com
gmail.google.com is an alias for www3.l.google.com.
www3.l.google.com has address 172.217.7.14
www3.l.google.com has IPv6 address 2607:f8b0:4006:819::200e
root@kali:~# host mx.google.com
Host mx.google.com not found: 3(NXDOMAIN)
```

DNS zone transfer

DNS zone transfer allows the copying of the master file from a DNS server to another DNS server. There are times when administrators do not configure the security settings on their DNS server properly, which allows an attacker to retrieve the master file containing a list of the names and addresses of a corporate network.

Microsoft RPC Endpoint Mapper

Not too long ago, CVE-2015-2370 was recorded on the CVE database at `https://cve.mitre.org`. This vulnerability took advantage of the authentication implementation of the **Remote Procedure Call (RPC)** protocol in various versions of the Microsoft Windows platform, both desktop and server operating systems. A successful exploit would allow an attacker to gain local privileges on a vulnerable system.

A detailed list of operating systems can be found on Microsoft's website at the following URL: `https://docs.microsoft.com/en-us/security-updates/securitybulletins/2015/ms15-076`. Further information on the CVE-2015-2370 vulnerability can be found at `https://cve.mitre.org/cgi-bin/cvename.cgi?name=CVE-2015-2370`.

SMTP

SMTP is used in mail servers, as with the POP and the **Internet Message Access Protocol (IMAP)**. As mentioned in `Chapter 2`, *Network Ports, Protocols, and Topologies*, SMTP is used for sending mail, while POP and IMAP are used to retrieve mail from an email server. SMTP supports various commands, such as `EXPN` and `VRFY`. The `EXPN` command can be used to verify whether a particular mailbox exists on a local system, while the `VRFY` command can be used to validate a username on a mail server.

An attacker can establish a connection between the attacker's machine and the mail server on port 25. Once a successful connection has been established, the server will send a banner back to the attacker's machine displaying the server name and the status of the port (open). Once this occurs, the attacker can then use the `VRFY` command followed by a user name to check for a valid user on the mail system using the `VRFY bob` syntax.

SYN flooding

One of the protocols that exist at the Transport Layer is TCP. TCP is used to establish a connection-oriented session between two devices that want to communication or exchange data. Let's recall how TCP works. There are two devices that want to exchange some messages, Bob and Alice. Bob sends a TCP **Synchronization (SYN)** packet to Alice, and Alice responds to Bob with a TCP **Synchronization/Acknowledgment (SYN/ACK)** packet. Finally, Bob replies with a TCP **Acknowledgement (ACK)** packet. The following diagram shows the **TCP 3-Way Handshake** mechanism:

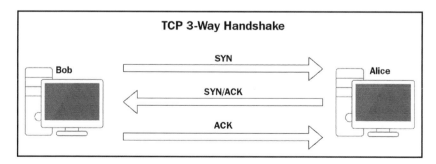

To further understand how TCP functions, please refer to `Chapter 2,` *Network Ports, Protocols, and Topologies.*

For every TCP SYN packet received on a device, a TCP ACK packet must be sent back in response. One type of attack that takes advantage of this design flaw in TCP is known as a **SYN Flood attack**. In a SYN Flood attack, the attacker sends a continuous stream of TCP SYN packets to a target system. This would cause the target machine to process each individual packet and response accordingly; eventually, with the high influx of TCP SYN packets, the target system will become too overwhelmed and stop responding to any requests:

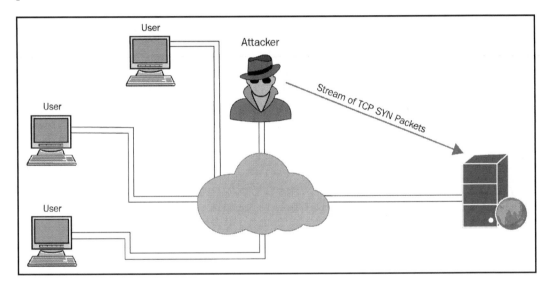

TCP reassembly and sequencing

During a TCP transmission of datagrams between two devices, each packet is tagged with a sequence number by the sender. This sequence number is used to reassemble the packets back into data. During the transmission of packets, each packet may take a different path to the destination. This may cause the packets to be received in an out-of-order fashion, or in the order they were sent over the wire by the sender.

An attacker can attempt to guess the sequencing numbers of packets and inject malicious packets into the network destined for the target. When the target receives the packets, the receiver would assume they came from the real sender as they would contain the appropriate sequence numbers and a spoofed IP address.

Vulnerabilities at the Internet Layer

The Internet Layer (TCP/IP stack) and the Network Layer (OSI model) are where the **Internet Protocol (IP)** resides. The Internet Layer and the Network Layer are responsible for IPv4 and IPv6 addressing, and routing IP packets; various routing protocols such as **Routing Information Protocol (RIP)**, **Open Shortest Path First (OSPF)**, **Intermediate System-Intermediate System (IS-IS)**, **Enhanced Interior Gateway Routing Protocol (EIGRP)**, and **Border Gateway Protocol (BGP)** operates here. There are many weaknesses/flaws which an attacker can leverage by simply exploiting the design of the **Internet Protocol (IP)**. In this section, we will take a look at a few notable ones.

Route spoofing

Route spoofing is where an attacker attempts to inject fake routes into the routing table of a device. The routing table is used as a forwarding database for a local device such as a computer, multiple layer switch, router or firewall to determine a path for sending traffic to a specific destination. If an attacker has successfully injected spoofed/fake routes into a target device, this will cause the victim machine to re-route its outgoing network traffic to another path, which may allow the attacker to intercept it.

On a Windows system, to view the routing table, simply use the `route print` command in Command Prompt:

```
IPv4 Route Table
===========================================================================
Active Routes:
Network Destination        Netmask          Gateway       Interface  Metric
          0.0.0.0          0.0.0.0     172.16.17.18    172.16.17.8     35
        127.0.0.0        255.0.0.0         On-link         127.0.0.1    331
        127.0.0.1  255.255.255.255         On-link         127.0.0.1    331
  127.255.255.255  255.255.255.255         On-link         127.0.0.1    331
      172.16.17.0    255.255.255.0         On-link       172.16.17.8    291
      172.16.17.8  255.255.255.255         On-link       172.16.17.8    291
    172.16.17.255  255.255.255.255         On-link       172.16.17.8    291
        224.0.0.0        240.0.0.0         On-link         127.0.0.1    331
        224.0.0.0        240.0.0.0         On-link       172.16.17.8    291
  255.255.255.255  255.255.255.255         On-link         127.0.0.1    331
  255.255.255.255  255.255.255.255         On-link       172.16.17.8    291
===========================================================================
```

To view the routing table of a Cisco IOS router, you can use the `show ip route` command, as shown in the following screenshot:

```
R1.TT#show ip route
Codes: L - local, C - connected, S - static, R - RIP, M - mobile, B - BGP
       D - EIGRP, EX - EIGRP external, O - OSPF, IA - OSPF inter area
       N1 - OSPF NSSA external type 1, N2 - OSPF NSSA external type 2
       E1 - OSPF external type 1, E2 - OSPF external type 2, E - EGP
       i - IS-IS, L1 - IS-IS level-1, L2 - IS-IS level-2, ia - IS-IS inter area
       * - candidate default, U - per-user static route, o - ODR
       P - periodic downloaded static route

Gateway of last resort is not set

      192.168.1.0/24 is variably subnetted, 2 subnets, 2 masks
C        192.168.1.0/24 is directly connected, GigabitEthernet0/0
L        192.168.1.1/32 is directly connected, GigabitEthernet0/0
      192.168.2.0/24 is variably subnetted, 2 subnets, 2 masks
C        192.168.2.0/24 is directly connected, GigabitEthernet0/1
L        192.168.2.1/32 is directly connected, GigabitEthernet0/1
```

However, it is recommended to ensure **route authentication** is turned on between routers that are participating in RIP, EIGRP, OSPF, and BGP routing. It is a good practice to ensure only authenticated routing information is exchanged between peer routers on a network.

 Authentication does not provide encryption.

IP address spoofing

An IP spoofing attack is where an attacker modifies the source IP address of traffic originating from his/her machine. The purpose of this attack is to either mask the attacker's identity and make the attack seem to originate from another source, or causes a reflective attack as described in the *Reflective* section in `Chapter 11`, *Network Security Concepts*.

Both IPv4 and IPv6 are vulnerable to IP spoofing attacks and the protocols that use the IP.

Internet Control Message Protocol (ICMP)

ICMP is a very helpful protocol that helps network professionals to determine whether there are any issues in a network segment and their possible causes. Even though one of the main functions of this protocol is to aid systems and networking professionals in their troubleshooting and diagnostics when checking connectivity on a network, this very protocol can be used for malicious activities by an attacker.

DoS vulnerability in ICMP

In 2004, a DoS security vulnerability was published by the **National Vulnerability Database** (`https://nvd.nist.gov`) with the ID CVE-2004-1060. This recorded security vulnerability allowed an attacker to cause a reduction in network performance by sending unsolicited and fake ICMP packets with a low next-hop **Maximum Transmission Unit** (**MTU**) value.

Further details of the CVE-2004-1060 vulnerabilities can be found at `https://nvd.nist.gov/vuln/detail/CVE-2004-1060`.

Smurf attack

A Smurf attack is a form of DDoS attack that takes advantage of the ICMP. In a Smurf attack, the attacker sends a continuous stream of ICMP messages to an IP network using an IP broadcast address as the destination, while spoofing the IP address of the potential victim's machine as the source IP address. Therefore, each device that receives an ICMP message from the attacker with the spoofed IP address will attempt to respond. If there are a lot of devices on the broadcast network, they all will be replying to the spoofed packets. This will result in a DDoS attack on the victim.

Teardrop attack

A teardrop attack is another type of DoS attack. It leverages the design flaw in the TCP/IP fragmentation reassembly process. In a teardrop attack, the attacker sends fragments of packets to a potential victim. As noted on older operating systems such as Windows 3.1 x, Windows 95, Windows NT, and versions of the Linux kernel 2.1.63, the receiving machine cannot reassemble the packets due to a bug in TCP/IP fragmentation reassembly. Since the receiving system cannot reassemble the packet, the packets will eventually begin to overlap each other, the host operating system will not be able to handle this type of fragmentation, and it will crash.

Ping of Death (PoD)

In a PoD attack, the attacker sends a specially crafted ping packet greater than 65,536 bytes to a victim machine. Since TCP/IP supports fragmentation of packets across a network, a malicious user is able to take advantage of this feature by breaking down a packet of 65,536 or more bytes into smaller pieces; this would allow the attacker to send these smaller pieces to a victim. When the victim's machine reassembles the pieces, many operating systems won't know how to process this large packet and will either freeze, reboot, or crash. This is another form of DoS attack.

Vulnerabilities at the Network Access/Link Layer

In this section, we will take a look at various vulnerabilities that exist at the Network Access/Link layer of the TCP/IP stack. As you learned in a previous chapter, the Network Access/Link Layer of the TCP/IP stack has the equivalence of the both the Data Link and Physical Layers of the OSI reference model:

OSI Model	TCP/IP Stack
Data Link	Network Access/Link
Physical	

As we learned in the early parts of this book, the Data Link Layer (layer 2) is responsible for the error checking, reassembly of frames, delivery of frames, **Media Access Control** (**MAC**) addressing, flow control of frames as they are sent and received on the network. The Physical Layer (layer 1) is responsible for the electrical and mechanical functions: for delivering the bits from one device to another. As the name suggests, the Physical Layer is the physical media used for transmission of the bits, such as the cables, hubs, radio frequency, and so on.

We will group the vulnerabilities under the Data Link and the Physical Layers of the OSI reference model.

Data Link Layer

Here, we discuss the vulnerabilities that affect the Data Link Layer.

Address Resolution Protocol (ARP) poisoning

The ARP was designed to resolve IP address to MAC addresses on a network. As we discussed earlier, all devices on a **Local Area Network** (**LAN**) use MAC addresses for communication between one device and another. However, there are times when a device has only the IP address of its destination; in this situation, the sender device would send an ARP request out on the LAN, and if a device has the IP address contained in the ARP request message, it responds with its MAC address. The IP is now bound to the MAC address in the local ARP cache of the sender.

To view the ARP cache of a Windows system, you can use the `arp -a` command.

An attacker may attempt to modify the ARP cache of a victim's machine by sending a **Gratuitous ARP** with an update containing a change to the MAC address of an existing entry within the victim's ARP cache. If the change is successful on the victim's machine, any traffic destined for the IP address will now be sent to the device that has the new MAC address specified in the Gratuitous ARP message. This would allow the attacker to either intercept traffic or re-route the victim's traffic on the network.

Sniffing

Sniffing is the monitoring of data packets as they pass through the network or between devices. A Sniffer is usually a software/application that has the ability to present raw network traffic as human-readable information for analysis. Sniffers are used by both the good guys and the bad guys. The good guys, such as network engineers, use a sniffer to help determine any problems on a network. A security engineer would use a sniffer to monitor network traffic for any type of security intrusion, such as malware traversing the network. However, an attacker would use a sniffer to determine the types of services that are being used on a victim's network and to find any confidential or sensitive information passing across the network.

Broadcast storms

A broadcast storm is an extremely concentrated amount of broadcast traffic being flooded either by one or multiple devices on a network. Each device on a network receives a broadcast message and processes it accordingly. Imagine there are hundreds of people within a single room (network) and everyone is shouting at another person (broadcasting); no one in the room will be able to process and communicate properly as there would be a lot overhead to process and noise. This is how a broadcast storm works on a network; eventually, after a few minutes, the network's performance will degrade gradually and it may eventually become crippled.

VLAN hopping

As mentioned in `Chapter 11`, *Network Security Concepts*, VLAN hopping allows an attacker to access the network resources and traffic of other VLANs that would normally be inaccessible. VLAN hopping attacks occur on switches with their physical ports configured to convert into a trunk port automatically. A trunk allows multiple VLAN traffic to pass across simultaneously. The Cisco **Dynamic Trunking Protocol** (**DTP**) is susceptible to VLAN hopping attacks. The attacker can established a physical connection to a switch and inject specially crafted **IEEE 802.1Q** frames into the switch port; if auto-trunking is enabled, the port will be converted into a trunk. This would then allow the attacker to access all VLANs on the network.

Physical Layer

Here, we will outline and discuss various vulnerabilities at the Physical Layer.

Wiretapping

Wiretapping is a type of sniffing that involves the monitoring of a telephone system and internet conversations. This allows an attacker to actively or passively monitor, intercept, and record any conversations on the wire. Wiretapping is done by placing a physical component inline, on the telephone wire or the network cable.

Other physical issues

The other physical issues are as follows:

- **Cable cutting**: The cutting of network cables can definitely cause a network outage, which will result in a physical form of DoS for legitimate users on a network.
- **Power instabilities**: Power outages are a critical concern for a business's daily operations. If a device's power supply blows out, the device will be down until the power supply is replaced. If the building loses power, all components will lose power. However, a lot of companies invest in **uninterruptible power supply (UPS)** for their core and mission critical network appliances and servers. A UPS can supply power to a component for a very short period of time. Therefore, a backup generator is recommended to counteract a power outage in a building or compound. Another type of power instability is an electrical surge, which can short out or blow electrical components. Using a power surge protector or an **automatic voltage regulator (AVR)** can protect network appliances from such abnormal spikes in electrical current.

Securing TCP/IP using a DiD approach

As mentioned in a previous chapter, one of the most valuable assets within an organization is their data. Some organizations are proactive in implementing cyber security controls and appliances to actively monitor and mitigate any threats to their network infrastructure, both internally and externally, while there are some organizations that believe they are safe without any network security appliances, a cyber-security team, or even being concerned about investing in improving their cyber security posture. One important point to note as a cyber-security or network security professional is that no matter how many network security appliances are currently deployed within a network, or how secure they are configured to restrict traffic, no network is 100% safe. This is due to advancements in cyber threats every day. One of the most critical threats is the **Advanced Persistence Threat** (**APT**), which is extremely stealthy and is challenging to detect.

In this section, we will focus on discussing various security controls and countermeasure techniques, which can be applied at each layer of the TCP/IP stack to reduce the risk of being a victim of a cyber-attack.

One of the most important questions we seldom ask ourselves is *how do we start locking down our network?* I would definitely recommend using a systematic approach when applying network security practices on a system or a network. Let's take a look back at the OSI reference model and the TCP/IP stack as a side-by-side comparison in helping us to decide on the best approach:

OSI Model	TCP/IP Stack
Application	Application
Presentation	
Session	
Transport	Transport
Network	Internet
Data Link	Network Access/Link
Physical	

You can begin to lock down your systems and network infrastructure using the following approaches:

- Top-down
- Bottom-top

Whenever a network professional is troubleshooting an issue, he/she usually applies one of these approaches. In applying network security, the approach is quite similar:

- **Top-down approach**: Using the top-down approach, a security administrator would apply threat mitigation techniques and countermeasures, starting at the Application Layer of the TCP/IP and working his/her way down to the Network Access/Link Layer. This approach is quite useful as it focuses on protecting the resources that are closest to the end user.
- **Bottom-top approach**: Rather than starting at the top of the TCP/IP stack or the OSI model, this approach starts at layer 1. Securing the Physical Layer is quite important as it will lead to the discovery of any unauthorized components connected to the network infrastructure, such as an **evil twin** access point.

Mitigating security threats

To get started securing an organization's network, one much first identify the assets of the company. Assets can be categorized into the following:

- Tangible
- Intangible
- Employees

Tangible assets are the physical components, such as computers, appliances, furniture, software licenses, and so on. **Intangible** assets are considered to be information resources such as financial accounting data, patents, and intellectual property. Lastly, we must not forget to protect our employees. Our employees are very valuable, as they are the ones who build trust and relationships with the clients, and they are the ones who have the experience within their departments and fields to get the job done right. Protecting our employees means providing training in various cyber security domains to ensure they are aware of indications of a security attack, threats, and potential incidents. This process will help identify critical and valuable resources, and reduce the risks of a cyber-attack.

Implement a next-generation firewall

A next-generation firewall has the capabilities of monitoring and filtering traffic at all layers of the TCP/IP protocol stack. Using a next-generation firewall has many benefits, such as the following:

- Built-in **Intrusion Prevention System (IPS)**
- **Virtual Private Network (VPN)** capabilities
- Botnet filtering
- APT filtering
- Prevent zero-day breakouts
- Deep packet inspection
- Malware and ransomware prevention

It's recommended for all organizations of any size and industry to implement a next-generation firewall at their network perimeter. A traditional, stateful filtering firewall isn't powerful enough to prevent the modern day threats that exist in the cyber security world. Each day, new threats are emerging; nowadays, hackers are not really as considerate about causing a disruption in service as a few years ago; now, they are interested in stealing the most valuable asset a company has, its data. Hence the rise of ransomware malware, which has hit the world quite hard over the past few years.

Implement an IPS

Another type of security appliance is an IPS. An IPS has the ability to detect and block attackers and other anomalies that other security appliances cannot find or have missed. Within an IPS, there are rules that govern how the appliance monitors and filters network traffic, and these rules can be customized by a security engineer to detect and stop certain activities that are of interest to a single organization. Since an IPS is usually placed behind a firewall, it blocks malicious traffic that was missed by the firewall appliance.

Implement Web Security Appliance (WSA)

Protecting our users also means providing web security for both outgoing and incoming traffic. A WSA is a web content security appliance that has the ability to mitigate threats, handles content filtering, and allow secure access to the web. When a user enters a URL in their web browser, data is sent to the WSA for further analysis and validation of the data, leaving the organization and the destination website/server. If the web traffic or website is harmful, the WSA will prevent the malicious traffic from entering the organization's network and restrict access to the malicious website/server.

Implementing Email Security Appliance

There are many types of threats for which attacker use email as their delivery platform; these threats are as follows:

- Spam
- Malware
- Phishing
- Spear-phishing

Using an Email Security Appliance will process both incoming and outgoing emails from an organization to help stop cyber-attacks that are delivered by email messaging. The incoming emails go through various processing and analysis stages, such as anti-spam filtering, antiviruses for virus detection, content filtering, and so on. The outgoing emails go through a very similar process to prevent any internally compromised systems within the organization from spreading malware or distributing any sort of threat.

Implement layer 2 security on switches

Securing layer 2, the switch network, is a very important aspect when implementing network security. Many people I've encountered within the IT industry, from IT techs to managers, have not realized the importance of securing a network using a layered approach, such as DiD. Having a next-generation firewall isn't going to stop all threats; what about preventing an insider threat, which a lot of us forget about? Over 90% of cyber-attacks happen from the inside, within a network, rather than originating from the internet.

The following are recommended network security practices:

- Applying **port security** on a switch's port will prevent a **Content Addressable Memory (CAM)** table overflow. CAM table has been mentioned in Chapter 3, *Ethernet.*
- Block all switch port negotiations to prevent an attacker from performing a VLAN hopping attack
- Remove all ports from VLAN 1 and do not use VLAN 1 for anything
- Implement **DHCP snooping** on the switches to prevent a malicious user or attacker from installing a rogue DHCP server on the network
- Implement **BPDU guard** to prevent an attacker from injecting specially crafted BPDU messages into a switch port to become the role of a root bridge
- Implement **Dynamic ARP Inspection (DAI)** to prevent ARP spoofing on the layer 2 network

Implement Virtual Private Networks (VPNs)

Implementing a VPN can help in protecting data in motion as it transits from one location to another. This will aid in preventing anyone who is attempting to eavesdrop on the network. A VPN allows secure access to a corporate network for members of staff who are traveling, work out in the field, or even work remotely.

Other important security checks

The other important security checks are as follows:

- Implement an **Authentication, Authorization, and Accounting (AAA)** server for user management on network and security appliances. AAA is used for central management of user accounts, privileges, policies, and log management in a single unified system.
- Train and educate employees to have a better understanding of cyber security.
- Install the latest updates to fix any bugs and security flaws in the software on a system.
- Keep regular backups of data in the event of a ransomware attack or system crash.
- Disable any unnecessary services on appliances and systems.
- Encrypt and apply passwords on sensitive data.
- Perform regular vulnerability assessments on the network infrastructure to determine risk rating and mitigation.
- Perform penetration testing regularly, both announced and unannounced, to find any hidden vulnerabilities on a system and network before a real attacker discovers and take advantage of them.

Summary

In this chapter, we took a look at many types of flaws within the TCP/IP stack, starting at the Application Layer and going down to the Network Access Layer. We saw how attackers can compromise a trusted website to simply steal sensitive data from the user's web browser, use ICMP to perform malicious activities, and create specially crafted TCP SYN packets that can be used to perform a DoS attack on the protocol and the system. Lastly, we've mentioned various cyber security appliances and controls that can be implemented to help prevent or mitigate these threats and attacks on a network, while protecting your assets in the organization.

In the next chapter, we will explore the topic of organizational security.

Questions

1. Using a VPN will assist in mitigating which of the following threats?
    1. Cross Site Scripting
    2. Cross Site Request Forgery
    3. Eavesdropping
    4. SMTP Enumeration

2. How can a network security professional prevent an unauthorized network device from gaining access to a network segment?
    1. Implement a firewall
    2. Implement port security
    3. Implement an IPS
    4. Implement a Web Security Appliance

3. Which layer of the OSI reference model does ARP spoofing occur at?
    1. Data Link
    2. Internet
    3. Network Access
    4. Network

4. Which type of network security appliance can prevent a zero-day attack?
    1. IPS
    2. Router
    3. VPN
    4. Firewall

5. An attacker is attempting to create a new user account on a database, which type of attack method is the attacker using on the system?
    1. Cross Site Scripting
    2. LDAP Injection
    3. SQL Injection
    4. CSRF

6. If an attacker is able to retrieve the master file containing all the records of an internal network or a DNS server, which type of attack is taking place?
    1. DNS Zone Transfer
    2. DNS Poisoning
    3. DNS Hijacking
    4. DNS lookup

13
Organizational Security

Within the field of networking, there will always be a bit of discussion regarding security. Most of the time, when we think of security, we think about locking down our network infrastructure by implementing various preventative measures and practices. We discussed these in the previous chapters. We must not forget about the topic at hand: organizational security.

Organizational security focuses a bit more on evaluating risks, implementing technical risk controls, and operational risk controls within a company. In this chapter, we will focus on the aspects that are aligned with CompTIA Network+ training.

The following topics will be covered in this chapter:

- Physical security
- Prevention techniques
- Authentication concepts

Let's begin!

Physical security

In your studies in the field of **Information Technology** (**IT**), there will be times during the discussion of security when the topic of physical security will be introduced. This is because it is just as important as digital/cyber security. In this section, we will discuss various physical security deterrents and prevention techniques for organizations.

Video surveillance

Often, you'll see surveillance cameras around an organization's premises or a residential property. These cameras are often interconnected to create a **Closed Circuit Television** (**CCTV**) network. Modern CCTV systems are now IP-based, which allows the video traffic media to be digitized and pass through an Ethernet network. This means that all of the video footage will be accessible through a single or multiple monitors.

These video surveillance cameras can be placed in areas that require constant monitoring; however, a CCTV system does not prevent intrusion, but rather acts as a deterrent. These cameras have various features—some have night vision, which gives them the capability to view objects in very low lighting or dark areas, while some have depth of field, which provides a focus range that detects whether something is near or far.

When placing cameras, one of the primary factors to consider the coverage of the area or the compound that you are monitoring. This might be a challenging task since cameras can't see around corners, and there may be some blind spots. In these situations, better placement of cameras is needed, or even more physical cameras on the site.

Some surveillance cameras are able to send alerts, stating that movement has been detection within the focal view of the camera. This is a benefit as you'll be notified of any movements within an area by the motion detection feature.

Asset-tracking tags

Within many organizations, the management team usually introduces asset management, a system for tagging company-owned equipment. This equipment could be network appliances such as switches, routers, cables, modems, and even end devices, such as laptops, printers, servers, and so on. These asset tags have unique tracking numbers that are associated with an inventory listing of components that belong to the company. Asset-tracking tags create a database of all the tag's components within the organization, where each tagged item has a list of important records such as model number, serial number, purchase date, location, and so on.

Sometimes, organizations use a bar code rather than a number, which makes it a bit simpler to check-in or check-out of a building.

Tamper detection

As an organization grows, there will be times where tracking and monitoring physical assets becomes a challenge. Having a tamper detection system implemented on a device will notify the administrator if someone has attempted unauthorized tampering. Some BIOS have alert systems, and networking appliances and servers have case sensors, which can detect if their cases are being removed.

Prevention techniques

In this section, we will discuss various prevention techniques.

Badges

ID badges are unique and are assigned to the employees of an organization. Each ID badge has a picture of the employee, their name clearly printed, and any other relevant details such as department or job title within the organization. Some organizations use smart cards, which they integrate in their physical security systems. Smart cards provide more features than a regular ID badge. These smart cards can be swiped through readers as an additional form of identification to access restricted areas.

A very important technique is to ensure that all employees are trained in their relevant areas of understanding and that they adhere to the organization's security policies. One type of training would be to train employees to be observant of anyone who is not wearing a company-issued ID badge and inquire about the abnormality.

Biometrics

Another form of authentication method is the use of biometrics. This is usually something that is on your body/person such as a fingerprint, iris, face, or voice. A biometric system stores a digitized version of your face, fingerprint, iris, or voice on the system. Biometrics is one of the best methods to ensure that a person can prove who they are. It's simple to change a password on a user's account, but you can't change a fingerprint on a person's finger.

Security tokens

A security token is an external device that can assist in proving your identity to a system. An example is the **Google Authenticator** application for smart phones. Many websites are enabling multi-factor authentication to improve the security of user accounts. After a user has entered their username and password on a website, the user is then prompted to enter their code from the Google Authenticator app, and this code changes frequently. If the user is unable to provide a valid code, access is not granted to the account.

Other types of security tokens are as follows:

- Smart card
- USB token—stores a digital certificate
- Key fobs—a hardware-based token such as the **Battle.net Authenticator** from Blizzard
- SMS—a code is sent to your mobile number

Locks

One of the most common forms of physical security is the use of a traditional door lock, which uses a key to open and lock the door. Another is a deadbolt, which is much stronger than traditional door locks, as it contains a physical bolt. Sometimes, you'll see electronic locks, which require a PIN to access the restricted area. This is a type of key-less entry. Other organizations use token-based systems such as RFID systems, in which the RFID card just needs to be within the proximity of the sensor to be activated.

Authentication concepts

Authorization, Authentication, and Accounting (AAA) is not a protocol, but a framework for ensuring access controls on a network by assigning policies and enabling the logging of activities. Authentication handles the mechanisms used to ensure that someone can prove their identity on a system before gaining access to the resource, such as providing a username (identity) and password combination. Authorization handles the assignment of privileges and policies to an authenticated user. Lastly, accounting is applied, which ensures that logs are generated for each action that is performed by the user.

Remote Authentication Dial-In User Service (RADIUS)

RADIUS is a client-server protocol that provides AAA services. RADIUS is supported on a wide range of network appliances, devices, and operating systems. A RADIUS server can be implemented on the network and is centrally accessible by all devices. This ensures that users are able to log in to their devices and systems.

A network may contain a lot of switches, routers, servers, **network access control** (**NAC**) servers, and firewalls, where user accounts would exist. Using a RADIUS server, all accounts can be centrally managed, policies can be applied, and logs can be created for the actions of each user.

Terminal Access Controller Access Control System (TACACS)

TACACS is another protocol that is similar to RADIUS, but this protocol is used on the older dial-up lines. Cisco created a proprietary version called **Extended TACACS** (**XTACACS**), which has additional features that add auditing and accounting functionality to the protocol. TACACS+ is the current version of the protocol and is not backward compatible with the other versions. TACACS+ is an open standard that utilizes the AAA framework.

Kerberos

Kerberos is a network authentication protocol that allows a user to log in once and gain access to all the resources the network has to offer without the user having to log in each time to access a different resource. In other words, the user is authenticated once and is trusted by the system. Therefore, they don't need to authenticate again to access another resource. Kerberos is an old protocol that was created by **Massachusetts Institute of Technology** (**MIT**) and is defined by RFC 4120.

 Kerberos is implemented in Microsoft systems.

Multi-Factor Authentication (MFA)

Most of the time, whenever we log in to a website, we provide our identity, that is, our username and a password, to authenticate with the site. If a hacker gains possession of your user account credentials, then your account is compromised. By adding an additional layer of security during the authentication phase, it makes it harder for an attacker to gain access. This is called MFA.

During MFA, the user enters their username and password, and if the account is found on the system, it prompts the user to enter one or more of the following:

- Something you know
- Something you have
- Something you are
- Somewhere you are
- Something you do

Afterward, the system will grant the user access to the resources.

The following are examples of each of the preceding factors:

- Something you know can be a password or PIN
- Something you have can be a token, such as a USB token or smart card
- Something you are can be a biometric, such as your fingerprint
- Somewhere you are can be a GPS location, such as being within the proximity range of a sensor
- Something you do can be something unique to you, such as a signature

Summary

As we have seen throughout this chapter, security is very important—not only in the digital world, but also in the physical world—to protect an organization's assets from potential intruders. We've discussed various physical controls that focus on detection and prevention. Then, we took a look at various authentication protocols that can be useful on a medium to large network infrastructure.

In the next chapter, we will be covering network troubleshooting methodology.

Questions

1. You would like to keep track of components within your organization. Which of the following would you use?
    1. CCTV
    2. Asset tags
    3. Tamper detection
    4. Badges

2. You would like to implement a technique that will indicate whether an employee has attempted to remove any tagging on the components. Which of the following would you use?
    1. CCTV
    2. Asset tags
    3. Tamper detection
    4. Badges

3. The IT department has implemented a lot of network appliances throughout the organization. The IT manager thinks that creating an unique account separately on each appliance is a bit tedious. Which of the following can they use to make the process easier?
    1. AAA
    2. RADIUS
    3. **Two-Factor Authentication (2FA)**
    4. Security token

4. Which of the following operating systems mostly uses Kerberos?
    1. Microsoft Windows
    2. Linux
    3. Unix
    4. macOS

5. Which of the following versions of TACACS is not backward compatible?
    1. TACACS
    2. TACACS+
    3. XTACACS
    4. ITACACS

14

Troubleshooting a Network

In this chapter, we will utilize all of the knowledge that you have garnered in the previous chapters in order to illustrate the entire network troubleshooting methodology. We will examine common hardware and software tools that are utilized to gather data on issues, and also discuss some everyday problems that plague both wired and wireless networks. Lastly, we will explore a number of typical network service issues that are prevalent across many networks. This chapter will aid you in connecting the concepts you've learned throughout this book to the real-life issues you'll face in administering a network, allowing you to quickly and confidently diagnose and resolve many of these issues.

In this chapter, we will cover the following topics:

- Network troubleshooting methodologies
- Troubleshooting tools
- Common issues on wired and wireless networks
- Network service issues

Let's get started!

Proper network troubleshooting methodology

Proper network troubleshooting follows a systematic approach. Rather than guessing solutions to problems based on scant information and random theories, network administrators who follow a proper troubleshooting methodology perform a specific, organized process that helps them to be more efficient in their problem-solving operations. In this section, we will discuss this methodology.

The first step in troubleshooting any network issue is to properly identify the problem that has arisen. In many instances, network administrators are presented with symptoms of the problem, through reports from other users, from automated reports by monitoring software, or from their own observations. Often, these symptoms do not provide all of the information on the issue. It is therefore essential for the administrator to gather as much data as possible regarding the problem. By gathering this additional data, administrators are able to better understand the root cause of the issue, and determine whether a single issue exists on the network, or whether the symptoms relate to multiple problems, which need to be segmented and worked on individually. Additional data can be gathered from devices involved in the issue, from log files in log management software, and from other reports stored either locally on the device or on remote management software. Data may also be gathered by questioning users involved in the issue, by attempting to duplicate the issue (while observing the network more closely), or by assessing what changes have been implemented on the network recently.

Once sufficient data has been gathered in relation to the problem that has manifested itself on the network, the administrator must then utilize the data they have gathered to establish a theory of probable cause or, in other words, to make an educated assumption about the cause of the issue. In establishing this theory, it is important not to overlook any of the obvious possible causes of the issue. Many issues that may appear complex at first glance may be caused by simple occurrences on the network. In order to formulate their explanation of the cause of the issue, administrators may follow several approaches, including segmenting the problem into multiple smaller problems, or working through each layer of the OSI model, either from top to bottom, or vice versa. These approaches may even be combined to form a more cohesive explanation of the cause.

Once a proper theory has been established, the administrator must then test their formulated theory concerning the cause of the issue. This test will then illustrate whether the theory was correct. If the theory was correct, the administrator can continue with the troubleshooting process to determine an appropriate resolution to the issue. If the theory was shown to be incorrect, the administrator must then return to the previous step to establish an alternate theory to test. At this stage, the administrator may also request help from other staff members, or escalate the issue if desired.

Once a theory regarding the cause of the issue is proven to be correct, the administrator must then move on to establish a plan of action resolve the issue. At this stage, sufficient data has likely been garnered to formulate a proper solution to the problem. However, the administrator may still need to consult with other staff members to establish a plan for the proper resolution of the issue. In many cases, the resolution process has the ability to affect business processes and, as such, the administrator must work alongside team members to identify potential repercussions of the resolution plan, and to both test the plan and schedule an appropriate time to implement it so that it impacts business processes as little as possible.

After establishing and verifying the plan of action, the administrator is finally able to implement the formulated solution. Depending on the anticipated impact on other processes, this plan of action may have to be implemented during off-periods, usually between the hours of 12 AM and 6 AM. It may also be necessary to request the aid of other personnel in the enterprise or to escalate the solution to other staff members for implementation. For example, if the plan involves a significant number of devices under the jurisdiction of another staff member, it may be appropriate to escalate the plan to that member.

Subsequent to the implementation of the plan of action, it is necessary to perform testing on all affected systems in order to verify full system functionality. This step ensures that no other business processes are unduly affected by the solution. Depending on the circumstance, it may also be necessary to implement preventative measures to prevent the issue from recurring. For example, if the issue that occurred involved power outages due to loose power cables, it would be appropriate to secure the cables to both the outlet and the PSU to ensure that the cable does not come undone again.

Lastly, it is important to keep a record of the entire process. Although the issue and its resolution may seem impossible to forget at the time of the incident, administrators often find themselves forgetting the issue entirely within the space of a few months. Through proper documenting of the issue, from the initial report all the way to the final testing of the implemented solution, administrators can save themselves a lot of stress by being able to simply reference their documentation when similar issues arise in the future.

In order to properly follow this methodology, administrators require a number of tools to aid them in troubleshooting issues and gathering data on their network. In the next section, we will discuss some of these tools.

Utilizing appropriate troubleshooting tools

In this section, we will examine some most common hardware and software tools that are used in troubleshooting and resolving network issues. We will first examine hardware-based tools, after which we will discuss a number of software-based tools that make the process of diagnosis easier.

Hardware-based troubleshooting tools

Let's first investigate some of the common hardware devices used to troubleshoot and repair both copper-based and fiber-based networks:

- **Crimper**: A crimper is a tool used to attach copper cables to connectors. In modern networks, this is most often used to attach twisted-pair copper cable to RJ 45 connectors, but crimpers also exist for other types of copper cables. The main purpose of a crimper is to both press electrical contacts down into the individual copper cables, thereby establishing electrical connectivity between the cables and the connectors, and to press the plastic hammer down onto the outer sheath of cable, thereby fixing the connector to the cable. However, crimpers usually also contain parts to peel the outer sheath and to trim the length of the individual copper wires. The following image shows an example of a crimping tool:

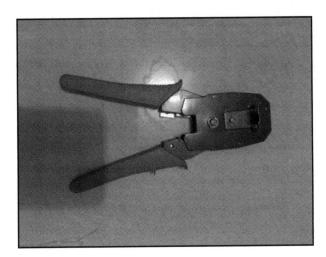

After copper cables are crimped on both ends, cable testers are usually used to ensure that proper electrical connectivity was established and that electrical signals can now traverse the cable properly. Most cable testers simply send a test signal from one end of the tester and verify that the signal is received on all pairs at the other end of the cable. More advanced (and more expensive) cable testers, however, can also measure and display the physical properties of the cable under test.

- **Punchdown tools**: Rather than crimping the ends of the copper cable, the ends may be attached to 66 or 110 blocks. Punchdown tools are used to both push individual cables from twisted-pair cables into their slots on the blocks, and to cut off excess wiring at the end of the slots. The following image shows an example of a punchdown tool:

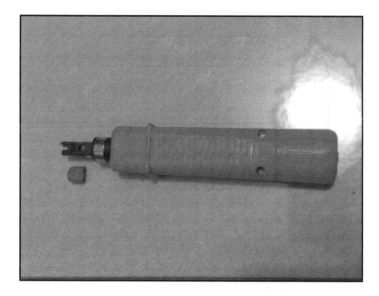

- **Tone and probe tool**: A tone and probe tool is a device used to help technicians trace copper cables. The tone generator is attached to the start of the cable, and the probe (which generates a loud sound once it is held in close proximity to the cable under test) is run along the cable, allowing the technician to easily follow the cable in dense wiring closets or racks, where it may be difficult to trace the cable visually.

- **Loopback adapter**: A physical loopback adapter is a device attached to equipment to feed a **transmitted (TX)** signal back into the **receiving (RX)** interface of the equipment. These adapters may be created for copper interfaces/cables by connecting the TX and RX cables, or for fiber cables by connecting the TX and RX connectors or cables in duplex fiber. Loopback adapters are useful for diagnosing physical layer issues. For example, a loopback adapter may be used at the end of a WAN circuit to demonstrate that the cables for the WAN circuit are operating correctly.

- **Multimeter**: A multimeter may also be used to test a number of parameters on copper cables. Multimeters can be used to test end-to-end continuity in cables, to check whether the cable is damaged, or to match cable ends as part of cable tracing work. They can also be used to test voltages in circuits such as **Power over Ethernet (PoE)** circuits and PDU outlets. The following image illustrates a multimeter tool:

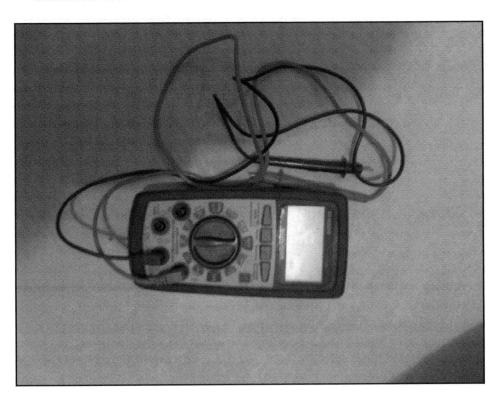

Several other tools are commonly used in diagnosing optical networking issues. One such tool is an **Optical Time Domain Reflectometer** (**OTDR**). OTDRs inject a series of light pulses into fiber cables and record the scattered or reflected pulses they receive in return. Based on these received pulses, they are able to characterize fiber cables. OTDRs are commonly used to document fiber cables and to estimate points at which fiber cables are damaged, allowing fiber repair teams to greatly increase their efficiency in repairing damaged cables. OTDRs usually require operators to select the wavelength of the test pulse, and display attenuation characteristics of the fiber according to the selected wavelength.

Another popular tool used for troubleshooting optical networks is a light meter, or optical power meter. These tools also require operators to select their desired wavelength, and this then allows them to measure the optical power received on a fiber. These tools are essential in optical networks, since equipment in these networks has particular minimum optical signal strengths, below which they are not able to establish links. Light meters therefore allow technicians to measure optical signal strengths and determine whether the signal meets the minimum threshold for the equipment. Optical signal strength is usually referenced in dBm.

Lastly, technicians often require the use of spectrum analyzers, which are used to examine **radio frequency** (**RF**) signals in the frequency domain, displaying the amplitude (strength) of signals with respect to their frequency. These analyzers are commonly used to test electrical signals, but may also be used to test other types of signals through appropriate transducers. Spectrum analyzers may be used to investigate interference or signal strength in a wireless network, the bandwidth of a particular signal across a wire, or the effectiveness of RF shielding in a particular cable.

In addition to these hardware tools, technicians also commonly use a plethora of software tools in their troubleshooting methodology. In the next section, we will examine some of these software tools.

Software-based troubleshooting tools

In this section, we will discuss some of the most common software tools and commands that technicians use to gather data within their network.

A **packet sniffer** is a program used to capture packets traversing a network. **Tcpdump** is one example of a command-line packet sniffer, while other packet sniffers may have a **graphical user interface (GUI)**. A packet sniffer is commonly combined with a protocol analyzer, so that technicians are able to both capture and analyze traffic using a single piece of software. Under normal network configurations, packet sniffers will only be able to capture unicast traffic directed at the host machine, or multicast and broadcast traffic on the network. Therefore, technicians usually configure monitoring ports on switches or utilize hubs to repeat traffic from other sources to their monitoring hosts. Packet sniffers and protocol analyzers can be used to perform in-depth investigations into networks, allowing technicians to view the protocols and payloads involved in conversations between host machines. The following screenshot shows an example of `tcpdump`:

A **port scanner** is a program used to identify open transport layer (UDP and TCP) ports on a machine. Port scanners are useful for assessing which services are running on a host machine, since many ports are associated with specific services. By utilizing port scanners, technicians can assess the attack surface on their host machines and ensure that only necessary ports are left open.

A Wi-Fi analyzer is an application that scans the wireless frequency ranges used with Wi-Fi devices, displaying information such as SSIDs, channels, Wi-Fi modes, and **signal-to-noise ratio (SNR)** from different APs within range of the host machine. These analyzers are an important part of wireless network planning, arming technicians with the knowledge required for tasks such as avoiding interference and scanning for rogue APs in the vicinity.

A bandwidth speed tester is an application used for testing the achievable throughput (speed) on a link. Speed tests are essential to ensure that links are performing as expected, and are an important part of ensuring that SLAs are being met. In running these speed tests, it is important to note the server used to perform the test, as many factors can affect the results of the tests, including the latency to the speed test server and the utilization of the link and server used for testing.

In addition to these applications, technicians also commonly utilize a number of command-line programs. These tools are called by entering their names in a command-line or terminal window, along with any necessary options for the tool. Common command-line tools may include the following:

- `arp`: The `arp` tool allows for viewing and modification of ARP table entries, allowing the user to understand and manipulate IP address to MAC address mapping on their host machine.
- `ping`: The `ping` tool is used to send ICMP echo request packets to remote hosts and process the corresponding ICMP echo reply packets, allowing for measurement of metrics such as **round-trip-time** (**RTT**), a measure of latency, jitter, and packet loss on a link. The following screenshot shows an example of the output generated by the `ping` tool:

```
rishi@linux-6w42:~> ping -n 5 8.8.8.8
connect: Invalid argument
rishi@linux-6w42:~> ping -c 5 8.8.8.8
PING 8.8.8.8 (8.8.8.8) 56(84) bytes of data.
64 bytes from 8.8.8.8: icmp_seq=1 ttl=121 time=88.4 ms
64 bytes from 8.8.8.8: icmp_seq=2 ttl=121 time=80.8 ms
64 bytes from 8.8.8.8: icmp_seq=3 ttl=121 time=79.6 ms
64 bytes from 8.8.8.8: icmp_seq=4 ttl=121 time=84.9 ms
64 bytes from 8.8.8.8: icmp_seq=5 ttl=121 time=51.6 ms

--- 8.8.8.8 ping statistics ---
5 packets transmitted, 5 received, 0% packet loss, time 4005ms
rtt min/avg/max/mdev = 51.676/77.097/88.409/13.087 ms
rishi@linux-6w42:~>
```

- traceroute: The tracert tool (traceroute in Linux hosts) utilizes the **time-to-live** (TTL) property of ICMP packets to map the path that a data packet takes to a particular destination, showing the IP address of every layer 3 node that the packet passes or *hops* through on its way to the destination, along with several measurements of RTTs for each hop. The pathping tool (available on Windows hosts) combines the functionality of both the ping and traceroute tools, first determining the path between a source and its destination, and then measuring RTT and packet loss to each of the nodes along the path. The following screenshot shows some example output from the traceroute tool:

```
linux-6w42:/home/rishi # traceroute 8.8.8.8
traceroute to 8.8.8.8 (8.8.8.8), 30 hops max, 60 byte packets
 1  192.168.100.1 (192.168.100.1)  1.477 ms  1.169 ms  1.278 ms
 2  179.60.213.150 (179.60.213.150)  8.989 ms  3.453 ms  4.553 ms
 3  179.60.213.149 (179.60.213.149)  13.390 ms  10.050 ms  12.130 ms
 4  179.60.213.194 (179.60.213.194)  57.578 ms  58.690 ms 179.60.213.66 (179.60.213.66)  49.402 ms
 5  179.60.213.57 (179.60.213.57)  53.666 ms  50.708 ms 179.60.213.61 (179.60.213.61)  60.937 ms
 6  179.60.213.97 (179.60.213.97)  59.698 ms  61.487 ms 179.60.213.81 (179.60.213.81)  50.453 ms
 7  172.31.13.14 (172.31.13.14)  50.178 ms  55.795 ms  51.298 ms
 8  108.170.235.183 (108.170.235.183)  53.901 ms 74.125.37.97 (74.125.37.97)  48.957 ms 108.170.235.183 (108.170.235.183)  54.824 ms
 9  google-public-dns-a.google.com (8.8.8.8)  56.730 ms  71.985 ms  62.730 ms
linux-6w42:/home/rishi # 
```

- nslookup: The nslookup tool (or the dig tool on Linux hosts) allow users to perform DNS resolutions, querying specific DNS entries to display their associated records. These tools can be used for tasks such as verifying that a host is able to resolve DNS entries correctly, or for querying specific DNS servers for records. The following screenshot shows an example of the output generated by the dig tool:

```
rishi@linux-6w42:~> dig google.com

; <<>> DiG 9.11.2 <<>> google.com
;; global options: +cmd
;; Got answer:
;; ->>HEADER<<- opcode: QUERY, status: NOERROR, id: 11697
;; flags: qr rd ra; QUERY: 1, ANSWER: 1, AUTHORITY: 0, ADDITIONAL: 1

;; OPT PSEUDOSECTION:
; EDNS: version: 0, flags:; udp: 4096
;; QUESTION SECTION:
;google.com.                    IN      A

;; ANSWER SECTION:
google.com.             194     IN      A       172.217.10.78

;; Query time: 76 msec
;; SERVER: 192.168.100.1#53(192.168.100.1)
;; WHEN: Sat Dec 01 08:36:57 AST 2018
;; MSG SIZE  rcvd: 55

rishi@linux-6w42:~> 
```

- `ipconfig`: The `ipconfig` tool (`ifconfig` in many Linux hosts) displays information about the interfaces on a host machine, displaying parameters such as the IP addresses and subnet masks configured on each interface. It is used as a way to verify the configuration on host interfaces.

- `iptables`: The `iptables` (or `ip6tables` for IPv6) tool is a Linux utility used to manipulate IP packets according to a set of defined rules. This utility allows users to manipulate firewall rules to accept or drop packets according to particular addresses or ports on the packets, or to manipulate packets to implement features such as **Network Address Translation** (**NAT**).

- `route`: The `route` tool is used to configure the routing table in both Windows and Linux hosts, allowing for manual manipulation of routes to specific networks from host machines. It allows users to statically define paths for traffic to specific networks, and is especially important on hosts with multiple **Network Interface Cards** (**NICs**).

- `netstat`: The `netstat` tool is used to list open TCP and UDP connections on a device, showing open ports, the addresses that those ports are bound to, and the states of the connections. This tool is useful in checking which services are bound to which sockets, allowing users to diagnose issues with services or to perform security audits on devices.
- `nmap`: The **Network Mapper (Nmap)** tool is used for scanning hosts or networks, allowing for the identification of available hosts, running services, open ports, operating systems, and a variety of other information pertaining to the target system or network. This tool is commonly used for security audits and network documentation, aiding users in discovering additional information about their networks.

By properly utilizing these tools, technicians can quickly troubleshoot variety of issues on both wired and wireless networks. In the following section, we will first explore some of the most common issues that exist on wired networks.

Common issues on wired networks

In this section, we will address some of the most common connectivity and performance issues that transpire on wired networks. As most of these issues exist at layer 1 and layer 2, higher-layer protocols will frequently exhibit issues as well when these problems exist, since these higher-layer protocols depend on the services offered by the lower layers. It is therefore recommended that technicians become familiar with the symptoms of these issues, and perform a bottom-to-top troubleshooting methodology when they suspect that these problems are present:

- **Link lights/status indicators**: Most equipment includes lights on each interface where links can be plugged into the equipment, which helps technicians to diagnose physical layer issues on those links. Lighting schemes differ between different vendors of equipment, but a lack of lights on an interface generally corresponds to no signal being received across the link for that interface. Technicians can therefore use the presence or absence of link lights on the interfaces to judge whether links are functioning properly, or whether troubleshooting is required.

- **Damaged cables and connectors**: The first step in troubleshooting a physical layer issue should always be to search for bends or breaks in the cabling or connectors (including in the pins of the connectors). These issues can be diagnosed through physical inspection, or by utilizing a multimeter to check continuity across cables and pins (to search for open circuits or shorts between circuits). These issues are usually remedied by simply replacing the damaged component in the link, or by replacing the entire link if deemed necessary.

- **Incorrect TX/RX alignment**: Rather than being linked to damaged cables or connectors, some issues can be traced to misaligned pins or connectors on equipment, resulting in the TX and RX sides of both ends not corresponding correctly. On copper cables, this may be due to wires being crimped improperly, while on fiber cables, this may be due to the incorrect placement of each duplex connector. For copper cables, therefore, the remedy is usually to recrimp the cables with the proper pin-out, or utilize ports with MDIX if required, while fiber cables simply require a reversal of the connectors at one end of the link. The following diagram illustrates this issue:

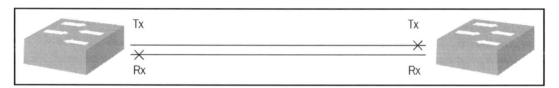

- **Attenuation**: Attenuation refers to the reduction in amplitude of a signal as it propagates through a system, due to the losses present in the system. Attenuation may be caused by a number of factors, including resistance in copper cables, absorption in fiber cables, and reflection in fiber connectors. Attenuation is the physical phenomenon that limits the maximum length of a link, since equipment requires a particular minimum threshold of signal power to communicate across the link. In diagnosing attenuation issues, it is important to observe whether link lights are present on equipment, to note the maximum link length for the cables/transceivers used in the link, and to utilize tools such as light meters to measure the received signal strength at both ends of the cable.

- **Crosstalk and EMI**: Crosstalk refers to the phenomenon whereby electrical signals transmitted in one circuit induce an undesirable electrical signal in another circuit. In the field of networking, crosstalk manifests itself most frequently in twisted-pair copper cabling. A number of techniques have already been employed to reduce crosstalk in these cables, including twisting the cables and wrapping the cables in shielding, but crosstalk may still occur as a result of cables being untwisted at the ends. In many newer Cat cables (for example, Cat7), it is therefore necessary to maintain the twists straight up to the connector end. While crosstalk deals with interference generated from within the cable, **Electromagnetic Interference** (**EMI**) deals with interference sourced from outside the cable, and which may be generated by a number of components, including microwave ovens and generators. Crosstalk and EMI problems may manifest themselves as cables not being able to support the speeds that they should, or as a high number of errors across the cables. These problems may be remedied by techniques such as ensuring that twists remain right up to the connector, by using cables with more shielding, or by moving the copper cables away from significant sources of interference.

- **Bad ports/transceivers**: There may also be cases where ports on equipment may be damaged or configured incorrectly. In the case of damaged ports, the link would be established properly by simply moving the cable to another port on the device. Bad ports are usually not easily repaired by technicians, and are commonly simply marked as damaged. In certain cases, the entire device may be returned to the manufacturer for repair. In some cases, ports may appear to be non-operational if they are not configured with the same speed and duplex settings on both ends. Ports must be configured with these settings matching on both ends of the link in order for the link to be established. Additionally, links may not be established due to the transceivers used at both ends. These transceivers may be incorrect for the type of link being established; for example, a transceiver designed for **multi-mode fiber** (**MMF**) may be inserted into a port while the link uses **single-mode fiber** (**SMF**) cable, the transceiver may be manufactured for a different device (many devices require transceivers manufactured from the same vendor), or the transceiver may simply be damaged. These situations can be remedied by sourcing the correct type of transceiver from the correct vendor, by ensuring that the same type of transceiver is used on both ends of the link, and by switching the transceiver to a known working module.

- **VLAN mismatch**: While troubleshooting connectivity issues on switches that support and employ VLAN tagging, it is important to check how the ports on both ends of a link are configured. VLANs segment broadcast domains, and are (usually) also implemented with different networks assigned to each VLAN. Therefore, is it important to check that the port undergoing troubleshooting is assigned to the correct VLAN. It is also important to ensure that the VLAN being tested has been created in all relevant switches in the network, as switches do not usually pass VLANs that have not been created on them.

- Sub-optimal performance: Even if connectivity has been established across a link, there may be cases where performance across the link is sub-optimal. For example, technicians may notice high amounts of latency (the delay between transmitting and receiving packets across a link) or jitter (the variation in latency across a link), which may be caused by factors such as the length of the link (since the signals used to transmit packets across a link take some time to travel) or interference across the link. Additionally, technicians may notice that links are not performing at their rated speeds due to the aforementioned factors, or due to incorrect cable types being used (for example, Cat6 cable may not be able to deliver 10 GBps across the full 100 m, as Cat6a cable might be able to do). Due to these links operating at lower speeds, bottlenecks may be created in the network. If a transmission is being performed across several links, the transmission would only be able to run at the speed of the slowest link in the chain. Many of these issues can be remedied by replacing copper cables with fiber cables. Since light pulses travel faster than electrical signals, latency in fiber cables is usually lower than in copper cables. Fiber cables also do not suffer from EMI or crosstalk. Additionally, fiber cables also have maximum link lengths that are much higher than copper cables, allowing speeds to be maintained across longer runs of cables. The following diagram illustrates a common bottleneck scenario:

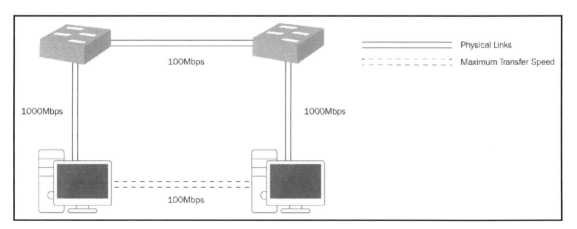

In this section, we have covered many of the issues that are commonly seen on wired networks in the hope that you will now be able to troubleshoot these issues much more quickly. In the following section, we will discuss some prevalent issues often exhibited on wireless networks.

Common issues on wireless networks

Wireless networks are becoming more and more ubiquitous around the globe, as they free us from a lot of the technical difficulties of wired networks. However, they also introduce a number of complications that must be considered. In this section, we will explore some of the most common issues that technicians face in wireless networks.

- **Physical layer issues**: Wireless signals face even more obstructions than signals in wired media, as these wireless signals are propagating in unguided media. RF signals between APs and client devices often have to propagate through a variety of objects and materials, including concrete walls, glass, and other electronic items. While propagating through these materials, these signals may undergo phenomena such as reflection (where the signals bounce off certain surfaces such as metallic objects), refraction (where the signals bend due to traveling through two dissimilar media), and absorption (where the signals lose a lot of their power while propagating through different materials). As a result of this, latency and jitter across wireless networks is often significantly higher than in wired networks, since RF signals may take a longer time to travel across wireless media and since each RF signal can take a variety of different paths (each with its own corresponding delay). Technicians must therefore properly assess the environment in which their wireless networks will be used, and try to minimize the number of obstructions present by positioning their APs appropriately. The following diagram illustrates some of these issues:

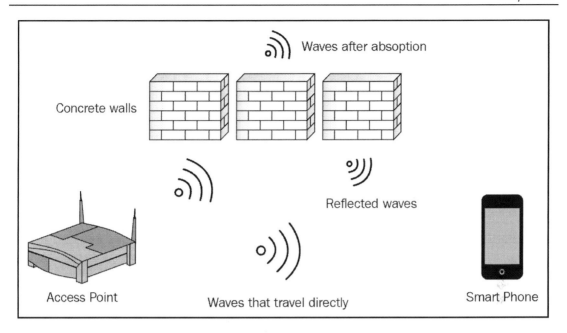

- **Antenna issues**: In order to mitigate some of these physical layer issues, technicians should properly plan their antenna choice and placement in the network. Omni-directional antennas are the most popular antennas supplied with APs, but they may not be the most appropriate for all situations. Omni-directional antennas radiate power approximately uniformly in all directions, and are thus well-suited to environments where wireless coverage needs to extend to fill an entire room and where the AP can be placed in the center of the room. However, there may be other environments that call for directional antennas, which radiate power in one direction only. In these types of environments, antenna placement becomes even more critical, as technicians must ensure that the signal is radiated in the proper direction.

- **Signal power issues**: Many wireless network issues are caused by clients simply not receiving sufficient signal power for proper operation. Wireless signals are attenuated by a number of factors, including the reflection, refraction, and absorption phenomena discussed previously. Additionally, wireless signals lose power as they propagate through physical media (air in most environments). Therefore, even in the absence of any objects to cause additional losses, signal power is reduced as the distance to the transmitter is increased, resulting in a particular maximum distance at which a client device can communicate with an AP. In order to increase this maximum distance, technicians may increase the power levels on their APs. However, this does not necessarily increase the range of the network unless the client power levels are also increased.

- **Interference**: In addition to signal power levels, technicians must also consider the levels of interference in their wireless networks. Wireless networks operate using particular frequency bands. For example, the 802.11n protocol (a popular Wi-Fi protocol in use today) commonly operates on 20 MHz channels, meaning that even though 11-14 channels (spaced 5 MHz apart) are available for use depending on the region in which the devices are operating, these channels cannot all be used, as channel overlaps will occur. For this reason, technicians must plan their wireless networks properly, ensuring that adjacent networks utilize channels with proper spacing to avoid overlaps and interference, thereby ensuring that clients meet or exceed their minimum threshold SNR, the ratio of the wireless signal power to the power of external noise and interference signals required for optimal performance. The following diagram illustrates the non-overlapping channels used in many 802.11n networks:

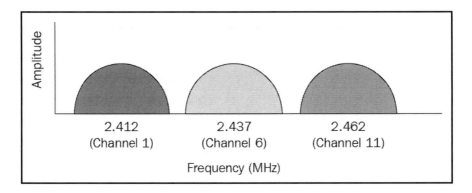

- **Client configuration issues**: In many instances, technicians may discover that their wireless networks are configured correctly, but that a single client is not configured properly for the network that they are trying to access. Some common client issues include the client device not being able to support the correct frequency (for example, the client device may only support 2.4 GHz networks, while the AP nearest to it only supports 5 GHz) the client device is connected to the wrong **Service Set Identifier (SSID)** (so that it is trying to access the wrong network) or the client device is configured with incorrect passphrases or security types, resulting in it not being able to authenticate and join the wireless network. These issues must be treated on a case-by-case basis, requiring the technician to compare the configuration on problematic clients with the desired configuration, and then re-configure the devices as required.

In this section, we've covered many common issues experienced while administering wireless networks. In addition to these wireless-specific issues, technicians frequently face several network service issues that impact clients on their networks. In the following section, we will describe some of these common issues.

Common network service issues

Many issues technicians encounter while troubleshooting networks are limited to particular client hosts. In these cases, technicians notice that all of the other clients on the network are operating properly, while the client in question exhibits issues. In these cases, technicians should examine the network configuration on the client machine itself, paying special attention to the possibility of the following:

- **IP address duplication**: In many networks with poor documentation practices, IP addresses may be reused by multiple clients, resulting in duplicate IPs on the network and poor/non-existent connectivity for the clients. For this reason, many technicians ping the IP that they intend to use before they configure the IP on a machine, in order to check whether any other hosts are utilizing the intended address. However, there are many firewalls that filter the ICMP messages used by the `ping` tool, resulting in the technician not receiving a response and reusing the IP address. This issue therefore reinforces the need for proper documentation.

- **MAC address duplication**: Although MAC addresses are not usually explicitly configured on host machines in the same way that IP addresses are, software exists that allows hosts to utilize MAC addresses other than those burnt into their NICs. Therefore, it is possible that rogue agents on the network may spoof MAC addresses of machines on the network for nefarious purposes, preventing communication to the original host machine. Technicians should thus be aware of this possibility, and actively search the network for rogue agents that might be spoofing their valid MACs.

- **Incorrect gateway and netmask**: IP addresses only form one part of a client's layer 3 configuration. The netmask/subnet mask and gateway form another critical part of the configuration, telling the host the size of the network that it is a part of, and letting it know which device it should communicate with to transport packets out of its own network. Therefore, it is important that technicians verify these configuration parameters and ensure that they match the network that the client is part of.

- **Incorrect DNS/NTP servers**: Client machines are usually configured to communicate with several servers that provide particular services that the client needs. Two of the most important services are name resolution services (provided by DNS servers) and time synchronization services (provided by NTP servers). Technicians must therefore verify that both of these servers are configured correctly on the client machine. DNS services can be verified through the use of the `nslookup` or `dig` tools. For time synchronization services, technicians should verify that the correct time zone is set on the client, and that the NTP server is responding.

In addition to these client configuration issues, some networks may suffer from DHCP-related issues. These issues may include the following:

- **Exhausted DHCP scope**: Technicians may notice that new clients connecting to the network are not being assigned addresses from the DHCP pool. In some of these cases, it may be that the pool is simply exhausted, and there are no more addresses to lease to new clients. In these cases, the technician may consider expanding the pool, adding additional pools, or reducing the lease time to ensure that addresses are available for use quicker.
- **Expired IP address**: In certain situations, host machines may not be able to communicate with DHCP servers to renew their IP address leases. In these cases, the address on the hosts may expire and the host will be forced to request a new address. In order to prevent these situations, reservations may be created on the DHCP server.
- **Rogue DHCP server**: In some instances, technicians may notice DHCP messages from servers other than the ones they configure. In these cases, it may be necessary to locate these rogue DHCP servers and disconnect the host machines manually, or explicitly configure particular ports on their networks to allow DHCP servers, and deny server messages from all other ports.

In some networks, misconfigured security policies may prevent proper network operation. Some of the most common security problems include the following:

- **Untrusted SSL certificates**: Web browsers may complain about untrusted SSL certificates for a number of reasons. In some cases, the certificate may be signed by a trusted CA, but may be rejected by the browser due to a number of issues, such as missing intermediary certificates, or misconfigured or expired certificates. In other cases, the server may be using a self-signed certificate that has not been imported into the client's certificate store. Most web browsers provide the technician with some information about the problematic certificate, which helps in the troubleshooting process.

- **Incorrect network or host firewall settings**: In some networks, firewalls at particular points may block valid traffic from reaching their intended destination. The firewalls (either host-based or network-based) may be configured with ACLs that drop traffic to valid addresses or ports, and will require the technician to trace the traffic through the entire path in the network, and determine which node along the path drops the traffic. The technician should always be aware of implicit denying rules that may exist in ACLs that may silently discard traffic on the network.

Lastly, some issues may be simply due to hardware or software failures. Many system processes and hardware devices often become stuck due to problematic software functions or components, requiring the technician to restart the particular software process or hardware device. In certain cases, these devices may need to be upgraded or replaced if the technician notices that they are becoming stuck and impacting services too frequently .

Summary

In this chapter, we discussed troubleshooting in depth, covering the steps of the troubleshooting methodology, some of the most popular tools used in diagnosing network issues, and some of the most common issues seen on both wired and wireless networks. This material was aimed at presenting a few practical examples to technicians, in the hope that they would better understand how to properly apply the troubleshooting methodology to issues on their network, and in the hope that technicians would be able to better relate the knowledge they have garnered in this book to the issues that they face in their workplaces.

Questions

1. A client has reported an issue with their machine connecting to the WLAN. A technician has just finished establishing a theory of probable cause for the issue. What is the technician's next step?
    1. Identify the issue
    2. Document the issue
    3. Test the theory to determine the cause
    4. Verify full system functionality

2. A network administrator has noticed that an end of one of their Cat5 cables is damaged. What tool will they require to remake the end of the cable?
   1. A crimper
   2. A light meter
   3. An OTDR
   4. A packet sniffer

3. A network technician has rebooted a server, and wants to verify that the server rebooted successfully and is alive again. Which of the following tools would best fulfill this task?
   1. Route
   2. Ipconfig
   3. Ping
   4. Wi-Fi scanner

4. An administrator has received reports that their web server is no longer serving traffic correctly. They have logged into the server and captured a minute's worth of requests to the server. What tool will now enable them to analyze these requests?
   1. Traceroute
   2. Wi-Fi analyzer
   3. Protocol analyzer
   4. Packet sniffer

5. A technician has received a request from a client to run 200 m of Cat6 cable. Which of the following phenomena must the technician discuss with the client to explain why signals cannot travel for 200 m across Cat6 cable without suffering significant degradation?
   1. Attenuation
   2. Incorrect pin-out
   3. Reflection
   4. Bottlenecks

6. A client is having issues with connecting to their Wi-Fi network. Upon further investigation, they have discovered that they are attempting to connect to the wrong network. Which of the following best describe this occurrence?
   1. Incorrect passphrase
   2. Incorrect security type
   3. Incorrect SSID
   4. Low power levels

7. A security administrator is analyzing a trace of some traffic on their network. They notice that several hosts on this particular wireless network have received IP addresses from a server that is not recognized. What is most likely present on this network?

    1. A malicious NTP server

    2. A rogue DHCP server

    3. A firewall

    4. An unresponsive service

8. A network administrator has configured a small WLAN with a DHCP server for a few HR personnel in an office. Several months later, the HR team triples in size. The personnel are now complaining that several of their devices cannot access the network. Which of the following is most likely the cause of the issue?

    1. A rogue DHCP server

    2. An incorrect ACL

    3. An exhausted DHCP scope

    4. Incorrect time

Further reading

Further information on the content for this chapter can be found at the following websites:

- **How to Crimp Rj45**: https://www.wikihow.com/Crimp-Rj45
- **Copper versus Fiber**: https://www.ecmag.com/section/systems/copper-vs-fiber

Assessment

Chapter 1: The OSI Reference Model and the TCP/IP Stack

1. 7
2. The Physical Layer
3. The Transport Layer
4. A switch
5. The MAC sub layer
6. Encapsulation
7. An L7 firewall
8. Segments
9. Physical
10. Physical

Chapter 2: Network Ports, Protocols, and Topologies

1. IP
2. UDP
3. DNS
4. SMTP
5. WAN
6. SCP
7. Physical, Data Link
8. 802.3
9. Mesh
10. POP

Chapter 3: Ethernet

1. 48
2. The Media Access Control
3. The Logical Layer Control
4. The CAM table
5. Frame
6. A file check sequence

Chapter 4: Understanding IPv4 and IPv6

1. 32
2. 254
3. 255.255.0.0
4. 6
5. 172.15.58.5
6. 172.19.5.63
7. 128
8. 11101011
9. 170
10. Unicast

Chapter 5: Routing and Switching Concepts

1. 1500
2. VLAN
3. IEEE 802.1D
4. Designated ports
5. Default
6. RIP
7. BGP

Chapter 6: Wireless and Cloud Technologies

1. 802.11b
2. 802.11n
3. Z-Wave
4. ANT+
5. SaaS
6. Gmail
7. Community

Chapter 7: Network Components

1. UTP Cat 5e
2. STP Cat 6a
3. SMF
4. QSFP
5. Bidirectional
6. Switches
7. Media converter
8. Router
9. RADIUS server
10. A UTM appliance

Chapter 8: Network Virtualization and WAN Technologies

1. Type 1 hypervisor
2. Saves cost on additional hardware, Reduces the storage spaces needed for additional servers
3. NAS
4. WAN
5. Mesh
6. VSAT
7. ATM

Chapter 9: Business Continuity and Disaster Recovery Concepts

1. Router
2. Physical
3. Inventory management system
4. SOP
5. SPoF
6. Hot site
7. 5
8. To ensure that business continuity is not affected
9. SNMP
10. Check the logs on the device

Chapter 10: Network Identity Management and Policies

1. Bring your own device policy
2. Acceptable use policy
3. User account policy
4. Site-to-site
5. SSH
6. ESP
7. Confidentiality

Chapter 11: Network Security Concepts

1. WPA
2. EAP-FAST
3. DOS
4. Social engineering
5. Logic bomb
6. Ransomware

7. MX
8. `arp -a`

Chapter 12: TCP/IP Security

1. Eavesdropping
2. Implement port security
3. Data Link
4. Firewall
5. SQL Injection
6. DNS Zone Transfer

Chapter 13: Organizational Security

1. Asset tags
2. Tamper detection
3. RADIUS
4. Microsoft Windows
5. TACACS+

Chapter 14: Troubleshooting a Network

1. Test the theory to determine the cause
2. A crimper
3. Ping
4. Packet sniffer
5. Attenuation
6. Incorrect SSID
7. A rogue DHCP server
8. An exhausted DHCP scope

Other Books You May Enjoy

If you enjoyed this book, you may be interested in these other books by Packt:

CompTIA Linux+ Certification Guide
Philip Inshanally

ISBN: 978-1-78934-449-3

- Understand the Linux system architecture
- Install, upgrade, and manage Linux system packages
- Configure devices and maintain the Linux filesystem
- Manage the Shell environment, write scripts, and manage data
- Set user interfaces and desktops in the Linux operating system
- Automate system admin tasks and manage essential system services
- Manage SQL server on Linux and log locally and remotely with rsyslogd
- Administer network and local security

CompTIA Security+ Certification Guide
Ian Neil

ISBN: 978-1-78934-801-9

- Get to grips with security fundamentals from Certificates and Encryption to Identity and Access Management
- Secure devices and applications that are used by your company
- Identify the different types of malware and virus and take appropriate actions to protect against them
- Protect your environment against social engineering and advanced attacks
- Implement PKI concepts
- Learn about secure coding techniques, quality control, and testing Troubleshoot common security issues

Leave a review - let other readers know what you think

Please share your thoughts on this book with others by leaving a review on the site that you bought it from. If you purchased the book from Amazon, please leave us an honest review on this book's Amazon page. This is vital so that other potential readers can see and use your unbiased opinion to make purchasing decisions, we can understand what our customers think about our products, and our authors can see your feedback on the title that they have worked with Packt to create. It will only take a few minutes of your time, but is valuable to other potential customers, our authors, and Packt. Thank you!

Index

W

Made in the USA
Middletown, DE
27 April 2019